Development with a body

Andrea Cornwall, Sonia Corrêa and
Susie Jolly | editors

Development with a body

sexuality, human rights and development

Zed Books

LONDON | NEW YORK

Development with a body: sexuality, human rights and development
was first published in 2008 by Zed Books Ltd, 7 Cynthia Street,
London N1 9JF, UK and Room 400, 175 Fifth Avenue, New York,
NY 10010, USA

www.zedbooks.co.uk

Cover designed by Andrew Corbett
Set in OurType Arnhem and Futura Bold by Ewan Smith, London
Index: ed.emery@thefreeuniversity.net
Printed and bound in Malta by Gutenberg Press Ltd

Distributed in the USA exclusively by Palgrave Macmillan, a division
of St Martin's Press, LLC, 175 Fifth Avenue, New York, NY 10010.

A catalogue record for this book is available from the British Library.
Library of Congress cataloging in publication data are available.

ISBN 978 1 84277 890 6 hb
ISBN 978 1 84277 891 3 pb

Contents

THREE | Changing mindsets

Figures

Boxes

Abbreviations

AALI	Association for Advocacy and Legal Initiatives
AHI	Action Health Incorporated
AIDWA	All India Democratic Women's Association
AKP	Adalet ve Kalkınma Partisi (Justice and Development Party, Turkey)
ANC	African National Congress
AOSI	Alliance for Open Society International
ATC	Anti Trafficking Centre
BPfA	Beijing Platform for Action
CATW	Coalition Against Trafficking in Women
CEDAW	Convention on the Elimination of All Forms of Discrimination Against Women
CHR	Commission on Human Rights
CIATON	Carnal Intercourse Against the Order of Nature
CLADEM	Comitê Latino-Americano e do Caribe para Defesa dos Direitos da Mulher
CPD	Commission on Population and Development
CPU	Cambodian Prostitutes Union
CREA	Creating Resources for Empowerment in Action
CSW	Commission on the Status of Women
CSWs	Commercial sex workers
CTA	Central de Trabajadores Argentinos
DfID	Department for International Development
DMSC	Durbar Mahila Samanwaya Committee
DoJ	Department of Justice
EGDI	Expert Group on Development Issues (Sweden)
EU	European Union
FGD	Focus group discussion
FGM	Female genital mutilation
FHP	Family Health Programme
FLHE	Family Life and HIV Education Curriculum (Nigeria)
FME	Federal Ministry of Education (Nigeria)
FWCW	Fourth World Conference on Women
GDP	Gross domestic product
GPI	Girl Power Initiative
GRUPAL	Grupo de Trabajo para la Participación en el Ámbito Local

HDRs	Human Development Reports
HERA	Health, Empowerment, Rights and Accountability
HIV/AIDS	Human Immunodeficiency Virus/Acquired Immune Deficiency Syndrome
HREP	Human Rights Education Programme for Women
IAWS	Indian Association of Women's Studies
ICCHRLA	Inter-Church Committee on Human Rights in Latin America
ICCPR	International Covenant on Civil and Political Rights
ICESCR	International Covenant on Economic Social and Cultural Rights
ICPD	International Conference for Population and Development
IDP	Internally displaced person
IDU	Injectible drug user
IFCVR	El Informe Final de la Comisión de la Verdad y Reconciliación
IGLHRC	International Gay and Lesbian Human Rights Commission
ILGA	International Lesbian and Gay Association
ILO	International Labour Organization
IOM	International Organization for Migration
IWHC	International Women's Health Coalition
KHANA	Khmer HIV/AIDS NGO Alliance
LBL	Landsforeningen for Bøsser og Lesbiske
LGBT(I)Q	Lesbian, gay, bisexual, transgender, (intersex) and questioning
MDGs	Millennium Development Goals
MDP	Millennium Development Project
MMS	Multi-media Messaging Service
MRTA	Túpac Amaru Revolutionary Movement
MSM	Men who have sex with men
NASCP	National AIDS Control and Prevention Programme (Nigeria)
NCE	National Council on Education (Nigeria)
NERDC	Nigerian Educational Research and Development Council
NGO	Non-governmental organization
NSWP	Network of Sex Work Projects
OIC	Organization of the Islamic Conference
PEPFAR	President's Emergency Plan for AIDS Relief
POA	Programme of Action
PRISM	People for Rights of Indian Sexual Minorities
PRSP	Poverty Reduction Strategy Process
PUCL-K	People's Union for Civil Liberties
SEE	South-eastern Europe

SIDA	Swedish International Development Cooperation Agency
SRHR	Sexual and reproductive health rights
STIs	Sexually transmitted infections
TAMPEP	Transnational AIDS/STD Prevention among Migrant Prostitutes in Europe Project
UN	United Nations
UNAIDS	Joint United Nations Programme on HIV/AIDS
UNDP	United Nations Development Programme
UNFPA	United Nations Fund for Population Activities
UNGASS	United Nations General Assembly Special Session
UNICEF	United Nations Children's Fund
USAID	United States Agency for International Development
WAS	World Association for Sexual Health
WHO	World Health Organization
WNU	Women's Network for Unity
WWHR	Women for Women's Human Rights

Acknowledgements

The support given by the External Group for Development Issues (EGDI) of the Swedish Ministry for Foreign Affairs made the writing and publishing of this book possible. We are immensely grateful to Ulrica Risso-Engblom, who was our main partner in this project, as well as to the other members of the EGDI Secretariat. The reflections developed by the contributors to this book and the other experts who were present at the EGDI seminar on 'Sexuality, Human Rights and Development: Making the Connections' in Stockholm in April 2006 greatly enriched the conceptual framework initially designed to address the intersections between development, sexuality and human rights. We also want to thank the other authors who were later invited to be part of this volume, as well as the IDS Bulletin for authorizing the reprinting of a number of these additional papers. In particular we would like to acknowledge the enthusiasm of those who positively responded to our invitation under a very stringent time frame, as was the case of Codou Bop, Cristina Pimenta and Melissa Hope Ditmore. We deeply regret that it was not possible for all these contributions to be included in the final edition. Lastly, we would like to acknowledge the editorial support of Jenny Edwards and Kirsty Milward, without whom it would have been impossible to finalize this book.

Figure 2.1 reproduced with permission of the Institute of Development Studies/Policy Briefing 29. Chapter 4 is a revised version of an essay that appeared in *Trafficking and Prostitution Reconsidered*, published by Paradigm, and in *SIECUS Report*. It is used with permission. Chapter 10 is a revised version of an article published in *Feminist Africa* and is used with permission. Figure 11.1 is reproduced with permission of the UCLA Moche Archive

Foreword

When I consider my human rights work of recent years, it seems to me that two issues have generated the most controversy and got me into the most trouble. One is sexual rights. The other relates to development. So I approach this Foreword with some hesitation, while warmly applauding the Swedish Ministry for Foreign Affairs' Expert Group on Development Issues for taking up the challenge of exploring the linkages between sexuality, human rights and development. I also congratulate the Swedish government for the recent adoption of its pioneering international policy on sexual and reproductive health and rights. Both initiatives will contribute to a more rational and human rights-based approach to these extremely important issues.

As I concluded in one of my 2004 reports, the rights to sexual and reproductive health have an indispensable role to play in the struggle against intolerance, gender inequality, HIV/AIDS and global poverty.[1] As is well known, while at least three Millennium Development Goals are directly related to sexual and reproductive health, unfortunately the goals do not explicitly refer to sexual and reproductive health. This refusal to name sexual and reproductive health is deeply regrettable. Thus, my report urges all parties to recognize *explicitly* the indispensable role of sexual and reproductive health in the struggle against poverty. Explicit recognition is important. We all know that what is unnamed is more likely to be unsupported, ignored and misunderstood.

Even where sexual and reproductive health is named, there is often another major problem. Listening to some states, you would think that sex does not generally precede reproduction. Some states try to bury or disguise sexual health and sexual rights within reproductive health and reproductive rights. Not only is this absurd, it is dangerous. Make-believe is never a good foundation for sound policy-making. In the context of reproductive rights, make-believe kills and maims, especially girls and women. Crucially, a focus on reproduction also ignores the fact of life that many expressions of sexuality are non-reproductive. Although constrained by the health focus of my UN mandate, my 2004 report observes that sexual and reproductive health must be understood in the broader human rights context that includes sexual rights.

There remains a long way to go, but in the last five or six years the international community has made significant progress towards understanding the relationship between human rights, development and poverty reduction. We now understand, at least in general terms, the basic 'value-added' of a human rights approach. The approach has a preoccupation with discrimination, inequality, participation, accountability and so forth. At root, the human rights approach brings entitlements, obligations and accountability. Today, this might seem rather trite. But that shows how far we have travelled in a relatively short time. A decade ago we simply did not have these insights.

Today the challenge is different – it is how to *operationalize* the human rights approach. In my view, it is very difficult to operationalize the human rights approach to poverty reduction or development *in general terms*. If we are to operationalize the human rights approach, we are best advised to focus on *particular* sectors – health, education, food, justice and so on. Of course, when applying the human rights approach to one sector, we must keep firmly in mind that many sectors are closely interconnected, as well as the interdependence and indivisibility of all human rights. Nevertheless, we have to graduate from the general and examine the particular. In this case, the devil is *not* in the detail – it is in the general.

So what do we learn if we examine, through the human rights prism, the intersections between sexuality and poverty? The right to equality and the principle of non-discrimination are among the most fundamental features of international human rights law. We know that discrimination on the basis of sexuality can cause – or deepen – poverty and hinder important public health initiatives. Thus, it is crucial to maintain, develop and apply the argument that discrimination on the grounds of sexual orientation is impermissible. The right to seek and receive information places a duty on governments to make publicly available information concerning governmental activities and services. This includes information in respect of education, health, employment, the administration of justice, political decision-making, and so on. This information must be available without discrimination to all, including sexual minorities and those living in poverty. Also, it must extend to issues concerning sexuality, such as safer sex. These are among the human rights, sexuality and poverty issues explored in this book.

All states have some binding treaty obligations in relation to the right to the highest attainable standard of health. As I outline in my report of 2004, this human right includes sexual and reproductive health and it encompasses freedoms and entitlements. By freedoms I mean the freedom to control one's health and body, as well as freedom from discrimination, including on the grounds of sexual orientation. By entitlements I mean, for example, equal access to contraceptives and information on sexual and reproductive health. The exercise of the right to education is instrumental for the enjoyment of many other human rights, including sexual rights and the right to the highest attainable standard of health. Education should be directed to the development of the individual's personality, talents and abilities to their fullest potential, and to preparation of the individual for a responsible life in a free society, in a spirit of tolerance and respect for human rights. The right to education is a primary vehicle by which children and adults can lift themselves out of poverty, as well as other forms of disadvantage.

The cumulative effect of human rights – non-discrimination, information, education, participation, accountability and so on – can empower individuals and communities. The challenge is to connect the powerless with the empowering potential of human rights. In other words, the challenge is to connect those 'who break rules around sexuality', and other disadvantaged individuals, with the empowering potential of human rights. In this way, they can break out of the vicious cycle of marginalization. Unfortunately, the world is littered with poverty reduction strategies that are not respectful of human rights. The world is also littered with poverty reduction strategies that fail to take into account sexuality. In my experience, sexuality is rarely raised as an issue in relation to poverty reduction.

A human rights approach to poverty reduction strategies has numerous benefits, one being that it demands due regard be given to issues of sexuality. As we have seen, a human rights approach to poverty reduction, with its various features of non-discrimination, access to information, active and informed participation and so on, is a vehicle for the promotion and protection of sexual rights, as well as sexual and reproductive health rights. Human rights are not a panacea. They are sites of dialogue – and sites of struggle. But at least they provide a site – a place for the most disadvantaged and 'invisible' to stand up and speak out. Human rights do not have to reinforce a single normative standard. Paradoxically, human rights norms can help to create a space without norms.

One view is that sexual rights signify a bundle of rights that are not yet – but should be – encompassed by contemporary international human rights. But there is another view. The rights to privacy, non-discrimination, equality, security of the person, bodily integrity, health, education, information and so on are already firmly established features of contemporary human rights. If these well-established, generic human rights concepts are applied, in a principled and consistent manner, to human sexuality, there might be no need to construct any new human rights. Rather, the term 'sexual rights' then becomes a useful shorthand for the bundle of specific norms that emerge when existing generic human rights are applied to sexuality.

Those who promote and defend human rights use the strategy of naming and shaming. Indeed, it is very important that, in relation to sexual rights, we name and shame human rights violators. But, in relation to sexual rights, we must also name *without* shame: we must clearly and firmly name sexual rights without hesitation. If we examine an issue and find it has a sexual rights dimension, we should name it as a sexual rights issue. Naming without shame will make the connections between sexual rights, human rights and development so evident that no one can pretend that they do not exist.

This book is a tool that can help those engaged in development and human rights to begin to make these vital connections.

Paul Hunt (UN Special Rapporteur on the Right to the Highest Attainable Standard of Health)

Note

1 E/CN.4/2004/49 dated 16 February 2004, para. 56. My various reports can be accessed via the website of the Right to Health Unit, Human Rights Centre, Essex University, www2.essex.ac.uk/human_rights_centre/rth/, and also the website of the UN Office of the High Commissioner for Human Rights, www.ohchr.org.

1 | Development with a body: making the connections between sexuality, human rights and development

ANDREA CORNWALL, SONIA CORRÊA AND
SUSIE JOLLY

'We used to talk about development with a human face. We should be talking about development with a body.' Arit Oku-Egbas, Africa Regional Resource Centre, Nigeria[1]

In Stockholm, in April 2006, an unusual combination of people gathered together with considerable excitement: an Argentinian lesbian activist, the Swedish Minister for International Development Cooperation, a South African sexuality researcher, a Turkish sexual rights NGO organizer and a UN Special Rapporteur, among others. This exceptional get-together, hosted by Sweden's Ministry for Foreign Affairs' Expert Group on Development Issues (EGDI), was the first of its kind, a seminar on making the linkages between sexuality, human rights and development.

The seminar provided a precious opportunity for exchange between sexual rights activists and government policy-makers, and for exploring the intersections between sexuality, human rights and development. It came soon after the adoption by the Swedish Foreign Ministry of a new policy on sexual and reproductive health and rights, which is the most comprehensive and far-reaching policy on sexual rights adopted by any development cooperation ministry so far, and a laudable move in the current climate of conservative backlash. Out of these discussions came this book, which draws together contributions from participants at the Stockholm seminar and from others who participated in a workshop entitled Realizing Sexual Rights, which had been held at the Institute of Development Studies in Brighton some months previously.

This introduction opens by briefly reporting on some of the 'sex wars' currently under way at local, national and global levels. These realities compellingly portray how sexual matters are key factors behind discrimination and injustice, and demonstrate how policy debates on sexuality are increasingly captured by conservative positions and ideologies that often escape the radars of progressive development actors. Then it moves towards a brief reminder that what is witnessed in today's world has many parallels with other times and places. This is followed by an examination of how the lack of critical systematic reflection about dominant conceptions of sexuality and gender – in particular heteronormativity – explains the silences and resistances observed in the development field in relation to 'sex'. Novel conceptual paths that may lead to a virtuous reframing of these connections are also explored, with a particular emphasis on the possibilities opened by a more consistent articulation of development and human rights. These new conceptual paths are not, however, exempt from paradoxes and challenges. While one example is the binary logic that still prevails in mainstream approaches to gender and development, another concerns the complexities of articulating rights and sexual identities. In a further step the pervasiveness and detrimental implications of existing sex and gender orders, as deployed in discourses and translated into realities, are scrutinized. The last section calls for the transformation of mindsets and provides inspiring illustrations of how this can be done.

Contexts and histories

Today's 'sex wars' – to use a phrase coined by Gayle Rubin (1984) – have a long history. In the current geopolitical order, they have taken on a new intensity. These wars have emerged acutely on the stage of the United Nations, which has become a veritable battleground (Girard 2001; Corrêa and Parker 2004; Sen and Corrêa 2000, among others). As Gita Sen (2005) observes, for all the talk of a 'clash of civilizations', there is little clash among those who for reasons of politics or religion oppose the possibility of granting sexual rights and freedoms to those who fail to conform to their prescribed norms. Faced with a perverse confluence of powerful reactionary actors, advocates of sexual rights reckon with an ever more hostile climate at the international level. Yet sexual rights activism has reached unprecedented levels of international connectivity, and continues to make advances in a number of settings.

While this book was being edited, hundreds of episodes took place throughout the world which illustrate the breadth and complexity of issues of sexuality. They also highlight the importance of addressing these through a human rights and development lens. A few are outlined below:

- In Lucknow, India, NGO activists doing HIV prevention work in a public place were caught by police and imprisoned, accused of infringing Article 377 of the Indian Penal Code – inherited from British imperial law – which criminalizes sodomy. In Nepal, the Blue Diamond society struggled for some days to secure the release of a group of *Metis* (transgender people) caught and abused by the police. They subsequently organized a demonstration in front of the Indian embassy to protest against the Lucknow arrests. Later in 2006, Indian debates gained greater global visibility, as a number of celebrities, including Nobel Prize-winning economist Amartya Sen, raised their voices in support of ongoing struggles to repeal Article 377.

- In Brazil, a sex workers' association launched a new fashion label with great media impact, in order to ensure its financial sustainability, which had been affected by the refusal of the Brazilian government and NGOs to sign the anti-prostitution clause attached to USAID funds for HIV prevention. In Italy, feminists and LGBTQ organized a big demonstration in Milan to contest the decision by the Berlusconi government which allowed right-to-life activists to become counsellors in abortion clinics, and in protest against the delays in approving same-sex marriage. This demonstration was particularly meaningful when we bear in mind that a few months earlier, in December 2005, Pope Benedict XVI had launched his first encyclical, *Deus Caritas Est* (God is love), which, once again, conflates human love (Eros) with heterosexuality, marriage and procreation. In May 2006, the Pope would morally condemn same-sex marriages and portray same-sex relations as 'weak love' because they do not fulfil the 'divine purpose' of biological reproduction.

- Meanwhile, in other parts of the world the abortion debate was heated. In Uruguay, the president kept refusing a provision legalizing pregnancy termination to be retabled in the parliament. Later in the year, in Nicaragua, a total ban on abortion, even if the mother's life is at risk, was imposed. But six months earlier, the Colombian Supreme Court had issued a decision that grants access to abortion under certain circumstances, including health risks. And in early 2007, in Portugal and the Federal district of Mexico, abortion was legalized and the European Court of Human Rights condemned Poland for its restrictive legislation.

- Last, but not least, when we started work on this book, the Nigerian government had moved to pass legislation to ban same-sex marriages, which included extremely repressive provisions regarding LGBT identity expression and social interaction. As a result of the unrelenting advocacy of Nigerian LGBT and human rights groups, by the time the book was being completed this provision was considered dead, at least for the time being. At the same time, calls came from Pakistan for international solidarity in support of Shahzima Tariq and Shamial

3

Raj, who were sentenced to three years each for committing 'unnatural acts and perjury', because they supposedly lied about Shamial being a transgendered male. Meanwhile, in Colombia, landmark legislation legalizing gay partnerships was passed and information and images came from Turkey telling of the marriage of two women in a distant rural area, which followed the local tradition in regard to ritual and clothing.

These flashpoints illustrate not only today's 'sex wars', but a pattern that can be observed over the course of centuries, intensifying whenever rapid reconfigurations of the economy, the state and private–public boundaries take place. The transition to modernity in Europe from the seventeenth to the nineteenth centuries – in particular the second half of the so-called Victorian era – is the most extensively scrutinized (Foucault 1980; Laqueur 1992; Weeks 1985, 2003). The reshaping of gender and sexuality in colonial and post-colonial non-Western contexts has also been extensively studied, as in the case of Gupta's study of 1930s Uttar Pradesh, India, Rago's (1991) analysis of prostitution in Brazil in the early twentieth century, and in Delaney's (1995) account of the transformation of the gender imaginary at the birth of the modern Turkish nation-state. Historical studies describe the control and punishment of 'loose' female sexuality and homosexuality in Europe long before the transitions to modernity in Europe and Asia (Crompton 2003; Van der Meer 2004), including of the part played by the Catholic Inquisition (Castañeda 1998; Mott 1992).

Parallels can, therefore, be drawn between what we are experiencing today and other historical realities. Practically all progressive political and social thinkers devoted to analyses of 'globalization' or 'late capitalism' identify shifts in gender and sex orders as one main feature of great transformations under way, even when their conclusions about the direction these shifts may take differ (Altman 2001; Castells 1996, 1997, 1998; Giddens 1991, 2000; Held et al. 1999). The current scenario, however, also presents some quite distinctive features. One is the implications of ever-increasing connectivity. The sparks generated by the episodes described in the brief list of events above flow around the world through electronic and other media, creating both connections and disjunctures across cultures and between global and local realities. The other feature is religion. Theorists of modernity have largely focused on the instrumental power of the secular state and its regulatory efforts, through the deployment of biomedicine and the law. Yet the resurgence of religion and the repositioning of religious discourses on sexuality at the very heart of today's contests over sexual rights and wrongs provide a very different landscape on which battles for equality and justice now come to be waged.

Sexuality and development: making the connections

So in today's context, how does development connect to sexuality? Mention the word 'sexuality' to people involved in development policy and practice and the reaction is often one of puzzlement – what does sexuality have to do with development? There are those who see sexuality as a private affair, something from which development should keep an appropriate distance – apart from helping to reduce the incidence of unwanted pregnancy and sexually transmitted disease. There are those who find the whole subject plain embarrassing. There are those who regard mention of sexuality and sexual pleasure to be a distraction from the 'real issues' of development, as a kind of frivolous add-on rather than something that is intimately entwined with core development concerns of poverty and marginalization.

Few of the development practitioners we have interacted with grasp the significance of sexuality for development. Yet while the word 'sexuality' barely makes an appearance in development policies, mainstream development agencies have always implicitly concerned themselves with issues of sexuality: with population, and, since the 1980s, with HIV/AIDS. For mainstream development sex is treated as a health issue, to be dealt with by experts in disease prevention and health promotion. The reasons why many people choose to have sex in the first place – for pleasure, as well as for the many other affective dimensions of intimate relationships – barely make it into the frame (Gosine 2004).

A positive approach to sex education or HIV/AIDS prevention that emphasizes the rights of women, men and transgender people to a pleasurable and safer sex life free of prejudice, risk or censure is one of the connections that might be made between sexuality, human rights and development (Corrêa and Jolly, Esiet, Ilkkaracan and Ronge, Lewis and Gordon, this volume). But the connections go further than this. For sexuality is about a lot more than having sex. It is about the social rules, economic structures, political battles and religious ideologies that surround physical expressions of intimacy and the relationships within which such intimacy takes place. It has as much to do with being able to move freely outside the home and walk the streets without fear of sexual harassment or abuse as it has to do with whom people have sex with. It is as much concerned with how the body is clothed, from women feeling forced to cover their bodies to avoid unwanted sexual attention

5

to the use of particular colours to mark the gender of infants and begin the process of socialization of boys and girls as different, as what people do when their clothes are off. And, where society and the state collude in policing gender and sex orders, it can be about the very right to exist, let alone to enjoy sexual relations.

Reframing the linkages

The perspective from development is that sexuality is a problem. Recasting sexuality as a positive force (Runeborg 2002; Jolly 2007), a source of pleasure and joy, or an embodiment of the rights that most development actors now profess to promote, is profoundly counter-cultural. For development thinkers and practitioners, engagement with sexuality as a development issue requires critical self-reflection in respect to deeply rooted assumptions. Nevertheless, several productive points of entry for making explicit the connections between sexuality, human rights and development can be identified.

Against a backdrop of the near-hegemonic hold of neoliberalism on mainstream development thinking, three significant shifts took place in the 1990s. The first was a move within mainstream development thinking beyond narrow income- and consumption-based measures of poverty towards a more multidimensional approach to the analysis and measurement of poverty. This came as influential development theorists persuasively argued that poverty should be redefined in terms of lack of opportunities, capabilities and freedoms (Sen 1995; Chambers 1997; Nussbaum 2000; Kabeer 2006). Many development agencies have come to adopt a more sophisticated approach to poverty analysis and measurement in the wake of this shift. Although sexuality is not mentioned in most policies and programmes on poverty, these broader understandings of poverty make possible considerations of how violence and discrimination around sexuality can intensify poverty, and how sexual fulfilment and autonomy can contribute to well-being.

The second shift was the rise of rights talk in development. Until the 1990s, human rights advocates themselves had little interaction with development agencies or practitioners (Uvin 2002). Most human rights work was concerned with the defence of civil and political rights, and efforts were primarily oriented at the legislative rather than the economic or social arenas. In the same manner, development thinkers and practitioners did not closely interact with the human rights field. But development and rights thinking increasingly converged around the post-cold war conferences: Vienna (1993), Cairo (1994), Copenhagen (1995) and Beijing (1995). The third shift was the increasing attention given to issues of gender by development actors, which was given impetus by the Beijing conference and the commitments made there. Gender advocates put questions of power firmly on the development agenda, and have prompted development thinkers to pay closer attention to the persistent inequalities that gender and sex orders produce.

The expansion of conceptions of poverty, the reframing of development in terms of human rights and the recognition of gender, power and difference prompted by these shifts open up new perspectives on the linkages between sexuality, human rights and development. Focusing on the intersection between poverty reduction and human rights, Paul Hunt argues in the preface to this book: ' ... a human rights approach to poverty reduction, with its various features of non-discrimination, access to information, active and informed participation and so on, is a vehicle for the promotion and protection of sexual rights, as well as sexual and reproductive health rights'. Sonia Corrêa and Susie Jolly apply Robert Chambers's (2005) analysis of the many dimensions of poverty to make these linkages evident. Henry Armas's chapter makes further connections, showing how rights to health, education, housing, employment and security are all compromised when those who seek them do not conform to normative expectations of sexuality – whether they belong to the heterosexual majority or sexual minorities.

Sexuality activists have not, by and large, engaged systematically with mainstream development agencies. Some are sceptical about the benefits of such engagement, given the depolicitizing effects that have been witnessed when development agencies have taken up demands for gender equality and participation. But, as Armas argues, the recent turn to a greater focus on rights in development – and, with this, issues of justice and power – can create entry points for more progressive forms of development practice. As these shifts in development thinking suggest, it is important to go beyond a monolithic view that equates 'development' with 'the development industry', and to look at what it takes to create an enabling environment for the achievement of human rights and well-being for all. It is this broader vision of development which underpins the connections that we seek to make in this book.

Sexual rights are human rights

Around the world, sexual rights struggles are evolving on the basis of citizenship and human rights claims to eliminate discrimination, stigma and state-sanctioned violence. The first section of this book explores paradoxes and challenges in conceptualizing sexual rights and in possibilities for their realization.

While secular and progressive development actors have been slow to engage with sex and sexuality, their reactionary counterparts in the growing number of 'faith-based' organizations and political interest groups internationally have had no such difficulty. Ultra-conservative interests have taken a strong position on sex, framed clear policies and deployed considerable resources to promoting those policies. In spite of such fervent opposition from religious and neoconservative forces, some enormously positive steps have been in taken in various countries around the world in recent years – from progressive legislation on civil partnerships to the legalization of abortion, even in Catholic majority countries.

Kate Sheill's chapter takes on the challenges of the current international climate. Sheill's analysis draws attention to the resurgence of resistance to the more progressive positions on sexual rights adopted and encoded in international agreements over the course of the 1990s. Drawing on examples from the Commission on Human Rights, the 49th Commission on the Status of Women (Beijing Plus Ten) and the Commission on Population and Development, she examines the obstacles to progress, the challenges of maintaining the hard-won gains of Cairo and Beijing and the opportunities we must seize if we are to realize the potential of sexual rights. Sheill's analysis suggests that in the difficult times we experience more than often, activists must combine defensive strategies and much courage to keep expanding the boundaries to claim political space for progressing sexual rights.

As mentioned before, one domain of policy where neoconservative ideological positions have been particularly influential is in relation to sex work and HIV prevention. Melissa Ditmore shows how the anti-trafficking measures adopted by the US government, for example, have leached into restrictions on funding any organizations who work with sex workers. This has undermined HIV prevention efforts, as well as efforts to address exploitation in the sex industry. The net effect of these policies has been to increase the vulnerability of sex workers: to police violence, trafficking, exploitation and infection with HIV. By conflating sex work with trafficking, the issues of labour rights and migration at the heart of the debate are obscured: sex workers' own agency is completely eclipsed, and their human rights are jeopardized.

Talking about sexuality in terms of human or sexual rights brings questions of identity, sexual expression, pleasure and risk into the domain of legal discourse. The law becomes a site for the recourse of wronged groups to pursue claims for justice. This presents a number of paradoxes. One such paradox arises from differences in the ways in which sexuality activists approach the role of the state in promoting, protecting and respecting sexual rights. On the one hand, feminist activism on violence against women has been instrumental in engaging the state in criminalizing gender violence and in enforcing punitive measures against offenders. Yet on the other hand, and for other groups, state intervention and punishment remain a major source of rights violations. Drawing attention to the extent of state-sanctioned and state-perpetrated violence against sexual minorities and sex workers, activists have sought legal reforms that decriminalize same-sex relations and sex work, as well as those that extend social and employment rights to LGBT people and sex workers (Sardá, Ditmore, Djordjevic, Armas, Baudh, this volume).

Successful mobilization by identity-based social movements since the 1960s and the development of the human rights framework, with its attention to the rights of specific social groups, has led to a situation in which an increasing number of social categories lay claim to their own, distinct, rights. This has permitted the advance of rights of those marginalized by gender, social and economic orders. But it has also produced another paradox: a tendency to ossify and essentialize the identities on which these rights come to be based. Perverse effects include fragmentation into myriad movements and interest groups, and subsequent difficulties in constructing productive alliances that can advance the rights of all humans. The crafting of the concept of sexual rights – one outcome of global human rights debates in the 1990s – has been identified by various authors as an opportunity to move beyond the limits of identity politics (Petchesky 2003; Corrêa and Parker 2004; Saiz 2004; Ilkkaracan, Jolly and Esplen 2007; Corrêa and Jolly, this volume). And yet, Jaya Sharma points out in her chapter, 'sexual rights' are often understood as referring specifically to the rights of sexual minorities who identify with the label LGBT (lesbian, gay, bisexual, transgender), 'women' and 'sex workers'.

The consequences of identifying sexual rights with particular categories of people are several. One is that this can lead to a failure to effectively address the sexual rights of those who do not fall into these categories, especially if the very recognition of the possibility of them having any sexual rights falls outside societal norms. Deevia Bhana's chapter addresses this in relation to a social category whose sexual rights are generally ignored unless they are subject to sexual abuse: young children. Drawing on research with seven- and eight-year-olds in a black township in KwaZulu-Natal, South Africa, Bhana shows how children of this age are far from 'innocent' about sexual matters: they already knew a great deal about sex and could talk to her comfortably about AIDS, sex and condoms. They had also learnt, however, that they were not supposed to talk about such things in front of teachers or parents, or they might be punished. A key strategy in the fight against HIV/AIDS is to safeguard the rights of those who are infected and at risk of infection. Yet such information, along with the positive sexuality education described by Nike Esiet later in the book, is generally denied to young children.

Defining sexual rights in terms that make them a property of particular social groups is not an adequate basis on which to address the rights of all humans to a sexuality of their choosing. It becomes too easy, Sharma argues, for rights talk based on categories of persons to become a discourse that distances and divides. It also becomes very difficult indeed to begin to talk about the sexual rights of those who are often seen as the violators of the rights of others: heterosexual men. Alan Greig's chapter highlights the need for a discourse on men's sexual rights that can take account of both gender norms and sexual hierarchies. Spelling out the perverse effects of heteronormative masculinity and patriarchal privilege, Greig calls for an approach that foregrounds 'a conception of accountability that is at once personal and political; the political accountability of duty-bearers to promote and protect the sexual rights of all rights-holders, men and women; and the personal accountability of men in relation to the ways in which their gender privilege serves to deny the sexual rights of others'.

A further consequence of the construction of sexual rights as the specific rights of particular groups is that people need to adopt labels in order to claim these rights. As Jaya Sharma points out, these labels define people in terms of their sexuality alone. This reduces the complexity of desires to a set of fixed and often essentialized categories. There is another paradox here. The logic of civil rights and political representation depends on the fixing of identities. Nancy Fraser (1989) argues that recognition matters precisely because without it issues of exclusion and the silencing of difference remain unresolved. Yet defining difference and fixing it in a set of legal categories lend an artificial rigidity to the fluidity of sexual desire and expression. As is evident from anthropological research in various parts of the world, the categories 'gay' and 'lesbian' – and indeed 'bisexual' and 'transgender' – are terms that arise from specific cultural contexts, and may fail to map the complexity of desires, identities and practices in other cultural contexts (Herdt 1994; Roscoe and Murray 1998; Samelius and Wagberg 2005).

In his contribution to this volume, Sumit Baudh explores a novel solution to this dilemma in the form of an argument for sexual autonomy as a human right. Baudh explores the basis on which sexual rights claims have been framed in human rights terms. He examines the archaic colonial law proscribing 'carnal acts against the law of nature' which forms the basis for Section 377 of the Indian Penal Code. Section 377 itself goes beyond identity to impose on the sexualities of all those in India, even if, as Baudh points out, it is largely applied to specific subjects – men who have sex with men. The right to sexual autonomy would be a fitting response, he argues, as it can be applied to all. As Baudh suggests, reframing the basis for claiming sexual rights as human rights in terms that can be applied regardless of sexual identity could ground activism in the longer run.

Gender and sex orders

Development perspectives on sexuality are generally limited to the problems associated with sexual relations such as unwanted pregnancy, sexually transmitted infections, rape and HIV/AIDS, and how to prevent them. But there are other important linkages that are implicitly made in the very way in which development interventions and models are structured, which are less visible. Many of the development implications of sexuality stem directly from the gender and sex orders that prescribe how we should live our everyday lives, what we do to earn a living and hold on to our jobs, what kinds of families we have and how we are treated in public, as well as in our private relationships. And while those whose sexualities depart from socially sanctioned norms suffer exclusion and prejudice – and, in some societies, often violent forms of repression – those who conform to these norms may also suffer the consequences of the limits to freedom and well-being that arise from the regulation of sexuality.

Most development interventions are premised not only on heteronormativity – assuming and enforcing heterosexuality as the norm – but also on marriage normativity (Sharma, Corrêa and Jolly, this volume). This serves to reproduce and reinforce prevalent social norms that restrict the choices available to women, men and transgender people. It finds tangible form in the restrictions and stigma experienced by non-married women seeking sexual and reproductive health services. It is encoded in the legal frameworks that persist in many countries which deny non-married partners the entitlements that married couples enjoy, whether rights to inheritance or to be considered next of kin. And it finds expression in restrictions women experience in many countries in pursuing independent lives, from being able to rent somewhere to live to being able to gain social acceptance as single women.

Gender and sex orders are constituted and reconstituted in every domain of our lives, from our most intimate relationships to relations

11

within the workplace, and more broadly in the political and economic spheres. Alan Greig notes:

> The violence of state laws and institutions is reinforced by violence at community level, ranging from discrimination to assault by peers, colleagues and family members. Those people who challenge norms of gender and sexuality through their sexual desires and practices and/or their gender 'presentation' face some of the most severe forms of social stigma and disapproval.

As Alejandra Sardá's account of the discrimination faced by lesbians in the workplace shows, the policing of gender identities at work produces forms of discrimination that currently lie outside the frame for equal opportunities legislation, yet have devastating consequences. She takes us beyond consideration of compulsory heterosexuality to compulsory *gender normativity*: as she shows, those who face the most blatant forms of discrimination are those who fail to conform to normative expectations of gender expression, women who adopt 'masculine' modes of dress and behaviour – irrespective of their sexual preferences. Greig describes how men who 'betray' their gender through their 'feminine' representation and/or sexual relations with other men may face violence and discrimination. Violence maintains the gender and sexuality hierarchy by keeping the men 'who are not men enough' in their place, and threatening men who strive to be 'man enough' with sanctions if they lapse. Furthermore, gender socialization may inhibit men's ability to experience joy, dignity, autonomy and safety in their sexual lives.

Progressive legal frameworks are a step towards breaking with gender and sex orders that hinder the realization of human rights and development. But where progressive laws depart from everyday beliefs and practices, challenges arise. Kopano Ratele's account of the conduct of the leading South African politician Jacob Zuma shows what can happen where legal provision meets socially embedded normativities. Appearing in a national media campaign encouraging more open discussion of sex, Zuma – who was at the time deputy president of South Africa – suggested during a public debate that oral sex was both unnatural and wrong. Ratele explains how this discursive act contravenes South Africa's progressive constitution, and how the effects of Zuma's 'ruling masculinity' imperil everyone's sexual rights.

Questions of 'culture' provide a common thread that runs through the different contributions in this section of the book. The law can both converge with or diverge from a societal culture. There are cases where constitutional principles and legal frames appear to be ahead of dominant social perceptions and practices – as in the case of South Africa. In other cases, the legal norms are more repressive than the realities of everyday sexual practices. In both cases arguments of culture are used to curtail social transformation or demand legal change. The chapters in this section suggest that everywhere the supposed cohesion of 'culture' is contested. Sexual practices and meanings vary widely across history, culture and individual trajectories, and are related with and transformed by economic and political processes (Parker and Gagnon 1994; Parker and Aggleton 1999). The boundaries of each and every 'culture' are being transformed by the power dynamics of today's globalizing world. Talk of 'culture', 'tradition' and indeed modernity comes to be selectively appropriated by powerful political actors to impose their particular views on societies. It becomes all the more important to ask 'which culture?', 'whose tradition?' and in whose name appeals to 'culture' and 'tradition' are made.

In many parts of the world, today's gender and sex orders are, as Giuseppe Campuzano's chapter reminds us, artefacts of processes of colonization. Campuzano contextualizes transgender identities in contemporary Peru in indigenous cultural forms that were virtually obliterated as Spanish colonial conquest sought to remodel Peruvian society. The fluidity of gender and sexual expression that preceded colonization came to be remoulded to conform with the colonizers' rigid binaries. In this context, the very visible contestation of binaries of gender and sexuality by *travestis*, as they create alternative cultural repertoires, becomes the focus for violent repression. What we see in Campuzano's account is a convergence between legal norms, religious frames and cultural constructs.

The societal enforcement of sexual and gender normativities finds its most brutal expression in the policing of non-normative expressions of gender and sexuality, but it also has consequences for those who conform. Sabina Faiz Rashid's chapter explores the lives and choices of young Bangladeshi women living in poverty in a Dhaka slum. In a nuanced account of the limits of and possibilities for agency, she shows how the very absence of alternatives may make marriage the only resource for poorer women. As one adolescent woman with a young child explained: 'If one's husband is not there, then what work will I do? How will I look after my child and bring him up? If one does not have a husband then one is always in tension – what will happen to me? Will someone harm me?' With limited room for manoeuvre, young women are able to exercise tactics that may marginally improve their lot within the existing order, rather than fundamentally challenge it. Rashid shows how the

13

gender order is beginning to shift, and the tensions and dilemmas that new manifestations of sexualities provoke for women. What becomes evident from her account is the need not to underestimate the security, and occasionally even pleasures, that people may find in compliance with prevailing gender and sex orders, not least in a context of extreme poverty where so much else is at stake.

Efforts to institutionalize 'gender' in development have sought to address the pervasive inequalities experienced by women in gender and sex orders the world over. But, paradoxically, they have often done so through the reinforcement of binary notions of gender and the sub-stitution of one set of stereotypes for another, rather than challenging stereotyping itself (Cornwall et al. 2007). 'Gender' is commonly used as shorthand for 'women'; women appear as an undifferentiated mass of vic-tims, men become the 'problem', and the complexity of gendered power relations is reduced to a simple equation in which women are always at a disadvantage (Cornwall 2000). This is not to deny what Connell has termed the 'patriarchal dividend' (Greig, this volume; Connell 1995). Yet it signals the conceptual and political limits of Gender and Development discourse, which has done little to disrupt the repressive effects of gender binaries, nor their heteronormativity. Gender and Development has yet to take on the theoretical developments of the 1990s, which highlight the mutability of sex and gender (see, for example, Butler 1990, 1994) and the oppressive effects of societal pressure to behave 'like women' or 'like men'. By casting women as victims and men as predators, narratives on female and male sexuality in development leave little space for the possibility of female sexual desire or male sexual vulnerability, let alone for pleasure.

Nowhere are these narratives of victim and predator more visible and potent than in relation to trafficking and sex work. Recourse to punitive measures – prosecuting either the provider or the purchaser – is often seen as a way of curtailing the sale of sex. As Jelena Djordjevic's account of the experiences of Serbian sex workers shows, however, criminaliza-tion can simply exacerbate the vulnerability of women in sex work to abuse: police violence, in this context, poses a far greater hazard to the lives and well-being of sex workers than most face in relation to clients. Global measures adopted to address the traffic in women for sex work are having, Djordjevic and Ditmore suggest, damaging effects at the local level which may end up exacerbating women's vulnerability to traffick-ing. Shireen Huq describes the Bangladesh government's forceful evic-tion of sex workers from a large cluster of brothels just outside Dhaka. Without any warning, truckloads of police descended on the nearly two thousand women and children living in the brothels, forcibly taking many to 'vagrant homes'. What these and other studies suggest is that increase in state powers over sex workers can result in increased police violence, and that interventions that seek to 'save' sex workers can end up making their lives more difficult and dangerous. These accounts have worrying implications for policies, such as those pursued by Sweden, which seek to export a model of abolishing prostitution by criminalizing clients, rather than starting from the realities and priorities of sex workers themselves.

Changing mindsets

What does it take to bring about the kinds of change that the contributions to this book argue are so urgently needed? The third section addresses a range of ways in which those working in the field of sexuality have brought about change, from which valuable lessons can be drawn.

As we argued earlier, some of the paradoxes that efforts to link sexuality, human rights and development need to grapple with are those of identity policies and gender essentialism. Making alliances beyond the restrictions of identity politics and gender binaries can provide avenues for overcoming these dilemmas. Shireen Huq provides an inspiring account of two different constituencies becoming '*attiyo*' or related, when evicted sex workers sought support from Naripokkho, a national women's network in Bangladesh. With nowhere to live, several moved into the network's offices and homes of staff. The new alliance went beyond political solidarity to evolve into friendships emerging over endless cups of tea. Discussions developed Naripokkho's analysis of sexual freedom, and the presence of transgender sex workers led them to question the sex/gender dichotomy, and eventually admit transgender groups into their networks.

Another pathway to change is through remodelling existing programmes and institutions to make them better fit complex realities. Nike Esiet's chapter addresses questions of institutionalization, in the complex and contradictory context of contemporary Nigeria. In the intensely hostile environment for the promotion of a more open approach to sexuality education, what the programme she describes managed to achieve is nothing short of remarkable. Esiet's account reminds us of the very real challenges that exist in those political contexts where good policy guidelines are in place which openly conflict with prevailing institutional and financial conditions, as well as dominant mindsets. Sexuality education, Esiet argues, is fundamental if young women and men are to enjoy safer sexual relations, particularly in Nigeria, where the

15

rates of HIV/AIDS and teenage pregnancy are very high. Though excellent guidelines have been adopted by the federal government and some states, implementation is extremely difficult because opposing views – such as the abstinence-only arguments pushed by USAID – are also strongly at play in the same policy context.

It is not only the young who can benefit from transformative learning about sexuality, as Jill Lewis and Gill Gordon (this volume) illustrate. Drawing on their experience of working with sex and sexuality in workshops for adults, they find new ways to talk about sex as pleasurable, rather than shameful, and as a source of joy rather than only in terms of disease and death. Their hands-on experience facilitating these workshops yields lessons about context and power which emphasize the importance of exploring how pleasure is constructed, as well as the diversity in what people find pleasurable. Understanding when pleasure-seeking leads to taking risks, and promoting the pleasures of safer sex, is a much-needed part of HIV/AIDS prevention, and can also be empowering in itself.

Henry Armas's call for a 'democracy of sexuality' implies reflection on issues of power and respect in our own sexual relationships, as well as the meaningful participation of those with non-conforming sexualities in policies and programmes. Sexuality matters for democratic citizenship, Armas argues; if people are to enjoy the very right to have rights, then their rights to participation, inclusion and non-discrimination need to be promoted and protected. For some marginalized groups, the opportunity to participate in determining what might make a difference to their lives generates very different solutions to those of external agencies. Ditmore gives the example of the slogan used by Cambodian sex workers: 'Don't talk to me about sewing machines, talk to me about workers rights', and cites the much-praised Sonagachi project in India, which involves clients and relatives of sex workers, as well as sex workers themselves, in making sex work safer – with significant impacts on HIV prevalence. Armas reminds us, however, of the need for caution in the embrace of participation as a panacea. Conservatism within communities can remain unchecked by the naïve uses of participatory methodologies. Armas shows how the human rights framework can offer normative underpinnings that can help to guide the process of participation – as it provides, at the same time, a set of non-negotiable principles that include non-discrimination. Because sexuality is an issue that enables people to work with politics at a personal level, he argues, the very intimacy of working with issues of citizenship and rights through the lens of sexuality makes space for a transformative process of self-reflection that can lead to social action.

In a similar vein, Pinar Ilkkaracan and Karin Ronge's chapter shows how for those who have never been given the opportunity to voice their experiences, simply creating spaces in which it becomes possible to talk and listen can be enormously empowering. It is also a reminder of the importance of understanding the context from the point of view of those within, of retracing the historical path of existing legislation, and of recognizing that most national struggles for sexual rights are crossed by transnational trends. Ilkkaracan and Ronge describe the incredible momentum that was generated as women came together to demand – and succeed in bringing about – changes to the conservative Turkish penal code. The chapter complexifies the analysis in regard to secularity and religion, as the penal code being reformed was not a *shar'ia*-based law, but rather a legacy of the secular state established by Atatürk, inspired by the Italian code of the Mussolini fascist period. It also underlines how the internal legal debate cannot be fully understood without taking into account Turkey's desire to join the European Union, and European assumptions that the main sexuality issue is honour crime, a view that sidelines many other sexual rights claims.

One lesson emerging from the diversity of examples this book brings together applies across the board to development policies and interventions: the need to pay closer attention to what works for particular contexts, rather than superimposing normative categories and prescriptions on vastly dissimilar settings. Development agencies have barely begun to grapple with the challenge of contextualizing their policies and interventions. Lip-service may be given to the significance of understanding what works in any given social, cultural or political setting. But in practice, mainstream development agencies are fonder of one-size-fits-all 'magic bullets' that can be 'scaled up' irrespective of the setting.

Important differences in state and social formations preclude readily transferable solutions. This is particularly the case in relation to sexuality. Different configurations of social, statutory and religious institutions lend an entirely different complexion to struggles to secure greater sexual rights and well-being. To complicate matters further, there may be little uniformity within any given context in the way in which particular dimensions of sexuality intersect with development and human rights. Take, for example, Brazil, a country with some of the most progressive legislation on sexuality in the world, considerable openness when it comes to talking about sex, and an increasingly visible and vocal presence of LGBT people and sex workers. For all its progressive laws and policies on the rights of these groups, Brazil denies women basic reproductive rights and homophobic-motivated human rights violations constitute a daily reality.

In any given context, the particular mix of openings and blockages will differ. Sometimes these opportunities are very localized; at other times, pathways to change may be circuitous and complex, as longer-term goals come to be pursued through incremental progress.

Political realities shape ways of taking action and constraints to action. Here the human rights framework can be especially valuable, as an analytical tool that permits situational analysis of entry points for progressive change. This is precisely because the human rights principle of indivisibility permits a more integrated and holistic approach, which in turn facilitates the kind of 'out of the box' thinking that is needed to address the preconditions for the realization of rights. The normative dimensions of human rights are also important, even if they present their own challenges – such as the potential generation of restrictive norms by human rights discourses themselves. Human rights norms can, however, also provide the scope to contest the way in which 'culture' is used politically to close down debate on sexuality. They offer legal instruments that can allow for challenges to states that contravene conventions they have signed. And they provide a powerful moral basis on which to contest violations of rights and freedoms of all people, and, as Paul Hunt puts it, 'to name without shame'.

Conclusions

'Sexuality lies at the core of human life, of what makes us fully human – it is the key to our capacity to contribute positively and fully to the societies we live in.' Carin Jämtin, former Swedish Minister for International Development Cooperation[2]

The linkages between sexuality, human rights and development constitute a vast landscape, one that is complex, heterogeneous and constantly contested. Approaching sexuality through a human rights and development lens builds on the connections that have been increasingly made in recent years between development and human rights. Adding sexuality to the equation takes us further, to reframe development itself as fundamentally concerned with the promotion of the well-being of people as *whole people* – not just in relation to their utility or capacities, their economic or social needs or their civil and political rights, but in terms of all that makes us fully human.

Sexuality matters for development precisely because it has become such a battleground. Neoconservative forces have staked out positions into which millions of dollars are being funnelled. They promote abstinence, the denial of contraception to young people and non-married women, the prohibition of abortion, the repression of homosexuality, and cutting off funding to those who work with sex workers. These agendas deny the realities and dilemmas of sexual relationships. They shore up, rather than seeking to transform, existing gender and sex orders. And they hinder efforts to reduce HIV infection.

What's needed, we argue, are efforts by progressive development actors to reclaim sexuality as an important area of human experience. Extending analyses of poverty to encompass sexuality and using the human rights framework to 'name without shame' – as Paul Hunt puts it in his preface to this volume – are steps forward. Development can take account of sexuality beyond the associations between the denial of sexual rights and deprivation, discrimination and injustice. Breaking the silence on sexuality opens a space for a more positive, affirming approach to development: one that can take up terms that have never been part of the development lexicon – love, pleasure, respect, tolerance – as well as recover those, like solidarity and mutuality, that have been lost in the passage of time. There are no easy solutions, no models, no blueprints. But there are experiences that inspire and ways of thinking about these connections that can help to orient action. This book seeks to offer both.

Notes

1 In discussion at the Realizing Sexual Rights workshop at IDS, September 2005.

2. Address given to the Stockholm seminar on 'Sexuality, Human Rights and Development: Making the Connections', 6 April 2006.

References

Altman, D. (2001) *Global Sex*, Chicago, IL: University of Chicago Press.

Butler, J. (1990) *Gender Trouble: Feminism and the Subversion of Identity*, New York and London: Routledge.

— (1994) 'Gender as performance: an interview with Judith Butler', *Radical Philosophy*, 67, Summer, pp. 32–9.

Castañeda, C. (1998) 'Historia de la sexualidad, investigaciónes del período colonial', in I. Szazs and S. Lerner (eds), *Sexualidades en Mexico, Algunas Aproximaciones desde la Ciencias Sociales*, Mexico City: Colégio de México.

Castells, M. (1996) *The Rise of Network Society*, Malden, MA: Blackwell.

— (1997) *The Power of Identity*, Malden, MA: Blackwell.

— (1998) *End of Millennium*, Malden, MA: Blackwell.

Chambers, R. (1997) *Whose Reality Counts? Putting the First Last*, London: Intermediate Technology Publications.

— (2005) 'Participation, pluralism and perceptions of poverty', Paper for conference on 'The many dimensions of poverty', Brazil, August, <www.undp-povertycentre. org/md%2Dpoverty/papers/ Robert_.pdf> (accessed 20 May 2007).

Connell, R. W. (1995) *Masculinities*, London: Allen and Unwin.

Cornwall, A. (2000) 'Missing men? Reflections on men, masculinities and gender in GAD', *IDS Bulletin*, 31(2): 18–27.

Cornwall, A., E. Harrison and A. Whitehead (2007) 'Gender myths and feminist fables: the struggle for interpretive power in Gender and Development', *Development and Change*, 38(1): 1–20.

Corrêa, S. and R. Parker (2004) 'Sexuality, human rights, and demographic thinking: connections and disjunctions in a changing world', *Sexuality Research and Social Policy*, 1(1): 15–38.

Crompton, L. (2003) *Homosexuality and Civilization*, Cambridge, MA: Belkap Press/Harvard University Press.

Delaney, C. (1995) 'Father, motherland and the birth of modern Turkey', in S. Yanagisano and C. Delaney (eds), *Naturalizing Power*, New York: Routledge.

Foucault, M. (1980) *The History of Sexuality*, Part 1, Harmondsworth: Penguin.

Fraser, N. (1989) *Unruly Practices: Power, Discourse and Gender in Contemporary Social Theory*, Minneapolis: University of Minnesota Press and Polity Press.

Giddens, A. (1991) *Modernity and Self-Identity: Self and Society in the Late Modern Age*, Cambridge: Polity Press.

— (2000) *Runaway World*, New York: Routledge.

Girard, F. (2001) 'Reproductive health under attack at the United Nations', *Reproductive Health Matters*, 9(18): 68.

Gosine, A. (2004) 'Sex for pleasure, rights to participation, and alternatives to AIDS: placing sexual minorities and/or dissidents in development', IDS Working Paper 228, Brighton: IDS.

Held, D., A. McGrew, D. Goldblatt and J. Perraton (1999) *Global Transformations: Politics, Economics and Culture*, Cambridge: Polity Press.

Herdt, G. (1994) *Third Sex, Third Gender: Beyond Sexual Dimorphism in Culture and History*, New York: Zone Books.

Ilkkaracan, P., S. Jolly and E. Esplen (2007) *Gender and Sexuality Cutting Edge Pack*, Brighton: BRIDGE.

Jolly, S. (2007) 'Why the development industry should get over its obsession with bad sex and start talking about pleasure', IDS Working Paper 283, Brighton: IDS.

Kabeer, N. (2006) *Inclusive Citizenship*, London: Zed Books.

Laqueur, T. (1992) *Making Sex: Body and Gender from the Greeks to Freud*, Cambridge, MA: Harvard University Press.

Mott, L. (1992), 'Justicia et misericordia – a inquisição portuguesa e a repressão ao nefando pecado da sodomia', in A. Novinsky and M. L. Tucci Carneiro (eds), *Inquisição: Ensaios sobre Mentalidades, Heresia e Arte*, São Paulo: EDUSP.

Nussbaum, M. (2000) *Women and Human Development: The Capabilities Approach*, Cambridge: Cambridge University Press.

Parker, R. and J. Gagnon (1994) *Conceiving Sexuality: Approaches to Sex Research in a Postmodern World*, London: Routledge.

Parker, R. G. and P. Aggleton (eds) (1999) *Culture, Society and Sexuality: A Reader*, London: UCL Press.

Petchesky, R. (2003) *Global Prescriptions: Gendering Health and*

Human Rights, London and New York: Zed Books.

Rago, M. (1991) *Os Prazeres da Noite; Prostituição e Códigos da Sexualidade Feminina em São Paulo*, São Paulo: Paz e Terra.

Roscoe, W. and S. Murray (1998) *Boy-Wives and Female-Husbands: Studies of African Homosexualities*, New York: St Martin's Press.

Rubin, G. (1984) 'Thinking sex: notes for a radical theory of the politics of sexuality', in C. Vance (ed.), *Pleasure and Danger: Exploring Female Sexuality*, London: Pandora Press.

Runeborg, A. (2002) *Sexuality – a Super Force: Young People, Sexuality and Rights in the Era of HIV/AIDS*, Stockholm: Sida.

Saiz, I. (2004) 'Bracketing sexuality: human rights and sexual orientation – a decade of development and denial at the United Nations', *Health and Human Rights*, 7(2): 48–81.

Samelius, L. and E. Wagberg (2005) *Sexual Orientation and Gender Identity Issues in Development: A Study of Swedish Policy and Administration of Lesbian, Gay, Bisexual and Transgender Issues in International Development Cooperation*, Sida Health Division Document, <www.ilga-europe.org/europe/guide/country_by_country/sweden/sexual_orientation_and_gender_identity_issues_in_development.html> (accessed 21 May 2007).

Sen, A. (1995) *Inequality Re-examined*, Cambridge, MA: Harvard University Press.

Sen, G. (2005) 'Neolibs, neocons and gender justice: lessons from global negotiations', UNRISD Occasional Paper 9, September, Geneva: United Nations Research Institute for Social Development.

Sen, G. and S. Corrêa (2000) *Gender Justice and Economic Justice: Reflections on the Five Year Reviews of the UN Conferences of the 1990s*, Calabar, Nigeria: DAWN Inform.

Uvin, P. (2002) 'On high moral ground: the incorporation of human rights by the development enterprise, PRAXIS', *Fletcher Journal of Human Security*, Development and Human Rights issue, XVII: 19–26.

Van der Meer, T. (2004) 'Pre-modern origins of modern homophobia and masculinity', *Sexuality Research and Social Policy*, 1(2): 77–90.

Weeks, J. (1985) *Sexuality and Its Discontents: Meanings, Myths and Modern Sexualities*, London: Routledge and Kegan Paul.

— (2003) *Sexuality* (2nd edn), New York: Routledge.

2 | Development's encounter with sexuality: essentialism and beyond

SONIA CORRÊA AND SUSIE JOLLY

Conceptualizing 'sex': essentialism and constructivism

Exploring the connections between sexuality, development and human rights requires that the dominant conceptualization of sex as a natural force be critically revisited. As is widely recognized, in the Western philosophical and religious tradition this view of sex has been and remains pervasive and compelling. Suffice to remind: the essentialist conception of sex underlies Aristotle's and Kant's ideas – which are foundational references to contemporary ethics and human rights. It is also of crucial relevance to Darwinist and post-Darwinist interpretations of social realities, and to the recurrent imbrications of sex and sin in Christian doctrine.

Though from the late eighteenth century onwards sexuality became a highly contested political terrain, this natural conception of sex was not so easily shaken. Rather, the development of science reinforced naturalistic assumptions, further crystallizing the widespread idea that sex is a unified domain of human experience (Weeks 1985, 2003). This formulation is at the core of biomedical discourses and practices and its imprint is unmistakable in psychoanalysis, sexology and social psychology and the early twentieth-century libertarian sexual theories and politics, which deeply influenced the 1960s cultural revolution.[1] Last but not least, though in a much subtler manner, the idea of sex as drive also lurks behind economic and educational theories.

Over the past few decades, however, sex essentialism has been systematically challenged by a wide range of philosophers, historians, social anthropologists and interactionist sociologists, and also feminists and queer theorists (Plummer 2000; Weeks 1985, 2003). These various streams of sex thinking can be loosely grouped as constructivist theories of sexuality which emphasize the culturally and linguistically constructed characteristics of sexual identities and meanings, and the embeddedness of sex taxonomies and practices in the power at play in institutional and social discourses. They argue that sexuality interweaves in complex ways with several crucial dimensions of human lives and is transformed by economic and political processes (Parker and Gagnon 1994; Parker and Aggleton 1999).

Though this epistemological shift has been evolving since the mid-1970s, it remains far from complete. Biological interpretations of sexual behaviour and gender roles have not lost ground in the last thirty years. Rather they have gained sophistication, depth and public appeal, repositing sex as a unified domain of human experience and militating against recognizing the ample evidence of variations in sexual practices and meanings within and between cultures (see, for example, Herdt 1987; Morgan and Wieringa 2005).

Conceptualizing women, men and sex as fundamentally determined by unchangeable natural laws leaves no room for transformation, plasticity or re-creation. This greatly compromises the articulation of sexuality, social change, democracy and human rights, and of 'development' conceived as the cumulative improvement of human subjectivities and relations. It also obscures the ways in which power operates through sex both through the construction of sex hierarchies on the basis of 'natural' sexual conducts and by a still resonant colonial discourse on sexuality which affirms the civilized nature of the colonizer. Anthropological research since the 1970s on same-sex relations throughout Western history and in a wide variety of cultural contexts (Parker and Aggleton 1999; Weeks 1985, 2003) has also revealed how sex hierarchies intersect with other forms of stratification – such as race, class, ethnicity and age – and translate into power differentials, socio-economic inequalities, stigma, discrimination and abuse.

A constructivist approach to sexuality, on the other hand, can allow for recognition of great variations in sexualities across cultures, moving beyond the easy supposition that the same fixed set of sexual identities are reproduced in every context (Samelius and Wagberg 2005). It challenges the hierarchy of 'natural' and 'unnatural' itself, instead of just shifting the place of certain sexualities within that hierarchy. Most importantly it creates a solid ground for sexual pluralism as a democratic value, and for the expansion of sexual rights claims as in the 1990s and early 2000s.

The adoption of constructivist theories of sex does not imply, however, the erasure of bodies and biology. It emphasizes instead how sexual identities, desires and practices are constituted through a complex and unstable interweaving of biology, anatomy, intellect and discourses. Petchesky's (2005) reconceptualization of body politics provides a possible frame to further examine these connections. She seeks to move beyond the constantly resurfacing binary logic underpinning feminist theorizing and practices – male/female, sex/gender, body/social construct – to articulate a vision of bodies that are sexualized and desiring, but which also labour, reproduce, experience hunger and illness and consume. Supported by the work of the radical biologist Fausto-Sterling, Petchesky explores how the subtle articulations between the body (the external image), biology (the inside) and social construction and contingencies (the outside) operate. She concludes, in line with Butler, that bodies and 'sex' 'simultaneously produce and are reproduced by social meanings'.

Development's encounters with sexuality

Sex essentialism, often interpreted as silence on the subject, has been and continues to be a recurrent subtext of development theories, values and applications. In the post-Second World War period, for example, much thinking was devoted to understanding and promoting fertility decline. It is not possible to intervene in fertility without acknowledging the complexities of heterosexuality, in particular power inequalities between women and men. Yet for more than forty years population policy recommendations managed to ignore these, as if they were a part of the natural order that could not be challenged or changed. Thousands of pages have been written on population that address complex demographic and macroeconomic aspects without ever mentioning the word sexuality, even when women's status eventually began to be taken into account. In terms of policy prescriptions, an obsession with technological fixes to bypass naturalized fertility preferences has dominated the field.

Related to this is the implied assumption in liberal economic thinking that sexuality is a natural and individual preference which does not need to be factored in. As pointed out by Nussbaum (1999), faith in the given nature of preference obscures the distortions of choice and desire that result from cultural constructs such as gender and sexual norms. While the bulk of liberal economic theory does not spell out its assumptions about sexuality, it is reasonable to suggest that sexuality is assumed to be a natural individual preference or behaviour, and that within this naturalization, sex is fundamentally heterosexual and related to the construction of the family as a main 'economic unit'. The classic household model, for example, assumes a heterosexual family, with the man as the head, hence invisibilizing other kinds of relationships. If a woman lives in a lesbian relationship, the household would be likely to be categorized as a 'female-headed household' – a term which generally applies to single women with children/other dependants since it is assumed that a woman cannot head a household in which a man is present. Given that the household still remains the basic unit of economic analysis, for example by economists involved in Poverty Reduction Strategy Processes (PRSPs), this is not a minor problem.

Nevertheless, in recent years development's encounters with sexuality have – in limited ways at least – become increasingly open across a variety of contexts, and deserve further investigation.

Public health, population and HIV/AIDS Public health is one crossroads at which 'development' and 'sexuality' have intersected for some time. The otherwise divergent progressive and liberal economics approaches have found in public health a certain amount to agree on – for example, the principle of promoting the public good in terms of reducing death tolls and bodily suffering. Yet public health frameworks, while indispensable to promoting social equity and well-being, also imply a series of risks and distortions in relation to gender and sexuality. They tend, for example, to naturalize gender, constantly pushing women back to reproductive roles, and deploying epidemiological taxonomies that easily lapse into sex-based discrimination and stigma.

This tendency is illustrated by research recently carried out by SOS Corpo, a feminist NGO, in the city of Recife in Brazil, which found, for instance, that female sex workers and male homosexuals were often denied access to services by the Family Health Programme (FHP) that constitutes the country's main primary health strategy. Additionally observations of FHP consultations and counselling revealed conventional assumptions of men being active and women passive in the discourses and conducts of health teams. The research also concluded that FHP teams – including the community health workers – often function as 'family police'. Mothers effectively relied on these professionals to control their daughters' sexuality and inform them when something 'wrong' happened.

In the field of population and women's health, progress has been tangible, but with equally worrying limitations. After the previous 'sexual silence' in population and reproductive health discourses, the outburst on the issue of sexuality in the Cairo process deeply astonished many actors. The feminist critique that made possible this outburst had targeted distinct but related dimensions: the coercion and objectification of women; male–female power differentials with regard to reproductive decisions; and the negative or sidelined health effects of contraceptives. This examination was a key element behind the call for sexual health and sexual rights in the International Conference for Population and Development (ICPD) and in the Beijing Platform for Action (PFA), which finally led to the PFA's famous Paragraph 96:

> The human rights of women include their right to have control over and decide freely and responsibly on matters related to their sexuality,

including sexual and reproductive health, free of coercion, discrimination and violence. Equal relationships between women and men in matters of sexual relations and reproduction, including full respect for the integrity of the person, require mutual respect, consent and shared responsibility for sexual behaviour and its consequences.

The Cairo and Beijing conceptual breakthroughs must be lauded. It is also necessary, however, to underline the hybrid nature of Paragraph 96. While its first sentence opens the ground for a malleable perspective on sexuality and rights, the second sentence has a strong heterosexual imprint (Petchesky 2000, 2003; Corrêa and Parker 2004). That women's sexual rights are exclusively placed in the health chapter is also significant, in particular because it has not been possible to adopt language condemning discrimination on the basis of sexual orientation in the section of the platform that addresses human rights. These caveats have been correctly criticized by LGBT and sex worker advocates in the last ten years. At the same time they have been extensively manipulated by conservative sectors as tools against further policy advancements in the realm of sexual rights. Most importantly, in the aftermath of Beijing, the concept of sexual rights has been predominantly used in mainstream policy discourse in limited senses, in relation to violence, disease and abuse (Corrêa and Parker 2004). As sharply identified by Petchesky (2000), Paragraph 96 was mainly driven by a victimization framework that restricted the application of sexual rights to a positive perspective that would also address pleasure and well-being.

In contrast to the public health field and the population debate, in the case of HIV/AIDS modes of transmission and the identity of the first visible 'victims' made it virtually impossible to entirely sideline sexuality. But not surprisingly, this has immediately triggered streams of epidemiological and behavioural research as well as policy responses characterized by stigma and denial. The icons of these trends are the 'gay cancer' discourse of the early 1980s and the systematic refusal by a wide range of governments to recognize the existence and effect of the epidemics.

HIV/AIDS-related discrimination and stigma have many sources. But in their multiple manifestations they are related to naturalized assumptions about sex and the taxonomies and hierarchies that follow. Indeed, the three decades of HIV/AIDS responses can be portrayed as a continuous confrontation between essentialist and constructionist streams of thought. In mobilization around HIV/AIDS the connections between bodies that are sexual, desiring, labouring, reproducing, experiencing hunger and illness and consuming appear under a new light (Petchesky

2003). In the intervention she made at the 2006 Toronto AIDS Conference, Petchesky noted that even today three major policy challenges must be addressed: to place sexuality at the core of the responses to HIV/AIDS; to recognize that sexuality is integral to a matrix of social, economic, cultural and relational forces; and to recognize that a human rights approach has the potential to accommodate the social, cultural and economic complexity of the epidemics.

Unfortunately, however, rather than using these powerful lenses to move forward, biomedical approaches remain dominant, tending to desexualize the pandemic and focus on technological fixes rather than social change. Paradoxically, conservative forces have done their best to bring sexuality back into the HIV/AIDS agenda as a dangerous and damaging force to be controlled and constrained, once more obscuring how HIV infection rates and 'risks' are defined by social, sexual and gender power relations (Sember and Corrêa 2006).

Human development, poverty and participation The human development discourse, with its overall emphasis on equity and empowerment, constitutes a privileged terrain to further expand the connections between sexuality, human rights and development. A brief overview of Human Development Reports (HDRs) (UNDP 1990–2005) provides insights into how these potential articulations have thus far been made.

Via attention to the HIV/AIDS epidemics, which have been addressed by practically all reports since 1990, the ground for exploring these connections has been somewhat prepared. The reports have variously emphasized the impact of HIV/AIDS on human development and human security, the devastating effects of the epidemics on productive generations and life expectancy, and problems of health infrastructure and constraints in health funding as the main obstacles to policy responses. At least one report (1992) mentions behavioural change and condom distribution. The 1993 report focusing on 'people's participation' made a key shift by calling attention to local participatory initiatives working on HIV/AIDS prevention. The 2002 report, *Deepening Democracy*, highlights the campaign for treatment access led by Doctors without Borders, which shifted the focus from participation at local to global arenas, and from national policy barriers to macroeconomic obstacles to responses to the crisis. In the 2005 report, *Aid, Trade and Security*, HIV/AIDS becomes a central topic of human development and the analysis strongly underlines the epidemics as a key factor behind identified falls in human development indicators, particularly in Africa.

Nevertheless, direct references to 'sex/sexual/sexuality' are much less abundant and uneven, although not absent. These terms are almost non-existent in the 1990s reports, including, surprisingly, the 1995 report, *Gender and Human Development*, except in reference to statistical data. But they appear more frequently in three of the HDRs of the new millennium. The 2000 Human Development and Human Rights Report analyses situations of infringement of rights in respect of the sexual abuse of girls, sexual orientation and sexual minorities. The 1994 decision of the UN Human Rights Committee on sexual orientation (Toonen vs. Australia) and the non-discrimination constitutional clauses adopted in Ecuador, Fiji and South Africa are also highlighted. Sexuality is also openly addressed – albeit discreetly in relation to other cultural identities – in the 2004 report, *Human Development and Cultural Liberty*. This publication expands the terminology adopted in 2000 to include the notion that 'living modes' do not justify discrimination, as well as using other key terms such as 'gender difference', 'bisexual', 'non sexist society' and 'hate crimes'. This report is remarkable in its balanced but extremely sophisticated exploration of the thorny challenges posed by the linkage of human development, human rights and multiculturalism and, given the policy climate, it should be credited for not entirely sidelining sexuality. The 2005 report, while raising the status of HIV/AIDS to macro policy levels, is also peppered with sexual terms. But here the tone is different: the report refers exclusively to coercive sex, sexual exploitation of women and girls, sexual abuse in conflict situations.

But despite these connections, the caveats remain deep. Significantly, when the discourse focuses on inequality, sexuality simply vanishes. Equally significantly, no mention is made of sex in discussions on rights-based approaches to poverty. This sudden disappearance is a symptom of what the Mexican human rights activist Claudia Hinojosa identifies as the false dichotomy between the 'seriousness' of the problem of poverty and the 'frivolity' of sexuality which tends to prevail among progressive thinkers of development. Hinojosa suggests this dichotomy can be dismantled by documenting the 'invisible' links between sexual exclusion and poverty; economic deprivation and sexual violence; compulsory heterosexuality and homophobia; and hegemonic masculinity and various forms of violence (Rojas 2001).

The apparent resistance to recognizing the connections between sexuality and poverty is particularly significant in the recent context of the Millennium Development Goals (MDGs), which have firmly foregrounded poverty. The process leading up to the formulation of the MDGs, and the subsequent process of mapping their implementation, has been contaminated by the persistent incapacity of poverty thinking to acknowledge the

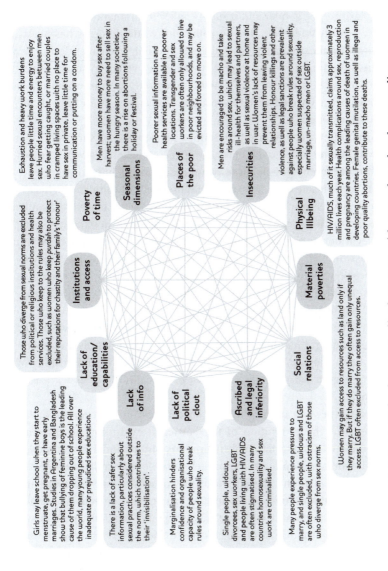

FIGURE 2.1 Web of poverty's disadvantages, with examples related to sexuality

The following are the text labels and boxes that appear in the figure:

Exhaustion and heavy work burdens leave people little time and energy to enjoy sex. Hurried sexual encounters between men who fear getting caught, or married couples in cramped living spaces with no place to have sex in private, leave little time for communication or putting on a condom.

Men have more money to buy sex after harvest; women have more need to sell sex in the hungry season. In many societies, there is a rise on abortions following a holiday or festival.

Poverty of time

Seasonal dimensions

Poorer sexual information and health services are available in poorer locations. Transgender and sex workers are often only allowed to live in poor neighbourhoods, and may be evicted and forced to move on.

Places of the poor

Those who diverge from sexual norms are excluded from political or religious institutions and health services. Those who keep to the rules may also be excluded, such as women who keep purdah to protect their reputations for chastity and their family's 'honour'.

Institutions and access

Men are encouraged to be macho and take risks around sex, which may lead to sexual ill-health for themselves and partners, as well as sexual violence at home and in war. Women's lack of resources may prevent them from leaving violent relationships. Honour killings and other violence, as well as legal sanctions are prevalent against people who break rules around sexuality, especially women suspected of sex outside marriage, un-macho men or LGBT.

Insecurities

Physical Illbeing

HIV/AIDS, much of it sexually transmitted, claims approximately 3 million lives each year. Health complications around sex, reproduction and pregnancy are among the leading causes of death of women in developing countries. Female genital mutilation, as well as illegal and poor quality abortions, contribute to these deaths.

Girls may leave school when they start to menstruate, get pregnant, or have early marriages. Studies in Argentina and Bangladesh show that bullying of feminine boys is the leading cause of them dropping out of school. All over the world, many young people experience inadequate or prejudiced sex education.

Lack of education/ capabilities

There is a lack of safer sex information, particularly about sexual practices considered outside the norm, which contributes to their 'invisibilisation'.

Lack of info

Marginalisation hinders confidence and organisational capacity of people who break rules around sexuality.

Lack of political clout

Single people, widows, divorcees, sex workers, LGBT and people living with HIV/AIDS are often stigmatised. In many countries homosexuality and sex work are criminalised.

Ascribed and legal inferiority

Many people experience pressure to marry, and single people, widows and LGBT are often excluded, with ostracism of those who diverge from sex norms.

Social relations

Women may gain access to resources such as land only if they marry. But if they do marry they often gain only unequal access. LGBT often excluded from access to resources.

Material poverties

meaning of sexuality in the lives of the poor. Feminist efforts were made to preserve the 1990s breakthroughs in relation to sexual and reproductive health and rights. In the conservative political climate following the hegemony of neoconservatives in the USA, however, and in response to a quest for tangibility which dramatically reduced the scope, depth and complexity of the gender and sexuality policy recommendations adopted in the 1990s conferences, the outcome of the MDG process has been a document almost entirely desexualized. The only clear mention of sex in the Millennium Project Report (UNDP 2005) refers to sexual education. Moreover, human rights – as the one policy area in which major advancements have occurred in relation to sexuality – were entirely left out (Robinson 2003).

Given the trajectory briefly described above it is not surprising that the MDG framework did not make a proper connection between sexuality and poverty even though these two dimensions of human experience are, in fact, closely linked. Sexual and reproductive health and rights are increasingly recognized as both cause and consequence of poverty (Family Care International 2005). Less recognized are the ways in which social and legal norms and economic structures based on sexuality constrain the possibility of people shaping their own lives, and impact on physical security, bodily integrity, health, education, mobility and economic status. In turn, these factors have an impact on people's opportunities to live out happier, healthier sexualities.

The intersections between sexuality and poverty can become visible by adapting Robert Chambers's framework 'Web of Poverty's Disadvantages' (Chambers 2005: 46), which identifies several possible dimensions of poverty. Figure 2.1 provides examples of sexuality linkages with each dimension.

One further site of encounters between development and sexuality has been in the promotion of the participatory approaches increasingly adopted by international institutions and national governments. Participatory development approaches were not generally intended to address sexuality, and the emphasis on consensus and on taking the lead from communities' own priorities can certainly effectively exclude minority positions and reinforce existing power relations, particularly around non-normative sexualities (Gosine 2004). Nevertheless, the opportunities these approaches sometimes create for people to raise issues important to themselves and to assert their own interpretations of their lives have in several instances led to the emergence of sexual politics within participatory spaces. This is particularly the case in HIV/AIDS policy and programmes, which created spaces for public conversations on sexuality and for the participation of groups and individuals usually excluded.

In 2003, for instance, the World Bank approved a loan to support the Brazilian HIV/AIDS programme which included funds for NGOs and community organizations working in public education and prevention. Civil society organizations supported by these resources cover a very wide spectrum, ranging from Catholic religious institutions that provide care to orphans and the sick, to lesbian, gay and feminist groups, as well as sex workers and transgender/*travesti* associations, the landless peasant movement, urban unions and a wide variety of community associations. This complex and contradictory web of civil society initiatives is organized into local forums and meets every two years in regional and national HIV/AIDS conferences. These are key locations for reconstructing sexual identities and struggling against discrimination, as well as for prevention work and policy monitoring. Civil society is represented on the National AIDS Commission, which was instrumental in 2005 in bringing about the suspension of the bilateral US–Brazil agreement providing funds for HIV/AIDS prevention: neither the government nor the NGOs would accept the US requirement to condemn prostitution as a precondition for receiving funds.

The success of the Brazilian HIV/AIDS national policy in terms of stabilizing mortality and infection rates is recognized internationally. At the same time, Brazil has witnessed a blossoming and public legitimization of LGBT politics, reflected in the geometric growth in participation of the São Paulo gay parade, which jumped from 2,000 people in 1997 to 250,000 in 2001 and to 2.5 million in 2005. It would be a mistake to say that participation in HIV/AIDS policy is the main cause behind this phenomenon, but it was undoubtedly one factor.

Human rights: the most promising estuary Human rights, and rights-based approaches to development, remain the most promising estuary for sexuality. The idea that rights could be claimed in relation to sexuality has been with us since at least the early nineteenth century. It was, however, immensely amplified in the libertarian atmosphere of the 1960s, the most immediate antecedent of the 1970–80 feminist and LGBT struggles against discrimination. By the late 1980s, in a wide variety of contexts around the globe, a first conceptual layer was settled from which ideas and practices relating to sexual citizenship would flourish. In the 1990s further crucial shifts occurred. Sexual matters were infused into human rights discourses and normative frameworks, projecting the possibility of prerogatives that are to be respected above and beyond nationally bounded legal definitions. Activists openly engaged in exercises aimed at transforming existing normative frameworks: constitutions; sub-constitutional legal frameworks; international law and human rights instruments such as UN treaty bodies' recommendations, resolutions and conference outcomes.

Saiz (2004) identifies the 1994–2004 period as the golden age of this normative breakthrough at the global level. It began with the favourable decision of the UN Human Rights Committee on the case Toonen vs. Australia, which asserted that the prohibition of same-sex relations was a breach of the right to privacy, and innovatively interpreted the principle of non-discrimination on the grounds of sex (of the 1948 Declaration) as including 'sexual orientation'. The same year witnessed sexuality breaking through the walls of population at the ICPD and the creation at the Human Rights Commission of the figure of the Special Rapporteur on Violence Against Women. This was followed by an extensive number of commentaries made by practically all UN treaty bodies on various infringements of the fundamental human rights of gays, lesbians, transgender, transvestite, transsexual and intersex persons, which helped consolidate the principle that sexuality legitimately pertained to international human rights laws.

Yet the more recent framings of rights-based approaches to development have yet to incorporate sexuality as a core dimension of freedom and well-being. This needs to be done, and done carefully. A key prerequisite for this project is to find ways of '... formulating claims to universal rights language that recognizes the significance of cross-cultural construction of sexuality', for example critically reflecting on strategies that 'appear to globalize essentialist and culturally specific notions of lesbian and gay identity' (ibid.). Although such identities have sometimes been an effective organizing principle in making claims for sexuality as a dimension of well-being, they have also excluded and restricted, and are not a precondition for claiming rights related to sexuality. Saiz views sexual rights as a concept that enables us to address the intersections between sexual orientation, discrimination and other sexuality issues and offers strategic possibilities for building bridges and coalitions across sexual identities.

Sharma (this volume) also underscores the potential of rights language to cut across identities and sustain claims about sexuality on the basis of ideas such as agency, accountability and indivisibility. But she also raises critical questions about sexual rights claims exclusively based on identities:

More often than not the assumption made is that sexual behaviour necessarily translates into identities based on that behaviour ... Drawing upon the Indian context, we know, however, that the number of people who identify as lesbian, gay, bisexual, transgender or even as indigenous identities such as *kothi*, *giriya* and *jogappa* is much smaller than the number of people who experience same-sex desire but do not identify themselves based on this desire. It is not only a question of numbers. The issue is a more basic one of how sexuality is being understood. An articulation only in terms of identities promotes a view that sexuality is fixed and that it can be fitted into mutually exclusive categories. We need to consider here a queer perspective of sexuality, according to which social processes of compulsory heterosexuality seek to stifle sexual diversity – not just in society at large, but even the potential for sexual diversity within each of us. If this is how we perceive sexuality, the dangers of a framework that is based only on identities become clear.

The same thread is pulled by Miller and Vance (2004) in a remarkable contribution to the disentangling of the interactions of rights claims and sexuality. It covers thorny issues such as the persistent re-creation of sex hierarchies and the complex implications of demanding state protection against sexual harms. They ask, 'How do we develop rights-based policies that foster the ability to experience chosen sexualities, without coercion, and allow more diverse public conversations about what can be desired and done, without inadvertently reinforcing a single normative standard of sexuality or pleasure?' (pp. 13–14). Moves to contextualize these conceptions and translate them into action are under way in a wide variety of settings (Campaña por una Convención de Derechos Sexuales y Reproductivos 2005; Cornwall and Jolly 2006; Parker and Corrêa 2003; CREA et al. 2005; Rojas 2001; Sharma, this volume). The following sections describe such efforts to advance sexual rights without presuming narrow identities, or (re-)enforcing normative standards of sexuality.

Contextualizing sexual rights frames

LGBT: supporting without imposing Western identity models As suggested above, the terms embraced by LGBT are themselves a particular interpretation of same-sex sexualities and transgender identities. These particular labels and models may indeed be welcomed by many in different Southern contexts, but they may also be combined with, or rejected in favour of, other indigenous ways of understanding same-sex sexualities. As Sharma (this volume) points out, sexual interactions between people of the same sex may be understood as a behaviour without any

33

implications for identity at all. The label 'men who have sex with men' (MSM) has been developed for this reason. This term was originally proposed to avoid presuming an identity, and has been widely adopted in HIV/AIDS work. While it may be worth using at times, however, it has been critiqued for its focus on physical interactions while ignoring love, emotions and desires (Gosine 2006), and because it is often used to describe transgender people who may themselves identify as women or a third sex rather than as men (Dowsett 2006).

Sexual rights provide a potential conceptual framework for action which can avoid such impositions. Identities need not be the basis for collective organizing and action. Instead of setting up an exclusive space for LGBT, for example, working with sexual rights may involve framing rights to express desire, or to choose your gender position more openly. The Coalition for Sexual and Bodily Rights in Muslim Societies has taken this approach to some degree. Founded in 2000, it is a network of more than sixty NGOs and academics from the Middle East, North Africa and South and South-East Asia involved in activism and advocacy for the promotion of sexual and bodily rights in Muslim societies. They bring together those working on women's rights, sexuality education, HIV/AIDS, sexual and reproductive health and 'LGBTIQ' (LGBT, intersex and questioning).

Like this coalition, the International HIV/AIDS Alliance in China sought to build common cause around different issues. Instead of separating people out into supposedly clear-cut and distinct identity groups, they ran trainings for peer educators from different groups – people living with HIV/AIDS, sex workers, men who have sex with men, and drug users – in an effort to reduce mutual stigma and promote solidarity in the face of general prejudice against 'high-risk groups'. This also created space for more open discussion with those with intersecting identities, such as lesbian sex workers, or people with HIV/AIDS who bought or sold sex (He 2005).

Challenging marriage normativity

> Tu Ekal Main Ekal (you are single, I am single). ... Did a woman not have a right to live outside the institution of marriage? Did she not have the right to an identity of her own? (Jagori 2004: 30)

As described above, development has in fact not been silent on sexuality, but instead has made implicit assumptions of sex essentialism. These have included assumptions that most people will live out their sexuality primarily in heterosexual and marital relations, as in the economic models of the household. These kinds of stereotypes reinforce normativities around marriage that do not even apply to many heterosexual people, let alone other people. Marriage itself, a social and economic structure related to sexuality, may be a prerequisite for economic and social survival, particularly although not exclusively for women. In some areas, being single is considered a tragedy. Breaking the rules, for example with adultery, can result in social censure, and even violence in some contexts, especially for women. Yet playing by the rules and getting married may also have its costs: marital rape remains unrecognized in many countries, and many women remain in unequal or unsatisfying marriages owing to family and social pressure.

At the same time, there are mobilizations challenging these positions. A Delhi NGO, Jagori, was made aware of the costs of marriage normativity by the people they were working with in a Delhi slum. They had focused on supporting women facing domestic violence within marriage. Widowed, divorced, unmarried and 'single' women, however, came forward to complain that they were vulnerable as a category of women outside the 'safety net' of marriage. One of the outcomes was the creation of a single women's collective which has become stronger over the years, and expanded to become a women's collective, taking on cases of violence in the community, other disputes, cases of corruption against civic and municipal bodies, struggles for civic amenities, and so on. Workshops on sexuality were held for single women, and materials produced, such as a book of profiles of single women. In this case the identity of 'single women' – including women who were divorced, widowed, unmarried, and lesbian – became an organizing principle for a broad coalition of those suffering under marriage normativity from the outside (ibid.).

Supporting greater equality in heterosexual relations In many societies, gendered ideas about sexuality encourage men to be macho and take risks, and women to be passive and ignorant. This can create obstacles to heterosexual sex that pleases both partners and is safe. Such norms are on a continuum with homophobia – because part of being seen as a proper woman or a proper man is being heterosexual, as well as conforming to structures of gender inequality, and marriage normativity.

A range of creative initiatives are challenging these stereotypes, and forging new possibilities for happier, more equal and diverse lifestyles – heterosexual or not. In Nigeria, for example, as elsewhere, there is great pressure on girls to have sex – from their boyfriends, their peers or in exchange for goods they need. Yet there is also huge pressure not to have sex – from parents eager for girls to remain virgins until marriage, from the churches, from teachers and from the abstinence programmes. Girl

Power Initiative (GPI) in Nigeria provides training for adolescent girls on sexuality – equipping them with the knowledge and confidence to make their own decisions. The first GPI classes were held in 1994 for sixteen girls. Now, GPI reaches over 50,000 girls every year through centres in four Nigerian states and outreach programmes in twenty-eight schools (Madunagu 2007).

There are also several such initiatives targeted at boys. One is Programme H, developed by four NGOs in Brazil and Mexico. They identified factors that made young men in low-income settings more likely to express gender-equitable attitudes and have safer sex, and less likely to inflict sexual and other violence. These factors were: having gender-equitable male role models and peer groups, and reflecting on the consequences of violence, for example by observing and thinking about the trauma caused by a father hitting a mother. Programme H then tried to re-create these factors through a manual of activities to be used with groups of young men, with more equitable men, who also served as role models, as facilitators. They also discuss and challenge homophobia, which is targeted not only at those with same-sex sexualities, but also at non-macho men and independent women. At the same time, a social marketing campaign using radio, billboards, postcards and dances to portray being more gender-equitable as 'cool and hip' was run in partnership with SSL International, the makers of Durex condoms.

Supporting sex workers without imposing particular interpretations of their experiences Similar to support for LGBT, initiatives aimed at improving the situation of people in sex work need to avoid imposing beliefs and understandings of what selling sex means to them. Neither should it be assumed that sex work always involves women selling to men. Though this form is predominant, other expressions of commercial and transactional sex exist, involving men and transgender selling, and women and transgender buying. Indeed, in many contexts transgender people are heavily involved in sex work. One survey of 147 transvestites in Buenos Aires found that 89 per cent were working in prostitution (IGLHRC 2001).

Essentialized views of sex work being a result of men's predatory urges, with women always as innocent and unwilling victims, predominate. Debates about consent should not slow action to respond to the real needs of sex workers themselves. The key question is not: Did sex workers choose this work and on what basis was that choice made? But rather: What do they want now and how can they be supported? There is a huge variety of situations and understandings of sex work. For example, the Chinese police system categorizes prostitutes according to a hierarchy of seven tiers ranging from second wives (top tier) to women who sell sex to transient construction workers from the countryside (bottom tier). The multiple and diverse voices of those engaged in sex work must be heard.

There are many pragmatic efforts to respond to sex workers' priorities, such as DfID's HIV/AIDS prevention and care programme in China. Chinese governmental approaches to sex work, MSM and drug users have in the past, and sometimes today, generally consisted of police harassment, arrests and re-education. The DfID programme worked with and trained police at different levels to encourage them to leave these groups alone. Programme staff also engaged with pimps to gain entry to brothels and win their support for condom use by sex workers. Peer-education training programmes were started with sex workers themselves. While a key element of the training consisted of safety promotion and HIV/AIDS awareness, the programme also responded to sex workers' inputs and included more general healthcare, sex tips and some discussion of the sexual pleasure of sex workers themselves (Jolly with Wang 2003).

A real need in interventions relating to sex work is support for sex workers who are getting too old to continue in this youth-based industry and need viable alternatives, such as economic empowerment, saving schemes and skills training, based on a non-judgemental, non-victimizing view of sex work. Durbar, a collective of 60,000 female, male and transgender sex workers in India, has done some important work in this area (see <www.durbar.org/home.html>).

Increasingly, sex work is equated with trafficking. While there is a connection in that some people are trafficked for sex work, many sex workers are not trafficked, and many people are trafficked for other kinds of labour, such as domestic work. People trafficked for whatever purpose may suffer horribly. The idea underlying much of the concern, however, is that both sex workers and migrants are victims. Policies follow which continue to treat these groups as victims, rather than as people who may have the capacity to make their own decisions, and whose opinions should be respected. Accusations of trafficking are used to justify deportation of migrants, and denial of visas or entry into the country for young women. Other approaches have been recommended to tackle the problem of trafficking, which avoid falling into these traps: for example, mobilizing around 'migrant rights' and 'sex workers' rights', which would include challenging forced labour where this is occurring, but not assuming that these people are all victims.[2]

Moving to more positive approaches to sexuality As discussed above, development has generally seen sexuality as a problem needing to be controlled – related to population control, disease or violence – rather than as a source of affirmation, pleasure, intimacy and love. Attempts to deal with gender issues related to HIV/AIDS have focused on coercion by men and women's lack of choice. It is true that many women are pressured into unsafe sex by violence or economic dependency, and these problems must be tackled. The emphasis on violence and gender inequality as the causes of unsafe sex gives only one part of the story, however, and one that fits well with essentialist framings of men's sexual desire as uncontrollable, and with women as innocent. What about women's agency and desires in sex? If no space is allowed for this in development interventions, women will become even more sexually constrained, and efforts to deal with HIV/AIDS further hampered, as well as gender stereotypes entrenched.

Some practical initiatives are taking a different approach, promoting the pleasures of safer sex with the goal of reducing transmission of HIV/AIDS, or promoting women's empowerment. The Pleasure Project mapped initiatives taken around the world which use pleasure as a primary motivation for promoting sexual health. This included programmes that eroticize male and female condoms; sex-positive books for teenagers; work with churches to improve sex among married couples; safer sex erotica designed for HIV-positive people; and pleasure and harm-reduction counselling for sex workers (Pleasure Project 2004).

Empowerment is the goal in the training courses on women's human rights run by the Turkish organization Women for Women's Human Rights. These include a module on 'sexual pleasure as a women's human right', challenging the denial of women's rights to decide upon and enjoy their own bodies. Already over 4,500 women have been trained, and the sexual pleasure module generally proves to be the most popular part of the course (Ilkkaracan and Seral 2000).

Sexual pleasure is sometimes seen as men's prerogative. The pursuit of pleasure is in reality, however, not without obstacles for most men. The Group of Men Against Violence formed in 1993 in Nicaragua not only works with men to tackle violence perpetrated by themselves or others, but also, through workshops, encourages men to discover the pleasures of tenderness, intimacy and equality in both sexual and non-sexual relations (Jolly 2007).

Reflections and recommendations

We have argued that development has not, as is often perceived, been silent on the subject of sexuality. It has instead assumed an essentialist view of sexuality as a natural drive and a unified domain of human experience, with heterosexuality and gender difference as biological imprints. The very absence of explicit discussion of sexuality in development discourse, about, say, population or the household, implies that sexuality is classed as a natural individual preference which does not need to be taken into account.

These essentialist framings deny the plasticity of people's sexualities, and thus constrain and fix people. They deny variation in sexual practices and meanings. And crucially, they obscure the ways in which power in modern societies operates through sex. Hierarchies such as between women/men, natives/colonialists, North/South, heterosexual/LGBT are seen as natural, rather than as the inequalities resulting from power struggles.

Development–sexuality intersections have become more explicit in the past two decades. Public health is one such crossroads. But here again initiatives have served to regulate sexualities by keeping them in line with naturalized hierarchies, as much as to improve people's quality of life. In the Cairo and Beijing processes, sexuality gained new visibility in discussions on population and women's health. This was a major achievement, but nevertheless the final agreements remained heterosexist in their framings.

HIV/AIDS work has created further openings. Here the struggle continues between essentialist hierarchies of natural and unnatural behaviours, innocent and guilty victims, and constructivist approaches that see the challenge as combating stigma and promoting safety in the wide diversity of behaviours. This has meant new resources and visibility for men who have sex with men, at the same time as new regulation of this population.

Human development discourses have been slow to address sexuality. Yet they have paved the way for seeing sexuality as part of development, not just a frivolity to be enjoyed once the serious issues of poverty have been tackled. This opens the way for a consideration of how poverty and sexuality intersect, not just in terms of sexual ill health, but around the norms, social rules, economic and legal structures that regulate our lives, integrating some people into oppressive systems, and marginalizing others.

Human rights and sexual rights offer the most promising potential for progress, although rights-based approaches to development have yet to incorporate sexuality as a core dimension of freedom and well-being. This needs to be done, but not by basing claims on fixed and restrictive identities. Sometimes identity may be an effective organizing principle, if the identities are what people want and resonate with local context.

Identities can also exclude and restrict, however: HIV/AIDS funding, for example, has provided much-needed support for men who have sex with men, but women who have sex with women have been left out of the picture owing to their generally lower risk (Gosine 2004).[3] Such funding has increased existing inequalities between women and men with same-sex sexualities. More development funding for community building, social inclusion and justice work should be directed at empowering women in their sexuality, to increase possibilities for them to make their own choices, including to engage in same-sex sexual relations if they wish to do so.

Identities are also not necessary as a basis for rights. We need to seek rights for people in all our diversity, including the diversity in each individual; make universal claims to rights that recognize the cultural variation in sexual identities; call for rights for women to be free of violence without pandering to discourses on innocence and chastity. And in all of this we need to remember that sex can be a good thing, a source of well-being and joy, not just of violence, disease, discrimination and poverty. And some initiatives are putting these frames into action, building alternatives to marriage normativity, and to inequalities in heterosexual relationships, supporting LGBT and sex worker rights without presuming limiting identities, and promoting pleasure for all.

Notes

1 This influence came mainly through the writings of William Reich. But it is also identifiable in the writing of feminist thinkers who wrestled bravely with psychoanalysis, such as Kate Millett and Shulamith Firestone.

2 See discussions by the Global Alliance Against Traffic in Women at <www.gaatw.net>.

3 Although sex between women is by no means automatically safer than sex between men, or between different sexes. It depends on what kinds of sex is had. Women who have sex with women may also be subject to other risks of transmission – through needle sharing, unsafe blood transfusions, sex with men (owing to inclination or coercion), etc., just like anyone else.

References

Campaña por una Convención de Derechos Sexuales y Reproductivos (2005) *Memorias del seminario 'Prostitución, trabajadoras del sexo, transgeneridades, nuevas tecnologías reproductivas' – un debate a partir de los derechos sexuales y derechos reproductivos*, Lima, Peru, September, <www.convencion.org.uy> (accessed 20 May 2007).

Chambers, R. (2005) 'Participation, pluralism and perceptions of poverty', Paper for conference on 'The many dimensions of poverty', Brazil, August, <www.undp-povertycentre.org/md%2Dpoverty/papers/Robert_.pdf> (accessed 20 May 2007).

Cornwall, A. and S. Jolly (2006) 'Sexuality matters', *IDS Bulletin*, 37(5): Brighton: IDS.

Corrêa, S. and R. Parker (2004) 'Sexuality, human rights, and demographic thinking: connections and disjunctions in a changing world', *Sexuality Research and Social Policy*, 1(1): 15–38.

CREA, Sangama, TARSHI (2005) 'A conversation on sexual rights in India', New Delhi: Creating Resources for Empowerment in Action.

Dowsett, G. (2006) 'The way forward: knowledge development', Presentation at 'MSM in Asia' conference, Delhi, October.

Family Care International (2005) 'Millennium Development Goals and sexual and reproductive health', Briefing cards, New York: Family Care International, <www.familycareintl.org/en/resources/publications/6> (accessed 20 May 2007).

Gosine, A. (2004) 'Sex for pleasure, rights to participation, and alternatives to AIDS: placing sexual minorities and/or dissidents in development', IDS Working Paper 228, Brighton: IDS.

— (2006) '"Race", culture, power, sex, desire, love: writing in "men who have sex with men"', IDS Bulletin, 37(5): 27–33.

He, X. (2005) 'Sex and participation in a workshop in China', Presentation at 'Realizing Sexual Rights' Workshop, IDS, October.

Herdt, G. (1987) *The Sambia: Ritual and Gender in New Guinea*, New York: Holt, Rinehart and Winston.

IGLHRC (International Gay and Lesbian Human Rights Commission) (2001) 'The rights of transvestites in Argentina', <www.iglhrc.org/files/iglhrc/reports/Argentina_trans.pdf> (accessed 20 May 2007).

Ilkkaracan, I. and G. Seral (2000) 'Sexual pleasure as a women's human right: experiences from a grassroots training program in Turkey', in P. Ilkkaracan (ed.), *Women and Sexuality in Muslim Societies, Istanbul: Women for Women's Human Rights*, Istanbul: WWHR, pp. 187–96.

Jagori (2004) 'Living feminisms, Jagori: a journey of 20 years', <http:// jagori.org/about-jagori/our-history/> (accessed 20 May 2007).

Jolly, S. (2007) 'Why the development industry should get over its obsession with bad sex and start to think about pleasure', IDS Working Paper 283, June, Brighton: IDS.

Jolly, S. with Y. Wang (2003) 'Gender mainstreaming strategy for the UK-China HIV/AIDS prevention and care project', www.siyanda.org (accessed 20 May 2007).

Madunagu, B. (2007) 'Girl power initiative in Nigeria', *Gender and Development in Brief*, 18, BRIDGE, <www.bridge.ids.ac.uk/dgb18.htm#2> (accessed 20 May 2007).

Miller, A. and C. Vance (2004) 'Sexuality, human rights and health', *Health and Human Rights*, 7(2): 5–15.

Morgan, R. and S. Wieringa (2005) *Tommy Boys, Lesbian Men and Ancestral Wives*, Johannesburg: Jacana Media.

Nussbaum, M. (1999) *Sex and Social Justice*, Oxford/New York: Oxford University Press.

Parker, R. and S. Corrêa (2003) *Sexualidade e Política na América Latina*, Rio de Janeiro: ABIA.

Parker, R. G. and P. Aggleton (eds) (1999) *Culture, Society and Sexuality: A Reader*, London: UCL Press.

Parker, R. and J. Gagnon (1994) *Conceiving Sexuality: Approaches* to *Sex Research in a Postmodern World*, London: Routledge.

Petchesky, R. (2000) 'Sexual rights: inventing a concept, mapping an international practice', in R. Parker, R. M. Barbosa and P. Aggleton (eds), *Framing the Sexual Subject*, New York: Routledge.

— (2003) *Global Prescriptions: Gendering Health and Human Rights*, London and New York: Zed Books.

— (2005) 'Rights of the body and perversions of war: ten years past Beijing', *UNESCO's International Social Science Journal*, Special issue on Beijing+10, 57(2): 475–92.

Pleasure Project, The (2004) 'Global mapping of pleasure', <www.the-pleasure-project.org/Global%20Mapping%20of%20Pleasure.pdf> (accessed 20 May 2007).

Plummer, K. (2000) 'Sexualities in a runaway world: utopian and dystopian challenges', Paper presented at the conference on Sexuality and Social Change, ABIA (Brazilian Interdisciplinary AIDS Association), Rio de Janeiro.

Robinson, M. (2003) 'Mobilizing people to claim rights', in WICEJ (ed.), *Seeking Accountability on Women's Human Rights*, New York: Women's International Coalition for Economic Justice (WICEJ).

Rojas, L. (2001) '*El Debate sobre los derechos sexuales en México*', Reproductive Health and Society Programme, Mexico City: Cólegio de México.

Saiz, I. (2004) 'Bracketing sexuality: human rights and sexual orientation – a decade of development and denial at the United Nations', *Health and Human Rights*, 7(2) 48–81.

Samelius, L., and E. Wagberg (2005) 'Sexual orientation and gender identity issues in development: a study of Swedish policy and administration of lesbian, gay, bisexual and transgender issues in international development co-operation', Swedish International Development Cooperation Agency (Sida) Health Division, <www.ilga-europe.org/europe/guide/country_by_country/sweden/sexual_orientation_and_gender_identity_issues_in_development> (accessed 20 May 2007).

Sember, R. and S. Corrêa (2006) 'Contribution to Sexuality Policy Watch conference', <www.ciudadaniasexual.org/boletin/boletin20.htm> (accessed 20 May 2007).

UNDP (1990–2005) *Human Development Reports*, New York: United Nations Development Programme.

— (2005) 'Millennium Project Report', <www.unmillenniumproject.org/reports/fullreport.htm> (accessed 20 May 2007).

Weeks, J. (1985) *Sexuality and Its Discontents: Meanings, Myths and Modern Sexualities*, London: Routledge and Kegan Paul.

— (2003) *Sexuality*, (2nd edn), New York: Routledge.

ONE | Sexual rights/human rights

3 | Sexual rights are human rights

KATE SHEILL[1]

Across the world, there is much talk and action on sexual rights: individuals campaign; organizations run programmes; academics publish papers; activists lobby. We have learnt a great deal and enjoyed many successes. Yet in the international human rights sphere, ten years on from that first articulation of sexual rights in the Beijing Platform for Action, there has been little progress and much opposition. In this chapter, I will examine some of the dynamics of the human rights discourse on sexual rights at the international, intergovernmental level.

Sexual rights embrace human rights that are already recognized in national laws and international human rights standards. The treaties themselves do not explicitly refer to or define 'sexual rights', but they do include rights that have a direct bearing on sexual health and sexual rights, including: the right to life (International Covenant on Civil and Political Rights [ICCPR], Article 6); to liberty and security of person (ICCPR, Article 9.1); to enjoy the benefits of scientific progress (International Covenant on Economic Social and Cultural Rights [ICESCR], Article 15.1[b]); to freedom of expression, including the right to seek, receive and impart information (ICCPR, Article 19); the right to marry and found a family (ICCPR, Article 23); to health (ICESCR, Article 12); and the right of equal access for women to healthcare services, including family planning (Convention on the Elimination of All Forms of Discrimination Against Women [CEDAW], Article 12).

The concept of sexual rights was first articulated in a UN document in 1995, with the adoption by consensus of the Beijing Platform for Action (BPfA), the outcome document of the Fourth World Conference on Women:[2] 'The human rights of women include their right to have control over and decide freely and responsibly on matters related to their sexuality, including sexual and reproductive health, free of coercion, discrimination and violence ...' (Para. 96). Sexual rights frequently serve as a locus where civil, political, social and economic rights intersect – HIV/AIDS providing a good example (Klugman 2000). Sexual rights are not separate from the goals of the broader human rights movement. Human rights are universal, indivisible and inalienable. Realization of sexual rights requires gender equality in society. It challenges deeply seated racial prejudices. It calls on us to confront the limited conceptualizations of gender-conform-ing sexuality and social 'norm'-conforming sexual behaviour. Taking a rights-based approach to sexuality is an important part of the struggle to achieve equality, an end to violence and justice for all.

Timing and contexts

It is timely to look at the human rights discourse on sexual rights and the efforts and opposition to progress at the intergovernmental level. Most of this chapter deals with events in 2005, which presented several opportunities to further the sexual rights discourse – at the annual UN sessions of the Commission on the Status of Women (CSW), Commission on Population and Development (CPD) and the Commission on Human Rights (CHR) and the five-year review of the Millennium Development Goals (MDGs) – none of which was as successful as we might have hoped. The struggles to get human rights, much less sexual rights, on to the agenda for the UN World Summit and the failure of states to commit to almost all of the proposed meaningful human rights reforms, cast a shadow over the forums in which sexual rights will be debated in future.[3] What seems clear is that we will continue to face challenges in our efforts to set a progressive agenda for the realization of sexual rights.

The CSW in March 2005 undertook a ten-year review of the BPfA. Despite US-led opposition, coded as being against 'new international human rights', the BPfA was reaffirmed and several states, notably Nigeria speaking on behalf of the African Union, New Zealand on behalf of Canada and Australia, and the European Union, spoke of women's right to control their sexuality.

The CPD in April of the same year looked at two issues relevant to sexual rights: HIV/AIDS[4] and the Contribution of the Implementation of the Programme of Action of the International Conference on Population and Development (ICPD)[5] to the MDGs.[6]

The 61st Session of the CHR followed immediately after the CSW and ran concurrently with the CPD. In 2005, there were six resolutions at the CHR that addressed sexual rights concerns: access to medication;[7] the right to health;[8] education;[9] HIV/AIDS;[10] extrajudicial, summary or arbitrary executions;[11] and violence against women.[12]

While the MDGs do not speak directly of sexual rights, they address some of the effects of denying sexual and reproductive rights by attending to the crises of maternal health (Goal 5) and the HIV pandemic (Goal 6). Without taking steps to realize individuals' sexual rights and reproductive rights the MDGs cannot be achieved.[13] Indeed, sexual and reproductive rights are vital in the contemporary struggle against global poverty.[14]

So what are the obstacles to progress?

Several governments are attempting to retreat from human rights and the commitments they have made in signing and ratifying the international standards and joining consensus at world conferences. This goes beyond sexual rights – to the challenging, in the context of counter-terrorism, of the absolute prohibition against torture[15] – though efforts to reframe sexual rights issues only as sexual health demonstrate this trend clearly. For example, at the 2005 CPD, the resolutions on HIV/AIDS and the links between the Cairo (ICPD) consensus and the MDGs made almost no mention of human rights.[16] Perhaps this is not surprising given that the MDGs themselves do not use a rights framework. And we have struggled to put human rights at the centre of the review of these goals and the attempts at UN reform. But beyond the threats to the human rights framework, what are the specific obstacles we must overcome to advance sexual rights?

Much is written about the opponents of sexual rights active in UN forums (for example, see Buss and Herman 2003) but we also need to think about our own activities if we are to be successful in our goals. By and large, opponents of sexual rights outnumber us and are better organized and better funded than most sexual rights activists. Galvanized by what they saw as failures in the human rights conferences of the 1990s, conservative activists, organizations and states now form a vociferous opposition at every UN forum where sexual rights concerns are on the table. For ten years, they have been refining their tactics and now they set the rules of engagement.

The efforts to resist progress or to renege on existing commitments to sexual rights can be so strong that they overwhelm our own strategies and we find ourselves time and again solely on the defensive. Instead of focusing on what we want, including the need to build on the ground-breaking conceptualization of sexual rights, we can find ourselves spending virtually all our time reacting to our opponents' agenda.

We need to be more affirmative in our own agenda. What do we mean by sexual rights? Would we agree on the definitions and strategies we need to pursue? We are not a homogeneous movement. How could we best handle that diversity? At a 2004 activist/practitioner meeting to review the ten years since the adoption of the Programme of Action (POA) of the ICPD, there was strikingly little talk of sexuality and it was kept to a side track. In the plenary sessions, with one notable exception, there was no talk of sexuality and definitely no talk of non-conforming sexualities. What does that mean – is 'queer' cracking consensus? Can the gains made in those 1990s world conferences survive the full implications of sexual

47

rights? When lesbian, gay, bisexual and transgender (LGBT) rights were explicitly put on the table at the UN CHR in 2003, the reaction was so strongly negative that it threatened the very foundation of human rights – the concept of universality.[17]

Even when states are not explicitly against sexual rights, the controversy seemingly inherent in these rights gives them a value that can be a very useful bargaining tool in negotiations. Too often we have seen 'friendly' governments use the controversy of sexual rights as an implicit threat to be levered to gain agreement elsewhere, ensuring that their language on another issue is adopted.

Another big obstacle is the sheer breadth of debate. Aside from the international conferences, there are now so many UN meetings where sexual rights are at stake that the human, financial and time resource costs make participation at every meeting impossible, even for the bigger organizations with the required UN accreditation. We need to work together to develop strategies to ensure our presence across these many forums and to share feedback from them as opponent states and organizations often use the same strategies at the different meetings.

The challenges to and of maintaining the status quo

Even the BPfA gives us a formulation of sexual rights that applies only to women, speaks only in terms of violence and came about largely because of awareness of the impacts of disease (the HIV/AIDS pandemic). If we are to realize the full promise of sexual rights we also have to move beyond the violation-based protectionist model of human rights (see, among others, Kapur 2002; Mahoney 1994; Miller 2004). By this I mean the model that focuses only on the negative articulation of rights – the right to be free from rather than free to – and on protection from disease, harm and danger, which seeks only to limit sexual rights. We need to recognize different articulations of human agency and ensure that we find ways and means of promoting and protecting affirmative claims to and diverse expressions of sexuality. For example, ensuring that we have the conditions in place for people to enjoy sexual pleasure, if they wish: sexuality education, adequate and accessible health services, gender equality, anti-discrimination measures, partnership recognition, no sexual violence, etc.

Not only is our use of victimization rhetoric and the protectionist model of human rights limited in what it can deliver for sexual rights, but our advocacy strategies are beginning to rebound on us. The USA has attempted to contain efforts to promote sexual rights by opposing the creation of any 'new' rights, and positioning sexual rights as new.

Sexual rights activists have worked hard to reject this, by referring to the relevant clauses in international covenants to show that basic principles of sexual rights have already been implied in existing texts. The opposition are using 'our' own argument against us – that sexual rights are not 'new' rights – and are using it to demonstrate – and show that we agree – that if specific rights have not been explicitly codified in previously negotiated texts, then they are not endorsed by the international agreements and thus are 'new'. At Beijing plus 10, the US-based right-wing Catholic Family and Human Rights Institute used this refutation by activists to contest abortion rights, hence their headline assertion 'UN Abortion Advocates Admit Beijing Excludes Abortion Rights'.[18] Their argument could equally be extended to other sexual rights issues such as LGBT rights or sex worker rights, and indeed there was strident opposition to the inclusion of reference to men who have sex with men and sex workers in the political outcome document of the five-year review of the UN General Assembly Special Session on HIV/AIDS (UNGASS review) in May/June 2006.[19]

If sexual rights are not new rights, can we at least use new language? It would appear not. A tactic opposing states used at the CHR in 2005 was not to accept any language that had not previously appeared in an international negotiated resolution. Regional texts were not sufficient, which ruled out the only reference to sexual and reproductive rights in any negotiated regional text I know of, in the Mexico City Consensus.[20] Nor would they accept an expansion of the concept of sexual rights contained in the BPfA – the outcome document of a women's rights conference – to include men. If we can never use language that has not been used before, how can we ever progress?

Yet the attacks go deeper than that – it seems that we are not allowed to use any old language either. In 2005, in the CHR resolutions on both violence against women and HIV/AIDS, the opposition of some states to sexual rights issues was to be expected, but the opposition to the long-established concept of 'reproductive rights' was more surprising. The scope of, and language on, reproductive rights is long established, having been first set out in a UN document in the ICPD POA (1994), which informs the language on reproductive rights in the BPfA (1995). While we are used to post-vote statements clarifying governments' positions against abortion, following adoption of the violence against women resolution, Guatemala, Ecuador, Honduras and Costa Rica delivered strongly worded comments just on the term 'reproductive rights' – in spite of the clear support for sexual and reproductive rights at the Beijing plus ten Latin American and Caribbean preparatory conference.[21]

In the HIV/AIDS resolution, China and certain Latin American states were particularly vocal in their opposition to reproductive *rights* (as opposed to reproductive health). Both resolutions also saw a weakening of references to these progressive UN guidelines on HIV/AIDS and Human Rights,[22] even though the guidelines were adopted in 1997 and have been referred to in numerous Commission resolutions since then – indeed, the HIV/AIDS resolution came about *because* of the guidelines. The guidelines' attention to, among other issues, men who have sex with men; the repeal of 'sodomy' laws; same-sex marriage; and decriminalization of sex work were the likely triggers for this last-minute challenge to the guidelines, as evidenced by the USA 'Explanation of Position' on the HIV/AIDS resolution, in which they expressed their concern that Commission members had sought action 'on a number of highly controversial and deeply divisive issues relating to sexuality ... '[23]

This questioning of the gains made in the 1990s UN world conferences and elsewhere constitutes an attack on the human rights framework. The 2006 review of the 2001 Declaration of Commitment on HIV/AIDS marginalizes human-rights-based approaches. The Human Rights Caucus at the UNGASS review commented:

> ... we are concerned by the dearth of language stressing the necessity of rights-based approaches to HIV and AIDS policy, programming and services. We are concerned not only because this is an obligation of governments but also because it makes work more effective. Rights-based approaches require ensuring the participation of affected communities, non-discrimination in programme delivery, attention to the legal and policy environment in which interventions take place, and accountability for what is done, and how it is done.[24]

The opportunities we must seize

We have to seize opportunities such as the IDS workshop, which gave rise to this publication, to make connections between the many actors working on different sexual rights issues, including HIV/AIDS, LGBT rights, sexual health, whether from policy or practice, at local, national, regional and international levels. Only through such exchange can we end the compartmentalizing that prevents the sharing of lessons and of evidence that different practitioners could contribute to the debates and advocacy efforts. We must continue to challenge funding restrictions that silence so many sexual rights workers and result in the loss of these experts in negotiation spaces. We must ground our arguments and interventions in human rights and lobby for the inclusion of language using clearly articulated rights-based approaches.

Maybe we need to move the debate. The regional preparatory conferences for Beijing plus ten and Cairo plus ten saw more progressive language on sexual rights than we ever see at the international level. How can we maximize these regional organizing successes? Should we take our efforts to the regional human rights bodies (where they exist)? How can we internationalize our gains at the regional level?

We also need to spread the word. None of us can cover every meeting so we need to give others the tools to push our concerns, or at least stave off the worst attacks. There are many professional lobbyists working at the UN, they cover a huge range of issues, and we must ensure that they understand ours. We must also educate negotiators in our ally governments so that when they have opportunities to progress the human rights discourse they are able to do so.

We have the new opportunities presented by the Human Rights Council (which replaced the Commission on Human Rights in 2006). While we will always need to be vigilant against attacks on our previous gains, we must move beyond solely defensive tactics and develop holistic, coherent strategies so that we can push on to realize the full promise of that first articulation of sexual rights. Sexual rights are human rights – it is time to stay strong and be bold.

Notes

1 Kate Sheill is Amnesty International's Identity-Based Discrimination Campaign Coordinator in the Policy Programme of the International Secretariat. The views expressed here are the author's and do not represent those of Amnesty International.

2 A/CONF.177/20, 17 October 1995.

3 *UN Summit: Human Rights Betrayed by a Failure of Leadership*, Amnesty International (AI Index number: IOR 41/059/2005), 12 September 2005.

4 Population, Development and HIV/AIDS with Particular Emphasis on Poverty, E/CN.9/2005/L.4, 11 April 2005.

5 The ICPD Programme of Action was adopted by consensus in 1994 and addresses, among other issues,

reproductive rights and sexual and reproductive health: Chapter 7 of the ICPD POA is entitled 'Reproductive rights and reproductive health' and employs a model that encompasses sexuality; see in particular Paragraphs 7.2 and 7.3; <www.unfpa.org/icpd/icpd_poa.htm#ch7>.

6 Contribution of the Implementation of the Programme of Action of the International Conference on Population and Development, in all its aspects, to the achievement of the internationally agreed development goals, including those contained in the United Nations Millennium Declaration, E/CN.9/2005/L.5, 11 April 2005.

7 Access to medication in the context of pandemics such as HIV/AIDS, tuberculosis and malaria: Human Rights Resolution 2005/23.

8 The right of everyone to the enjoyment of the highest attainable standard of physical and mental health: Human Rights Resolution 2005/24.

9 The right to education: Human Rights Resolution 2005/21.

10 The protection of human rights in the context of human immunodeficiency virus (HIV) and acquired immunodeficiency syndrome (AIDS): Human Rights Resolution 2005/84.

11 Extrajudicial, summary or arbitrary executions: Human Rights Resolution 2005/34.

12 Elimination of violence against women: Human Rights Resolution 2005/41.

13 A/59, 27 September 2004, Report of the Special Rapporteur on the right of everyone to the enjoyment of the highest attainable standard of physical and mental health to the UN General Assembly, Paragraph 30.

14 Ibid., Paragraph 31.

15 See, for example, Amnesty International Report 2005, AI Index: POL 10/001/2005; *UK: Law Lords confirm that torture 'evidence' is unacceptable*, AI Index: EUR 45/057/2005.

16 While the resolution on 'Population, development and HIV/AIDS with particular emphasis on poverty', E/CN.9/2005/L.4, 11 April 2005, references rights on four occasions, the resolution on the Contribution of the Implementation of the Programme of Action of the International Conference on Population and Development, in all its aspects, to the achievement of the internationally agreed development goals, including those contained in the United Nations Millennium Declaration, E/CN.9/2005/L.5, 11 April 2005, makes only one explicit reference to

human rights, simply stressing the importance of promoting women's full enjoyment of all human rights and fundamental freedoms (Paragraph 7).

17 Amnesty International, *UN Commission on Human Rights: Universality under threat over sexual orientation resolution*, AI Index: IOR 41/013/2003, 22 April 2003.

18 Catholic Family and Human Rights Institute: UN Abortion Advocates Admit Beijing Excludes Abortion Rights, 4 March 2005, <www.c-fam.org/FAX/Volume_8/ faxv8n11.html>.

19 UNAIDS Statement on the Political Declaration on HIV/AIDS, http://data.unaids.org/pub/ PressStatement/2006/20060620_PS_ HLM_en.pdf>.

20 'Review and implement legislation guaranteeing the responsible exercise of sexual and reproductive rights and non-discriminatory access to health services, including sexual and reproductive health' – from Report of the Ninth Session of the Regional Conference on Women in Latin America and the Caribbean [regional preparatory meeting for Beijing plus 10]. Mexico City, LC/ G.2256 (CRM.9/6, 10–12 June 2004, Paragraph 6(xi).

21 Ibid.

22 UN guidelines on HIV/AIDS and Human Rights, <www.unaids. org/NetTools/Misc/DocInfo. aspx?LANG=en&href=http://gva- doc-owl/WEBcontent/Documents/ pub/Publications/IRC-pub02/JC520- HumanRights_en.pdf>.

23 Item 14: Human Rights and AIDS. Explanation of Position. Statement of Leonard A. Leo, United States Public Delegate. Delivered at the Commission on Human Rights, 21 April 2005.

24 Statement by the Human Rights Caucus at the High Level Meeting on HIV and AIDS, New York, 2 June 2006.

References

Buss, D. and D. Herman (2003) *Globalizing Family Values. The Christian Right in International Politics*, Minneapolis/London: University of Minnesota Press.

Kapur, R. (2002) 'The tragedy of victimization rhetoric: resurrecting the "native" subject in international/post-colonial feminist legal politics', *Harvard Human Rights Journal*, 15: 1–38.

Klugman, B. (2000) 'Sexual rights in southers Africa: a Beijing discourse or a strategic necessity?', *Health and Human Rights*', 4(2): 144–73.

Mahoney, M. R. (1994) 'Victimization or oppression? Women's lives, violence, and agency', in M. A. Fineman and R. Mykitiuk (eds), *The Public Nature of Private Violence. The Discovery of Domestic Abuse*, New York: Routledge, pp. 59–92.

Miller, A. M. (2004) 'Sexuality, violence against women, and human rights: women make demands and ladies get protection', *Health and Human Rights*, 7(2): 17–47.

4 | Sex work, trafficking and HIV: how development is compromising sex workers' human rights[1]

MELISSA DITMORE

When people imagine abuse of people who work in the sex industry, many immediately picture lurid images of so-called sexual slavery, and of women and children being forced to sell sex. Most sex workers, however, are not forced or tricked into their jobs, but choose sex work from the limited opportunities available to them. In the global North, sex workers are frequently students, who are typically preparing themselves for other work, and single mothers, who may find sex work supports their families in fewer hours than other available occupations, thereby freeing them to spend time with their children. Some are migrants (Thukral et al. 2005; Petro 2006; Zi Teng 2006). In the global South, sex workers often lack skills and other opportunities for employment, and many enter sex work when they first leave home (DMSC 2007; Ditmore and WNU 2006). Many sex workers belong to sexual minorities, including gay people and transgenders. Around the world, transgender people are among the most discriminated-against people in the job market, and many engage in sex work to earn their livelihoods (Thukral and Ditmore 2003; Thukral et al. 2005; Jenkins et al. 2005).

Sex workers are particularly vulnerable to human rights violations because their work is often stigmatized and, in many countries, illegal. This chapter examines the ways in which policies of development, combating trafficking in persons, the prevention of HIV, and working conditions in the sex industry affect sex workers. It shows how the conflation of sex work with trafficking finds shape in debates in international legal arenas and in the restrictions on funding for HIV prevention and development work introduced by the Bush administration. It explores the human rights and development implications of two key fields of intervention by international agencies in the field of sex work and trafficking. The first is in the international legal arena: the United Nations' Palermo Optional Protocol to Prevent, Suppress and Punish Trafficking in Persons, Especially Women and Children, which was adopted in 2000. The second is in relation to the conditionalities that have accompanied a major source of funding for HIV prevention and treatment: the President's Emergency

Plan for AIDS Relief (PEPFAR). Through an analysis that explores the actual and potential effects of these interventions on those who work in the sex industry, the chapter suggests that existing measures may do more harm than good.

The conflation of trafficking and sex work

Public concern about the issue of trafficking in persons has a long history. In the late nineteenth and early twentieth centuries, panics about 'white slave traffic' occurred in the context of rapid urbanization: women and men moved from rural areas to cities in search of work. Concerns over women's mobility were linked to moral concerns, particularly concerning female virginity (Pearson 1972; Walkowitz 1992), and led to the passage of legislation addressing sexuality: in the UK, the act that repealed the Contagious Diseases Acts in 1883 also raised the age of consent and criminalized homosexual acts[2] (Pearson 1972; Self 2003); the US Mann Act of 1910 addressed 'immoral acts' – it was most widely used to charge women who travelled to meet men with whom they would have sex, often their fiancés. Langum (1994) and Grittner (1990) document the selective use of the Mann Act in cases of interracial sex and against suspected communists.

The seemingly endless debate about trafficking focuses heavily on sex work, with a number of questions continually re-emerging: is all participation in the sex industry (particularly prostitution) trafficking? Is such participation an inherent violation of human rights? 'Trafficking' is now used to refer to situations involving force, fraud and coercion to exploit a person's labour or services. Legal definitions of trafficking focus on the use of force, deception and coercion, and debt bondage. While the term is popularly associated with forced prostitution, trafficking occurs in a wide range of industries beyond the sex industry, including in the supply of labour for agriculture, construction, manufacturing and domestic work. Because of the emphasis on coercion in the way trafficking is thought about, sex workers lose out when their work is conflated with trafficking: their agency is denied. By equating migration for sex work with the trafficking of women against their will, sex workers are made subject to further intrusions of legal authorities. Indeed, around the world, sex workers cite the state and its agents as the prime violators of their human rights (Schleifer 2006; Human Rights Watch 2003; Jenkins 2002; Jenkins et al. 2006).

Migration and work lie at the heart of the international traffic in persons. Trafficked persons are for the most part migrants – often undocumented – seeking work elsewhere who find themselves in untenable working conditions. A widely publicized trafficking case involved some dozens of Asian men and women relocated to the US Territory of the Northern Mariana Islands for work in sweatshops and brothels, for which they were either inadequately paid or not paid at all, and were brutalized by their employers if they dared to protest about their conditions. Sex featured in the Marianas case, in that some of those trafficked were employed in brothels, but many trafficked persons are not involved in the sex industry at all. Testimony to the US Congress by the Director of the Global Survival Network described thousands of people in debt bondage and slavery in the garment industry.[3] The crucial factors that determine a case of trafficking are the working conditions in which people find themselves, and the means – deception, coercion, outright enslavement – by which they are brought into those conditions.

The equation of sex work and trafficking leads to an overly simplistic analysis that neglects the core issues of trafficking, namely conditions of labour and migration, while refocusing discussion on other problems. Maintaining a lurid focus on sex allows the dull and intractable issues of labour and migration to be ignored in favour of a more politically popular and publicity-friendly condemnation of trafficking as if it only involved the traffic of women for sex work. This artificially narrow focus is doubly perilous. Punitive measures introduced with the aim of abolishing sex work altogether have led to the imposition of limitations on women's working and mobility in the name of protecting them against the twin evils of trafficking and prostitution. These limitations not only restrict women's freedom, but may even drive determined migrants, particularly those seeking work, into the arms of traffickers (see Djordjevic, this volume). Second, while notions of trafficking reflected in recent approaches have grown more sophisticated – as reflected by a move away from an exclusive focus on sex to one that also includes servitude and slavery in industries as disparate as sweatshops, domestic labour and construction – the influence of activists' agendas vis-à-vis sex work and trafficking has also expanded. Trafficking and migration are now discussed in the context of HIV/AIDS, development and public health. Sex work is now discussed as a development and labour issue in addition to the earlier conception of prostitution as a public health and law enforcement issue. In recent years sex worker activists have increasingly engaged in international negotiations that affect sex workers, from the International Conferences on HIV/AIDS to the Working Group on Contemporary Forms of Slavery (Ditmore 2007) and the negotiations of the Palermo Protocol (Doezema 2005).

Victimhood, consent and gender in the United Nations Palermo Protocol

The United Nations Palermo Protocol is a measure to address transnational organized crime. Its Optional Protocols, on smuggling and trafficking in persons respectively, reveal important differences in the way in which these two issues are framed. Trafficking in persons defines a victim of crime rather than an agent, while smuggling necessarily implicates the person who has engaged the services of a smuggler. A smuggled person, like a trafficked person, has clandestinely crossed a border or been transported, but unlike trafficking, smuggling is not linked to work. A smuggled person is not perceived as a victim but a criminal, an illegal immigrant, an undocumented alien, while a trafficked person is assumed to be an innocent victim. This conception of agency divides in the imagination – if not in reality – along gender lines. This division is reflected in the title of the protocol addressing trafficking, which is the Optional Protocol to Prevent, Suppress and Punish Trafficking in Persons, *Especially Women and Children* (emphasis added). The Smuggling Protocol has no such coda and no specific emphasis on gender. Smuggled migrants are assumed to be men seeking work elsewhere without proper documentation, while trafficked persons are assumed to be duped victims, usually women.

The UN protocols reinforce the idea that trafficking is something that happens to women while smuggling is the province of men. This gendered distinction follows long-standing stereotypes of women as victims and men as less liable to be victimized. As well as presenting a distorted view of women, this harms men. Trafficked men are invisible and their situations continue to be less recognized and therefore more difficult to address. These distinctions may also significantly affect enforcement, depending on the way they are interpreted. One of the most hotly disputed elements of the Palermo Protocol was the definition of trafficking in persons. Debates about the definition of trafficking typically centred on whether to include all sex work. For a small minority of feminists, sex work and the exchange of sex for goods or money, as in prostitution but also, in some contexts, even dating, are a reinforcement of male power and privilege.

In a United Nations protocol, definitions necessarily afford a certain interpretive leeway for enforcement by signatory nations, in order to allow consensus to be achieved in such a large meeting. The protocol does not prohibit additional measures and/or sterner enforcement, thereby allowing signatory nations to enforce additional domestic legislation regarding these crimes and to assess punishment for them as they see fit. Such an allowance for domestic legislation affords great variation in the possible enforcement of this document nation by nation. Thus nations are able to legislate prostitution as they see fit. Australia, Germany, the Netherlands and New Zealand, among others, were very clear that they would not sign a protocol that would require them to change their national laws to outlaw prostitution. Similarly, nations such as Iran, Iraq, the USA and the Vatican would not have signed a protocol requiring them to decriminalize prostitution in their jurisdictions.

The definition of trafficking adopted in the protocol specifies that the threat or use of force or deception is a necessary component of trafficking in persons into any situation. It goes on to make clear that consent is irrelevant when these means have been used. In other words, a person can consent to work but not to slavery or servitude. The definition additionally specifies that any recruitment, transportation or harbouring of a person under eighteen is to be considered trafficking in persons, regardless of the means used. The issue of consent came to be especially significant in framing competing definitions. Under international law, children – defined as any person 'under 18 years of age' – are not able to give consent. During the October 2000 meetings, a member of the Philippine delegation made an intervention (spoken suggestion) whose apparent intent was to redefine prostitutes as children. International Human Rights Law Group representative Melynda Barnhart summarized this statement by saying that the delegate '... essentially said that all women making decisions that [this delegate] doesn't agree with, i.e. prostitutes, others should have the legal ability to override'. The written proposal, distributed on 2 October 2000, had been significantly refined but seemed clearly to include people with disabilities: '"Child" shall mean any person under 18 years of age provided that those over 18 years of age but unable to fully protect themselves from abuse, neglect, cruelty, exploitation due to mental or physical incapacity be considered for the purpose of this protocol.'

Whatever the intentions behind this proposed definition, it is legally very dangerous. During the 1950s, women in the United States could be institutionalized for being 'promiscuous' (Keefe 1994: unnumbered). It would be all too easy, using the definition above, to see a return to that state of affairs, with adult women being judged unable to 'fully protect themselves' owing to 'mental or physical incapacity' if they engage in unapproved activities such as promiscuity or prostitution. The definition betrays a readiness to sacrifice many of women's hard-won gains, including independence, legal majority and the ability to make enforceable contracts, solely in order to render prostitution more criminal. Definitions of this kind, in which the normal presumption of adult autonomy can be overruled by a subjective, external judgement as to the desirability of an activity, are essentially perilous. They call to mind Rubin's 'brainwash theory', which '... explains erotic diversity by assuming that some sexual acts are so disgusting that no one would willingly perform them. Therefore, the reasoning goes, anyone who does so must have been forced or fooled' (Rubin 1984: 306).

The reasoning of people who want to abolish prostitution proceeds from the same point. Prostitution as a condition is assumed to be so inherently intolerable that no rational person could freely choose it for themselves; therefore if anyone appears to have chosen it for themselves, it can indicate only either that they are not rational or they are victims of coercion or deception, that is to say victims of trafficking. The perils of such an argument lie precisely in the way that it opens the door to a paternalistic interpretation of 'what is best for women'. Such interpretations have historically had a very negative impact on women; the gains made by the modern feminist movement have been in large part concerned with escaping from such paternalism and forcing the recognition of women's autonomy and their ability to make their own decisions. To roll back those gains in the interests of pursuing a war on prostitution is perilous indeed.

But there are further costs of a short-sighted policy on trafficking. Despite a continuing tendency to see trafficking simply in terms of slavery, it is a complex issue that involves issues of migration and labour. New restrictions are evident throughout the world, whether they take the form of an increase in scrutiny of young women leaving certain nations, such as Thailand and other Asian nations, or entering them, as in the case of Japan, or simply increased control of borders in general, as in the case of the United States. Policies that restrict travel, and especially women's travel, actually encourage the practice of trafficking in persons by closing legal avenues of migration. Would-be migrants of both sexes are forced to fall back on the services of people who can help them cross borders and find work, increasing the potential risks that they run when others take advantage of their vulnerable situations (Meillón 2001; Kwong 1997).

The shift from anti-trafficking to anti-prostitution in development funding

The USA also passed an anti-trafficking law in 2000, a law including services and assistance for people in the USA who were trafficked. Under the Bush administration, US funding policy reflects the repressive US attitude towards sexuality in general and sex work in particular. Money has been earmarked in the US federal budget for anti-trafficking efforts to prevent modern slavery and to assist people who have suffered in untenable working conditions in the USA and abroad. This money is administered through a number of agencies, including the Office for Victims of Crime and the Office of Refugee Resettlement for work in the USA, and the US Agency for International Development (USAID) for work abroad. The Bush administration has included little-noticed but very politically effective constraints on this funding so that none of this money will go to projects that do not explicitly condemn 'prostitution and sex trafficking'. This policy has had adverse effects on international organizations and NGO operations, particularly those promoting HIV prevention for sex workers. The Bush administration's policies demand that organizations receiving certain funds must have an official position opposing prostitution. These stipulations began with anti-trafficking funds and quickly and quietly moved to HIV-prevention monies.

Under these restrictions, even while trafficking is a key concern, it is sometimes precisely those sex work projects that are recognized for their excellent and effective anti-trafficking projects and HIV-prevention efforts which have found themselves under attack. The US administration has been very clear in its determination that projects that 'promote prostitution' will not receive further anti-trafficking funds from USAID. Unfortunately, this seems to include projects that work with sex workers in productive ways to promote both their human rights and their health, including working to prevent the spread of HIV. This restriction is now applied to all HIV-prevention money from the USA.

The shift in focus from trafficking in persons to attacking funding for sex work projects indicates an interest in promoting anti-prostitution ideology at the expense of health and human rights, particularly the health and human rights of women and others in the sex industry. Whatever the nature of the ongoing debate, ideology should not be permitted to override effective HIV-prevention efforts or to interfere with treatment of people living with HIV. Unfortunately, that is exactly what is occurring. Sex workers are put at risk by being denied services, sometimes in accord with the pledge and at other times by service providers using the pledge to justify denying services. For example, male sex workers in Cambodia were told that for doctors to answer their questions about anal sex would be in violation of the US funding policy.[4] Sex workers are not the only people to be adversely affected by such misguided policy: the children and families of sex workers and their clients will all be affected, and this broadly affects public health.

This ideological agenda has affected successful projects whose efficacy has been widely recognized. Projects that involve sex workers are the most successful at combating abuses within the sex industry around the world, but because such projects often advocate legalization of prostitution, they may find themselves cut off from funding. An example of a project that may suffer under this new policy is the Durbar Mahila Samanwaya Committee (DMSC) of Kolkata, more widely known as the Sonagachi Project. This is considered one of the strongest success stories of HIV prevention among vulnerable populations in South Asia. The Sonagachi Project is one of many projects that exemplify pragmatic and effective approaches to reducing not only transmission of HIV but also abuses such as trafficking within sex work. The Sonagachi Project's anti-trafficking initiative relies on the participation of red light district residents, especially sex workers, to prevent trafficking into the red light districts. At the International Conference on HIV/AIDS in Toronto in August 2006, Sonagachi personnel reported that this programme had assisted over a thousand people to leave the red light areas where DMSC is active. Their anti-trafficking initiative relies on the participation of red light district residents, especially sex workers, to prevent trafficking into the red light districts.

Shifting farther away from sex workers' rights

Trafficking in persons is an enormous issue but it affects far fewer people than HIV and AIDS. In 2003, the USA announced PEPFAR as the guiding policy document for all US foreign assistance relating to the global HIV/AIDS pandemic. Under PEPFAR, fifteen focus countries in Africa and the Caribbean, as well as Vietnam, have received a concentrated influx of funding for prevention, treatment and care in the hope of turning the tide in parts of the world facing the worst of the pandemic.

The USA is to be applauded for the creation of the US Global AIDS Fund and for targeting areas most affected by HIV and AIDS. Unfortunately, the Bush administration incorporated the following amendment into the text of the act that allocated PEPFAR funds: '(f) LIMITATION. – No funds made available to carry out this Act, or any amendment made to this Act, may be used to provide assistance to any group or organization that does not have a policy explicitly opposing prostitution and sex trafficking.' The irony that the man initially charged with enforcing this policy resigned amid scandal after media reports in April 2007 that he hired the services of an escort agency was not lost on sex workers around the world (Sex Workers Project and NSWP 2007).

PEPFAR has numerous restrictions, which apply only to PEPFAR monies. President George W. Bush has, however, recently proposed twice as much funding – US$30 billion – for the four years after PEPFAR ends.

This funding may have similar restrictions attached. There are, however, two court cases pending and one bill proposed that may change aspects of PEPFAR's restrictions. The PATHWAY Act would remove restrictions on funding for reproductive health and rights, including access to abortion and information about abortion. The lawsuits brought by DKT, a social marketing company that sells condoms in the developing world, and AOSI/Pathfinder International contest the anti-prostitution policy. The Department of Justice (DoJ) initially warned that applying these restrictions to US groups would raise free speech issues and suggested that the requirement should be applied only to overseas groups, but in 2004 DoJ revoked this policy and said that the administration could apply the rule to US groups. To date, these have not been definitively decided as appeals proceed. Unfortunately, these court decisions will not affect organizations based outside the United States.

Anti-trafficking policies have leached into HIV-prevention programming, preventing work that sex workers themselves prioritize – labour rights and improved working conditions – in favour of politically palatable but ineffective police raids. I am sad to report that even intergovernmental organizations without US funding have followed this trend. The United Nations Fund for Population Activities (UNFPA) has the mandate to address sex work, in part because it is the sole UN agency that receives no funding from the USA. In 2006 UNFPA held a global consultation on sex work with representatives of UNAIDS member organizations, sex workers from nearly every region, and public health and development professionals. The overwhelming message from all but four of the presentations was that sex workers' rights – with an emphasis on workers' rights for sex workers of all genders – are the key to HIV prevention in the sex industry. The draft guidelines developed and circulated following this consultation, however, emphasize preventing female people entering the sex industry, and getting female people out of the sex industry, without support for the promotion of good working conditions within the industry. The strongest recommendation on working conditions for sex workers is the recommendation to 'promote access to decent work and alternative employment', language that itself stigmatizes the sex industry. These draft guidelines are counter to the global consultation from which they were supposedly derived and counter to the principle of meaningful involvement of people living with HIV/AIDS and people vulnerable to HIV/AIDS. Such an approach is ineffective for HIV prevention among sex workers and promotes rights violations of sex workers by further stigmatizing their work.

It is easy to declare that one is 'against traffic in women' or 'anti-prostitution' but immensely more difficult to determine what would be helpful to those deemed in need of help. By excluding sex workers from the process of determining solutions and denying funds to their organizations and to those who work with them, these policies undermine efforts to improve their situations. A number of effective programmes have rejected such highly restricted funding. Brazil turned down approximately US$40 million offered by the US government in opposition to these restrictions. Pedro Chequer, Brazil's National AIDS Commissioner, said 'sex workers are part of implementing our AIDS policy and deciding how to promote it. ... They are our partners. How could we ask prostitutes to take a position against themselves?' (Kaplan 2005). And Sonia Corrêa, an AIDS activist in Brazil and co-chair of Sexuality Policy Watch (previously known as the International Working Group on Sexuality and Social Policy), commented, 'This would be entirely in contradiction with Brazilian guidelines for a programme that has been working very well for years. We are providing condoms, and doing a lot of prevention work with sex workers, and the rate of infection has stabilized and dropped since the 1980s' (Boseley and Goldenberg 2005).

Putting ideology first: who's selling out?

Trafficking in persons has a long history of conflation with the sex industry. Responses to trafficking that exclusively focus on the sex industry affect a broad range of people and issues, sometimes in unanticipated ways. The people who are hurt by the policies described here are not policy-makers, lobbyists or activists: they are poor people far from the spaces where these decisions are made, women, men and transgender persons whose voices and needs were not considered when these decisions were made. These ideological policy shifts are not abstract or without consequences: they translate to a very real human impact, and the potential to cause significant suffering to real people.

Sex workers are members of communities, some of whom are the clients or dependants of sex workers. Any decision that affects their health or economic options also has an impact on others. The issues that arise in relation to policies that seek to eradicate this industry have a complex and much broader relationship with the labour market as a whole, particularly with respect to gender and migration. Sex work is a significant portion of the economy: the ILO estimates that the sex sector accounts for between 2 and 14 per cent of GDP of four Asian countries, for example (Lim 1998: 7). But the sex sector does not exist in isolation, and sex workers are not the only group likely to be affected by policy formulated on a conflation of prostitution and trafficking. As a

63

consequence, any policy that targets the sex industry will necessarily have a much broader impact, as measures proposed to address one particular sector 'spill over' to affect other areas. In common with other economic sectors of marginal legality or low social acceptability, the sex industry employs many undocumented workers. A crackdown on sex work may be implemented through a more general attack on sectors employing undocumented workers or, conversely, broad initiatives to crack down on undocumented labour may gain impetus from a policy that favours repression of sex work. If organizations working with migrants are seen (rightly or wrongly) to be facilitating clandestine or illegal employment, they too are likely to be singled out for increased scrutiny, legal harassment or withdrawal of support.

Everyone loses out if reproductive health, anti-trafficking and HIV-prevention efforts are undermined because sex workers are deliberately deprived of access to friendly and supportive services. Sex workers' groups are at the forefront of proposing specific, practical solutions to the many problems faced by sex workers. Policies that inhibit these projects harm the health of sex workers, their human rights and their ability to organize. The most effective sex work projects are precisely those which address sex work as labour, such as the much-heralded Sonagachi Project, commended as a best-practice project by UNAIDS (Jenkins 2002). Cambodian sex workers use the slogan 'Don't talk to me about sewing machines, talk to me about workers rights' to emphasize the need to address working conditions within the sex industry. Their voices – incompatible with an ideological stance that is unable to accommodate the inclusion of better conditions within the sex industry as a valid human rights issue – have been ignored by the people who have crafted these policies.

When sex workers are asked what would make a difference to their lives, they call for improvements in their working conditions, including but not limited to freedom from violence, the right to refuse a client or a request, freedom of movement, and sanitary conditions conducive to protected sex. The simplest, most efficient and effective way to know how people of all genders who work in the sex industry would improve their conditions is to ask them. Policy-makers and development experts would do well to listen to sex workers on issues related to sex work instead of overriding their concerns and thereby jeopardizing their human rights.

Notes

1 Excerpts from this essay appeared in *SIECUS Report* 33(2), 2005, pp. 26–9. An earlier version of this essay appeared as 'Trafficking in lives: how ideology shapes policy', in K. Kempadoo with B. Pattanaik and J. Sanghera (eds), *Trafficking and Prostitution Reconsidered*, Boulder, CO: Paradigm Publishers, 2005. Used with permission.

2 This was used most notoriously against Oscar Wilde.

3 Testimony by Steven R. Galster, Global Survival Network, before the House Committee on Energy and Natural Resources, 16 September 1999, Concerning the US Commonwealth of the Northern Mariana Islands, <www.house.gov/resources/106cong/fullcomm/99sep16/galster.htm>.

4 In *Taking the Pledge* (2006), a thirteen-minute film, in English, Khmer, Thai, French, Portuguese and Bengali, with English subtitles, featuring sex workers from Bangladesh, Brazil, Cambodia, Mali and Thailand describing the problems created by the 'anti-prostitution pledge' required to receive USAID and PEPFAR funds, produced by the Network of Sex Work Projects. Available on <http://sexworkerspresent.blip.tv/file/181155/>.

References

Boseley, S. and S. Goldenberg (2005) 'Brazil spurns US terms for Aids help', *Guardian*, 4 May, <www.guardian.co.uk/aids/story/0,7369,1475965,00.html> (accessed 4 June 2007).

Ditmore, M. (2007) 'Feminists and sex workers: working together', in J. Klaehn (ed.), *Women across Borders*, Toronto: Black Rose Books.

Ditmore, M. and WNU (Women's Network for Unity) (2006) *Structural Stigmatization of Sex Workers in Cambodia*, Phnom Penh: Women's Agenda for Change, Women's Network for Unity.

DMSC (Durbar Mahila Samanwaya Committee) (2007) 'A survey of the vrious [*sic*] types of social, physical and occupational oppressions heaped upon our sex workers before and after their entry into sex work', <durbar.org/new/Survey_2007_Report.html> (accessed 4 June 2007).

Doezema, J. (2005) 'Now you see her, now you don't: sex workers at the UN trafficking protocol negotiation', *Social and Legal Studies*, 14(1): 61–89.

Galster, S. R. (1999) 'Testimony before the House Committee on Energy and Natural Resources', 16 September, <www.house.gov/resources/106cong/fullcomm/99sep16/galster.htm> (accessed 4 June 2007).

Grittner, F. K. (1990) *White Slavery Myth, Ideology, and American Law*, New York and London: Garland.

Human Rights Watch (2003) 'Ravaging the vulnerable: abuses against persons at high risk of HIV infection in Bangladesh', 15(6[c]), <www.hrw.org/reports/2003/bangladesh0803/> (accessed 15 June 2007).

Jenkins, C. (2002) *Sex Work and HIV/AIDS*, UNAIDS Technical Update, UNAIDS Best Practice Collection, Geneva: UNAIDS.

Jenkins, C., P. Ayutthaya and A. Hunter (2005) 'Katoey in Thailand: HIV/AIDS and life opportunities', Washington DC: USAID, <www.alternatevisions.org/publications.htm> (accessed 4 June 2007).

Jenkins, C., CPU (Cambodian Prostitutes' Union), WNU (Women's

Network for Unity), and C. Sainsbury (2006) 'Violence and exposure to HIV among sex workers, Phnom Penh, Cambodia', Washington DC: Policy Project and USAID, <www.researchforsexwork.org/> (accessed 4 June 2007).

Kaplan, E. (2005) 'Just say não', *The Nation*, 30 May.

Keefe, T. (1994) *Some of My Best Friends are Naked*, San Francisco, CA: Barbary Coast.

Kwong, P. (1997) *Forbidden Workers*, New York: New Press.

Langum, D. J. (1994) *Crossing over the Line*, Chicago, IL: University of Chicago.

Lim, L. L. (ed.) (1998) *The Sex Sector*, Geneva: International Labour Organization.

Meillón, C. (ed.) in collaboration with C. Bunch (2001) *Holding on to the Promise: Women's Human Rights and the Beijing + 5 Review*, New Brunswick: Rutgers.

Pearson, M. (1972) *The £5 Virgins*, New York: Saturday Review Press.

Petro, M. (2006) 'I did it ... for the money', *Research for Sex Work*, 9: 19–21, <www.researchforsexwork.org> (accessed 4 June 2007).

Rubin, G. (1984) 'Thinking sex', in C. Vance (ed.), *Pleasure and Danger*, Boston, MA: Routledge & Kegan Paul.

Schleifer, R. (2006) 'Human rights', in M. Ditmore (ed.), *Encyclopedia of Prostitution and Sex Work*, Westport, CT: Greenwood Press.

Self, H. J. (2003) *Prostitution, Women and Misuse of the Law. The Fallen Daughters of Eve*, London: Frank Cass.

Sex Workers Project and NSWP (Network of Sex Work Projects) (2007) 'Advocates criticize moralistic policy that Randall Tobias enforced', Joint press statement, 1 May, <www.sexworkersproject.org> (accessed 4 June 2007; audio file: <www.sexworkerspresent.blip.tv/file/216631/>, accessed 4 June 2007).

Thukral, J. and M. Ditmore (2003) *Revolving Door*, New York: Urban Justice Center Sex Workers Project, <www.sexworkersproject.org> (accessed 4 June 2007).

Thukral, J., M. Ditmore and A. Murphy (2005) *Behind Closed Doors*, New York: Urban Justice Center Sex Workers Project, <www.sexworkersproject.org> (accessed 4 June 2007).

Walkowitz, J. (1992) *City of Dreadful Delight*, Chicago, IL: University of Chicago.

Zi Teng (2006) 'Chinese migrant sex workers in Hong Kong', *Research for Sex Work*, 9: 22–5, <www.researchforsexwork.org> (accessed 4 June 2007).

5 | The language of rights

JAYA SHARMA[1]

Rights language can be used in a myriad of ways. As Alice Miller (2004) argues, the manner in which rights are claimed can range from being status quo-ist to being transformatory. There has, however, been insufficient reflection and dialogue regarding the limitations of rights language. Too often there has been an unquestioning acceptance that rights language will always ultimately promote the quest for justice.

The reflections shared in this chapter draw upon my experiences as a member of PRISM (People for Rights of Indian Sexual Minorities), a queer activist forum based in New Delhi, India, which works on issues related to same-sex sexualities.[2] This is a context in which many 'progressive' movements still view sexuality as a 'luxury' cause, one not to be prioritized. PRISM has sought to highlight the ways in which a range of dominant ideologies and institutions (such as those relating to patriarchy and religious fundamentalism) deploy constructions of sexuality to maintain inequitable distribution of power, resources, suffering, pleasure and spaces, to the detriment of full and free expression of human sexuality and people's human rights. PRISM's work seeks to bring into question basic notions and norms of sexuality. It seeks to problematize enforced heterosexuality and heteronormativity and the idea that sexual identity and behaviour are fixed from birth, and focuses on issues relating to same-sex desire and gender transgression. We seek to make these issues visible in mainstream society, to respond to human rights violations, and to engage with progressive movements with issues of marginalized sexualities as an intrinsic part of their mandate.

In PRISM, we have used the language of rights to demand legitimacy and freedom from violations faced by same-sex-desiring people, particularly vis-à-vis the state. Many of us, however, find that the rights discourse is insufficient to articulate and act upon a queer feminist perspective on sexuality. In this chapter, I draw on experiences from PRISM's work and discussions within the forum with other activists to examine the language of rights from a queer perspective.[3] I seek to unpack some of the underlying premises of rights language and the directions that these premises push us towards when it is deployed. I explore the limits of rights language in the context of the realities and needs of queer activism, especially in relation to dialogue with other progressive groups. The chapter suggests that the articulation of queer issues only in terms of rights might limit the discourse on same-sex desire, and that alternative, feminist, framings might offer more potential for developing strategies for achieving justice and equity.

Queer thoughts on the rights language

The issue of identity Talk of rights by a range of players in the Indian context – including people's movements, NGOs and the state – is almost always in terms of identities based on gender, race, ethnicity, class, dis/ability, age, sexual orientation, etc. Even when broader terms such as human rights and sexual rights are used, the manner in which they are drawn upon is in terms of identities. For example, when human rights are evoked, it is the human rights of particular sections of society which are demanded, such as the human rights of tribal people, children, women, etc. There could be other ways of evoking human rights. As Susan Jolly commented in her response to a draft of this chapter, heteronormativity itself could be argued to be a human rights violation! Yet rights are almost never articulated in this manner.

Even in the case of sexual rights, while the concept itself is a universalistic one, in the manner in which I have encountered it in dialogue or negotiations there is a tendency to articulate these rights as they relate to specific groups, such as 'sexual minorities', 'women' or 'sex workers'. The potential that the language of sexual rights holds to cut across identities is most often not drawn upon in the manner in which even activists engaged with issues of sexuality use the term.

That the logic of rights pushes us into a framework based on identities is a source of concern, particularly in the context of same-sex desire. At the outset, it needs to be clarified that there is no denying that the assertion of identities is important, particularly in a context such as that in India, where there is such silence around same-sex desire. Identities are also important in order to be able to experience a sense of belonging to a community, the value of which cannot be overestimated, particularly in the face of severe stigma and isolation. It needs to be underlined, therefore, that the concerns outlined below do not constitute a rejection of identities based on sexual behaviour. It is, however, important to recognize that identities capture one aspect of the existing reality with respect to same-sex desire and the dangers of assuming that it is the entire reality.

More often than not the assumption made by activists in contemporary urban India who address issues related to same-sex desire, including a vast majority of activists who identify as LGBT, is that sexual behaviour necessarily translates into identities based on that behaviour. Therefore, for example, the assumption is that every woman who experiences desire for women will identify/can be identified as a lesbian. In the Indian context we know, however, that the number of people who identify as lesbian, gay, bisexual, transgender or even as indigenous identities such as *kothi*, *aravani* and *jogappa*, indigenous identities that have their own sets of norms related to gender expression and sexual behaviour, is much smaller than the number of people who experience same-sex desire.

It is not only a question of numbers. The issue is a more basic one of how sexuality is being understood. Speaking of sexuality only in terms of identities promotes a view that sexuality is fixed and that it can be fitted into mutually exclusive categories. We need to consider here a queer perspective of sexuality, according to which social processes of compulsory heterosexuality seek to stifle sexual diversity – not just in society at large, but even the potential for sexual diversity within each of us. If this is how we perceive sexuality, the dangers of a framework that is based only on identities become clear. If this is premised on predefined communities based on sexual orientation, we are faced with the issue of excluding those who do not identify and of promoting a view of sexuality that is rigid.

Intersectionality instead of 'othering' The discussion on rights and identity has another specificity when it comes to same-sex desire. In the case of race, caste or disability, there are clear markers of identity. As a queer perspective sees everyone as having potential for a diversity of sexual desire, including same-sex desire, however, it is difficult to draw boundaries. This in my view generates anxiety within those who identify as heterosexual in a manner that makes queer activism all the more challenging. In this context it becomes much easier, even for those who are liberal, to speak in defence of the rights of the 'other'. The language of rights then provides a safe distance with which to deal with same-sex desire.

Queer politics challenges this tendency to distance oneself from the issue. Instead it pushes other progressive individuals and movements to recognize the logic of incorporating issues of queer sexuality as being part of their own agenda. It is only by situating rights within the framework of intersectionality that this deeper alliance-building becomes possible. Such a framework articulates the fundamental linkages between the norms and structures related to compulsory heterosexuality, patriarchy, racism, casteism, religious fundamentalism and other ideologies that

69

seek to define and control people. It recognizes that any attempt to isolate one dimension will constitute a limited approach that fails to address the underlying interplay of forces.

Box 5.1 Activism Against Violence Against Women

An intervention was made by PRISM during the sixteen days of 'Activism Against Violence Against Women', three years ago. PRISM raised the issue of lesbian suicides with the women's organizations who were part of the campaign.[4] In the previous four months, there had been at least three cases of lesbian suicide reported in the press. The response of the women's groups to raising the issue of lesbian suicide was positive. They said, 'Why don't you raise the issue and we will support you.' We in turn asked the women's groups whether the issue of lesbian suicide was not intrinsic to the agenda of the women's movement. It was this approach which was articulated in the leaflet that was then jointly brought out by PRISM and a number of organizations including women's groups.

After sharing the three cases of lesbian suicides the leaflet stated:

'Apart from rape, sexual harassment, and bride burning, violence against women happens every time a woman is married against her will. It happens every time a woman feels guilty for wanting to be happy and every time that a woman must die because she is unacceptable to society.

'Lesbian suicides are a result of society's attempt to restrict women's choices and control their lives.

'We protest these deaths as Violence Against All Women.'

How can you claim human rights if you are not considered human? In addition to the limitations of a narrowly defined rights approach in building deeper alliances, there are also limitations in the capacity of such an approach to address the attitudes of those who are hostile to same-sex-desiring people. In a context in which queer sexuality is despised by many and also criminalized, rights language does not take us very far in the process of claiming justice. For hostile players to even grant that homosexuals are 'human', and therefore should enjoy 'human rights', becomes difficult. In more liberal contexts, there are those who grant that homosexuals, like other people, have rights that should not be violated.

Even here, however, if the discomfort aroused by and moral judgement against same-sex desire are not addressed, a mere assertion of rights will not suffice. There is no short cut to engaging with underlying beliefs and values.

Box 5.2 Prayas

Prayas, a 'high profile' child rights organization, based in New Delhi, in a concept note that it circulated in 2003 on Legalizing Homosexuality, stated:

'Freedom does not mean licence. Injectible Drug Users (IDUs), organized Commercial Sex Workers (CSWs), or Men having Sex with Men (MSM) can hardly take recourse to Fundamental Rights to persist in their behaviour unhindered.

'It is erroneous and imprudent to say that we have a "gay community". There are present hardly any of the accepted prerequisites of community. At best, gays make for a small discrete group of freaks or perverts. It would be unwise to ignore larger interests of society, in order to cater to the whims of these disparate microscopic groups.

'It is incorrect to assume that homosexual behaviour is not "unnatural". It is just not there in other species. It is not the natural order. Clandestine and subterranean, homosexuality cannot be taken to be in consonance with Human Rights.'

Addressing heteronormativity Another danger related to the rights language is that the way in which rights are articulated and claimed might not address underlying structural inequalities and norms. In the case of queer sexuality, this failure to address underlying norms is fatal. The violations experienced by same-sex-desiring people are often not of a tangible nature. These include the silence surrounding same-sex desire, in contexts such as India. Owing to this, same-sex-desiring people often feel, before/if they come into contact with others 'like them', that they are 'the only ones in the world' who are this way. The relentless assumption and assertion of heterosexuality as the only reality continuously marginalizes and seeks to invalidate the experience of same-sex-desiring people. If we were to focus only on more tangible violations, as the existing rights discourse pushes us to do, everyday, ongoing violations would be difficult to articulate or address.

Heteronormativity needs to be centrally addressed because all violations related to queer sexuality, tangible or intangible, stem from the threat that same-sex desire poses to existing norms and structures relating to compulsory heterosexuality. It is because of the perceived threat to societal norms that uphold heterosexuality that the violations that accrue are so severe.

The rights language, however, does not help 'unpack' heteronormativity – i.e. why these norms exist; how they serve the interests of existing power structures; and how these norms might be challenged. In fact, the language of rights and the related language of choice can sometimes take us away from addressing the underlying issues. For example, it runs the danger of limiting the issue of queer sexuality to the realm of 'personal' choice. This danger is compounded by the fact that the space that the rights discourse has historically occupied has been one of the individual, located in a liberal framework. Feminist critiques of the limits of law and human rights, by which we are all made rights holders, also point to the illusory nature of choice. These critiques also point to the related danger of the oversimplification of power relations. In the context of compulsory heterosexuality, the extent to which choice and rights can be exercised is severely limited, given the constraints to recognizing or acting upon the diversity of desire within us.

The limitations of rights language in addressing heteronormativity are similar to those outlined in the discussion on intersectionality – that is, that rights language by itself does not offer the tools that can enable an

---

Box 5.3 *Antakshiri*

A gender and sexuality training course was conducted by a New Delhi-based organization that works on gender and education. The participants were non-formal education teachers involved in an educational intervention in rural Rajasthan. One of the 'fun' activities included *antakshiri* (a song-based game in which participants divide up into teams and have to sing, picking up on the last alphabetical letter of the song sung by the opposing team). The men were on one side and the women on the other, singing romantic songs addressed to each other. While the activity was aimed at reducing some of the inhibitions related to sexuality, it was highly heteronormative. The experience was similar to the kind of heteronormative humour that is often exchanged with colleagues in workspaces.

analysis of how different axes such as gender, sexuality, class and so on intersect. It appears to me, therefore, that rights language is precisely that – a language, more than an 'approach' or an 'ideology' – in itself.

Side-stepping subversion That rights language does not generally engage with heteronormativity also means that it almost never engages with the subversive potential of queer sexuality. An important manifestation of this lack of engagement is the focus of rights language, in the manner in which it is most often deployed, on violations. In the context of same-sex sexuality, we find that it is sometimes easier for us as activists (whether same-sex-desiring or not) who are engaged with these issues to restrict the discourse to violations, and to generate a more limited consensus around these. On the part of others, too, there is a preference for limiting the engagement to violations of human rights. There is a reluctance to recognize and submit to the subversive potential that queer desire holds, which comes from the structures and ideologies that are threatened. Part of this reluctance also needs to be located in the anxieties that a deeper engagement with issues of same-sex desire generates, given middle-class (the background of the majority of the activists that PRISM has thus far engaged with) construction and experience of sexuality as an intensely personal, intimate realm.

Box 5.4 Sovereignty and Citizenship

Attempts were made to pass a resolution at the Indian Association of Women's Studies (IAWS) conference in Goa in May 2005. The theme of the conference was 'Sovereignty and Citizenship'. The resolution was drafted by feminist, queer (both same-sex- and other sex-desiring) individuals, including an activist who also works on issues of disabilities. The resolution was as follows:

'We in the women's movement have long recognized that constructions of what is "natural" and "normal" have been used to define and control us as women. We also recognize that rigid binaries of "man" and "woman", notions of what constitutes a "normal" body and notions of what constitutes "acceptable" sexual behaviour limit possibilities for all of us. They also stigmatize and deny citizenship rights to individuals and communities perceived to deviate from the "normal". These include, for example, people with disabilities, those who are same-sex-desiring, lesbian and bisexual women, transgendered people, *hijras* and sex workers.

'In this context, Section 377 of the Indian Penal Code clearly violates every principle of equity, justice and citizenship. Section 377 criminalizes a wide range of non-procreative sexual acts considered to be "against the order of nature". This provision is justified on the grounds that it provides legal redress against child sexual abuse. However, not only is it entirely inadequate in this regard, in practice it is used to harass, control and criminalize those who threaten patriarchal structures upheld by compulsory heterosexuality. We call upon the government to repeal Section 377 and to ensure that a separate law be enacted at the earliest to effectively deal with child sexual abuse. Legal provisions such as Section 377 violate the letter and spirit of the Fundamental Rights enshrined in the Constitution which guarantee equality and freedom to all citizens.

'IAWS commits to engaging with the experiences and emerging perspectives that communities perceived to deviate from the "normal" offer to the women's movement. Such an engagement would enable us to subvert and strike at prescriptive norms. It would also help evolve a framework of citizenship which is not merely a liberal framework of inclusion but one which is transformatory and liberatory.'

The only opposition to the resolution came from a member of AIDWA (All India Democratic Women's Association), a leftist party's women's wing, who said that the section of the resolution on Section 377 should remain but the section relating to the subversive potential of queer politics should be deleted.

Conclusion

This chapter has sought to highlight some of the premises underlying the language of rights and their implications, such as the dangers of being pushed into using a limiting framework of identities based on sexual orientation. Another set of implications relate to the nature of engagement with other progressive movements with queer issues. In a context in which there are fears and anxieties about a closer engagement with these issues, the rights language can allow others to offer support from a 'safe' distance. The chapter has also sought to draw attention to the limitations of rights language in taking account of intersectionality, which is required to undertake alliance-building efforts that are more deep rooted. Similarly, its limitations in terms of unpacking and therefore challenging heteronormativity have been highlighted. In fact, a narrow use of rights language offers an escape from addressing heteronormativity and its subversion.

I would like to reiterate here that I believe it is possible to use the language of rights and to address intersectionality, heteronormativity and subversion at the same time, and that is how effective claim-making needs to be undertaken. The IAWS resolution quoted above made an effort to use the language of rights in this manner. In order to work with a framework of intersectionality, to address heteronormativity and to highlight the subversive potential of sexual desire, we need to draw upon feminist and queer politics. The use of rights language comes into play in a *full* manner to make a claim only *after* such an engagement has been undertaken.

It is only queer/feminist ideological and analytical frameworks which have helped us as activists draw out the linkages between oppressions. As argued above, although the rights discourse provides us with important concepts such as the 'indivisibility of rights', it does not enable us to analyse precisely *how* these forces intersect to define and control the realities of our lives. Similarly, it is only the conceptual framework provided by queer politics which enables us to analyse and challenge heteronormativity and the social structures that uphold it and deem same-sex desire 'abnormal' or illegitimate. Heteronormativity is so pervasive, insidious and often intangible that it cannot be challenged only as 'a violation of sexual rights'. A queer articulation challenges and seeks to subvert the foundational norms of society – rather than focusing only on violations of rights.

More recent feminist critical engagement with rights language has highlighted the limitations of such a framing with respect to justice for women. I would argue that in the realm of queer sexuality, the critiques of status quo-ist rights discourses acquire even greater significance and that the advantages of rights language are more difficult to enjoy. Despite these limitations, the language of rights has made a significant contribution to the struggle for justice in a context in which same-sex desire is marked with silence, stigma and violations. We need, however, to be more specific in our analysis of its contribution in our struggle against heteronormativity. There is also a need to draw upon rights language strategically, while being firmly rooted in a queer, feminist framework that can offer more effective and liberating discourses and strategies for justice and equity.

Notes

1 This chapter draws upon ongoing discussions within PRISM on the rights language. Discussions with other activists and academics have been extremely valuable in formulating the arguments presented here. In particular, I would like to acknowledge the insights of Madhu Mehra, a feminist human rights advocate, and Dr Uma Chakravarthy, a feminist historian and civil liberties activist.

2 PRISM is a non-funded, non-registered, queer, feminist forum of individuals based in Delhi, India. PRISM is inclusive of all gender and sexual expressions and identities. We work towards raising issues relating to same-sex sexualities that fall outside the heterosexual norm, and to interrogate the norm itself.

3 By a 'queer perspective', I mean one that recognizes the dangers of narrowly defined identity politics, challenges heteronormativity and locates itself in a framework of 'intersectionality', which takes account of the connections between different types of struggle and the interplay of multiple identities. Being queer is not the same as having same-sex sexual desires; a same-sex-desiring person will not necessarily subscribe to queer politics, just as an opposite-sex-desiring person could, because of the nature of their politics, have a queer perspective.

4 There have been many such cases of young women who are driven to entering into a suicide pact with their lovers. These suicides are often in a situation in which the women are being pressured by their families to get married to men.

Reference

Miller, A. (2004) 'Sexual rights, conceptual advance: tensions in debate', Paper presented at the 'Sexual, Reproductive and Human Rights Seminar' organized by CLADEM, in Lima, Peru.

6 | Children's sexual rights in an era of HIV/AIDS

DEEVIA BHANA

Over five million South Africans are currently infected with HIV/AIDS, with women and young girls (aged fifteen to twenty-four) facing greater levels of infection (UNAIDS 2005). One of the primary strategies in the fight against HIV/AIDS is to safeguard the rights of those who are infected and who are at risk of infection. But the rights of young children are often peripheral to these strategies. This is because HIV/AIDS necessarily invokes sexuality, and sexuality and associations of sexuality and young people are usually considered problematic. Around the world, the question of child sex rights produces deep anxiety and is hotly contested (Waites 2005). Rarely does scholarship link children, sex, HIV/AIDS and rights (Silin 1995). Hegemonic versions of childhood view sexual knowledge as polluting innocence (Renold 2005). Such attitudes presuppose a developmental view: sexuality and sexual rights are accomplishments of maturity and the preserve of the adult world (James et al. 1998).

Child rights discourse calls for children to be treated as autonomous individuals. While they may benefit from adult protection, this discourse views them as capable, interactive social agents who engage with people and institutions (Prout 2000). The notion that children have rights that are not necessarily realized or claimed by all children has guided contemporary approaches adopted by UNICEF to development programming. Arguing for a 'Human Rights Approach' to development programming, UNICEF (2003) argues against development programmes based on agencies determining in advance the needs of children, and for more participatory approaches that focus on children having rights and being able to have their opinions taken seriously. Yet the voices of children in much research on early childhood, especially in so-called 'developing' countries, are usually mute. Even research informed by a concern for children's rights often addresses children as relatively passive, desexualized beings without the capacity to formatively and constitutively engage with sexual matters. There is very little information on the ways children themselves construct their knowledge of HIV/AIDS and sexualities, their freedoms and lack of freedoms, and whether they draw on rights discourses, and if so how.

This chapter argues that exploring children's understandings of HIV/ AIDS from the perspective of 'rights' can open a space through which to move beyond commonly found representations of African children as being either simply victims of HIV/AIDS or as subjects instrumentally exerting new 'rights' brought by South Africa's democracy. Based on a study of seven- and eight-year-old children's understandings of AIDS in a black township school in KwaZulu-Natal, South Africa, this chapter shows how boys and girls spoke about sexuality and HIV/AIDS and how, through this, they contested, affirmed and resisted rights. The research is influenced by a deep commitment to the rights of children to articulate their views and emotions and to be heard and taken seriously. Using ethnographic methods and group interviews, the research explored the extent to which sexuality characterized young children's narratives in a context of a severe AIDS epidemic. Rather than seeing children as victims, this research shows how in exercising, negotiating and adjusting what they see as their rights, children can be encouraged to raise and discuss issues about sexuality and about 'rights'. Allowing children to talk about such sensitive issues, this chapter argues, enables them to express themselves as sexual agents.

Race, class, gender in South African AIDS

South African AIDS is gendered and racialized. Apartheid and a racialized migrant labour system have worked to destabilize family structures and fuel the HIV/AIDS epidemic (Phillips 2004). At the heart of South African AIDS are gender inequalities, and there is considerable gender disparity in the rates of infection. The province of KwaZulu-Natal, where this research was conducted, has experienced some of the highest levels of infection in the country, with one-third of pregnant women now infected (Department of Health 2005). Young women's vulnerability to HIV/AIDS is increased by gender violence, rape and the gendered nature of their roles within heterosexual relationships (O'Sullivan et al. 2006). The current context in post-apartheid South Africa has seen rising unemployment and social inequalities, which have exacerbated HIV prevalence rates, especially among black men and women.

Combined with the history of apartheid and black male migrancy, the enduring racialization of poverty vividly materializes in the context of informal settlements in which the children in this study live. Ominously, the demographic patterns of HIV mean that people in poverty (and in South Africa they are predominantly black) bear a disproportionate burden. Informal settlements are rooted in unequal provision of housing for blacks under apartheid and have mushroomed in urban areas; they are testimony to the failure of the new government to provide adequate housing to the poor. These settlements have the highest rates of infection and the children here are at most risk of HIV/AIDS. The home context for many children is characterized by one-roomed shacks or *imijondolos* which are occupied by several people. Many children live in households where a parent or caregiver is HIV positive and where children are care-givers to parents. There are about 300,000 AIDS orphans and numbers are expected to grow. There are no accurate figures for the number of children aged between nought and nine years old who are infected with AIDS. The majority of infections occur through infected mothers during pregnancy or through breastfeeding (Whiteside and Sunter 2000). The extent to which sexual abuse contributes to HIV infection is not known, but the myth that sex with young children cures AIDS increases children's vulnerability.

Young children's emerging meanings of HIV/AIDS and sexuality are embedded within the broader context of South African AIDS and the specific social and cultural systems that shape and are important in shaping the structure of experience of sexuality. As HIV/AIDS decimates thousands of people, particularly those in informal settlements, there is increasing openness in sexual speech and overwhelming visibility of sex and HIV/AIDS education and prevention – to such an extent that many have become 'sick of AIDS' (Mitchell and Smith 2003). It is possible to argue quite easily that young children emerging from these social worlds are victims whose rights have not been realized, particularly as regards the poor provision of housing and poverty. I argue, however, that we must resist the tendency to view African children as innocents, victims of HIV/AIDS and poverty.

The question of HIV/AIDS, childhood sexuality and basic autonomy for young children remains complex but must be seen within the broader cultural context and overview of childhood sexuality. As I will illustrate, children's sexualities are nuanced, gendered, racialized and classed differences in identity and power. Children's emerging sexualities are redolent of their readings of the South African landscape, where power, wealth and health are so unevenly distributed in terms of these identities. In attending closely to the experiences of young children, the studies confirm that childhood sexualities can be understood only in relation to, and as part of, wider social relations. To understand childhood sexual-ity it is important to go beyond sexuality. It is precisely for this reason that age/race/class/gender play such an important role in the analysis of childhood sexualities.

Constructing sexual rights in the context of HIV/AIDS

How do young children construct knowledge of HIV/AIDS, especially when sexuality is seen as problematic? The literature on sexual rights and young people often constructs children primarily in terms of rights to protection, especially from sexual abuse and sexual contamination, while bodily autonomy and sexual knowledge and behaviour are generally seen as applying only to adults (Waites 2005). Recent years have seen shifts in knowledge of children's sexuality. Many commentators in the new sociology of childhood argue that children must be understood and accepted as sexual, rather than for their sexuality to be ignored and hidden (Weeks 2000). In South Africa, there is little literature on sexuality and early childhood. That which exists tends to point in the direction of constructing children as being in need of protection, despite laws that uphold the competency and rights of young children. In the following sections, children's understandings of gender, sexuality and HIV/AIDS are addressed. Children, as will be demonstrated here, are neither innocent nor ignorant about HIV/AIDS and sex.

Asserting the right to talk sexually about HIV/AIDS A dominant adult view in the construction of childhood is that children and sex should be kept apart. In contrast, discussions with seven- and eight-year-old children about their knowledge of HIV/AIDS shows how prominently sexual matters feature:

Researcher: How exactly is HIV/AIDS spread?

Mlondi: By kissing [giggles].

Wendy: They're naughty [laughs]. They take off their clothes and have sex.

Researcher: What's that?

Wendy: It's when you are going to make a child.

Wendy: By playing with boys.

Nosiphu: Sleeping with him. People get naughty in bed [laughs].

Scelo: By not wearing a condom.

In these discussions, seven- and eight-year-olds connect HIV/AIDS with sex and sexual behaviour and in doing so transgress the myths of sexual innocence. Enabled by support from their peers, and accompanied by laughter, these children could talk about sex within the wider constraints of sexual taboos and in ways that allow them to insert themselves into a sexual culture. Laughter acquires a symbolic significance in this context. Not only does it allow for the validation and support of childhood sexual cultures, it also allows them to speak of transgression. Their knowledge about condoms does not simply break the myth of childhood innocence, but also provides the young children with awareness of the safety that the condom is supposed to provide against HIV/AIDS. But while children are asserting their right to know sexually and enjoy the conversation, judgement is also passed on sex as 'naughty'. The significance of sex as 'naughty' highlights the ways in which young children take the meaning of sex – as both pleasurable (using the logic of laughter) and naughty (adopting an adult stance). In other words, young children assert their rights to talk about HIV/AIDS sexually but also adopt adult stances on the matter, distancing and rejecting child sex. In this way, they adjust and accommodate children's rights to know sexually.

Man-eaters: the gendering of HIV/AIDS and the violation of girls' rights It is widely acknowledged that gender is critical in understanding increased risk. In the next discussion, young girls show their vulnerabilities and demonstrate their lack of rights in contexts of violence and rape:

Phumzile: It's men that spread this disease, because we heard from women how it started. I know it's men, because usually they rape a girl, and go and keep changing and sharing this woman. And maybe she is already infected, and they go and rape other ones ... Men. They rape and rape and don't care.

Researcher: What is rape?

Phumzile: Rape is AIDS.

Nomusa: When an older person calls you and does bad things to you ... he puts his penis in you ...

Nontobeko: When somebody eats people, he is a man-eater and gets HIV.

Researcher: Eats people? What do you mean by that?

Nontobeko: One old man from near where I stay – he always threatened us, he tells us that he eats kids. If he sees us wandering in the road, he will take one and eat and show them.

Phumzile: They want to rape the children.

Hlengiwe: Because I know that from experience, because when we were walking home with my friends and this guy, he is a very old man, he came after us, he was running after us; I don't know about my friends, but I fled home. One of them was nearly caught by this man. I know that he is not good.

Anele: Sometimes he buys us chocolate.

Hlengiwe: We were a group of six and this same old guy came and bought us sweets. But we didn't eat them because our parents know

81

about him; they said if anyone who give us something we must throw it away, and we always throw it away.

Given the opportunity, the girls show how evocatively they can talk about their concerns, and the limitations of their rights. UNAIDS (2005) asserts that in a number of countries HIV-positive women were found to be ten times more likely to have experienced male violence that those that are HIV negative. Significantly the girls in this study point out that AIDS is rape. Sexuality is nuanced by other social differences. Within the context of danger and poverty in which they live, the young girls' sexualities are framed by the discourse of heterosexual danger (both real and imagined) – being vulnerable to HIV/AIDS, to older men and rape.

Unlike in the previous section, where the children in the group demonstrated knowing about sexuality in emotively pleasurable ways, the discussion here is ominous and serious. The material and social circumstances in South Africa's townships make black girls more vulnerable to rape and abuse. The myth of HIV/AIDS being cured by having sex with a virgin also underlies the concerns of young children. Given the legacies of apartheid, the history of inequalities, a violent and highly patriarchal system of government, and the calamitous socio-economic conditions in which black men continually are emasculated, it is no surprise that the girls are constructing their femininities and their sexualities by drawing upon discourses of fear of AIDS and men – 'men who don't care' and who rape.

Without attempting to diminish the fear through which sexualities are being constructed and the vulnerabilities of girls, it is also important to understand that the master identity of dangerous sexuality is being deployed by the girls whose vulnerability and status as 'victims' is reinforced by parents who warn them of men.

Resisting the right to know When young children were asked whether they should talk about HIV/AIDS in the classroom, the responses were overwhelming: 'No', 'It wouldn't be right', 'Sex is not to be discussed by small children':

Researcher: Are we supposed to talk about AIDS?
Nkanyiso: No.
Researcher: Why?
Nkanyiso: It doesn't make us feel good.
Researcher: Why?
Thabiso: We don't like talking about them.
Researcher: Why?

Mlungisi: We don't like to be taught bad things.

Silindile: It's not right.

Researcher: Why?

Mlungisi: We are going to do it too.

Researcher: You'll do it?

Silindile: Maybe a girl says to a boy, 'Come and have sex with me.'

Nkanyiso: We'll get smacked ... by the teachers.

Researcher: Why?

Silindile: Because it's old people's stuff.

By resisting the right to know about HIV/AIDS and about sex, the children were drawing upon discourses of childhood innocence despite the richness of their knowing. These contradictions show very clearly the constant struggle that young children have to endure in trying to present themselves as the ideal child. The deployment of childhood innocence is a strategic tool in the manufacture of the adult's version of childhood. To adopt the position of adult is to allow childhood innocence to flourish and to mark out hierarchies – those who assert the right to know suffer the effects of being excluded from the mythical (but powerful) version of childhood.

Discredited notions that children who know about sex do sex is also resurrected by Silindile, working to validate adult concerns about sexuality and young children. The rejection of the right to know and the negotiation around knowing is framed not only by dominant adult perceptions of childhood sexuality but also by the concrete knowledge that they will be 'smacked'. In South Africa corporal punishment has been banned since 1996, but its practice has not been completely eliminated, as suggested by other research and by the children themselves (Deacon et al. 1999). Corporal punishment thus induces fear, and limits and represses their sexual voices.

Conclusion

Attempting to promulgate and enforce the idea that children have sexual rights would be a difficult undertaking in South Africa. Yet this chapter shows how children are already 'doing' sexual rights and that these rights are marked by class, race and gender. It is through this complex matrix that rights are asserted, negotiated and rejected. Young children have an indefatigable sexual curiosity, but this is tempered, adjusted and negotiated. Their agency and thus the assertion and negotiation of their rights can be seen as shaped, created and constrained by their social contexts, but they too shape them and are enabled by them.

Complex social, cultural and economic forces in South Africa have shaped and are shaping the experience of sexuality and of sexual rights, and these condition the possibility for agency. Issues of power, gender inequality and sexual oppression are increasingly important to young girls and boys in this study, and are an indication of their later risk. Young children position themselves and their knowledge in relation to the world of adults in ways – as in the example of associating the connections between sex/AIDS and 'old people's stuff' – that have an impact on their right to knowledge and information and their freedoms.

The freedoms of young girls and their vulnerability to HIV show in the performance of their sexuality framed by discourses of danger and fear that are intimately linked to the contexts in which they live their lives. Despite arguing that rights are an active realm of rejection, appropriation and assertion, young girls will have very little choice to exercise their autonomy in contexts of male violence; neither will boy as well as girl children have much choice in the context of corporal punishment.

South African HIV/AIDS has made the domain of sexual struggles more visible, and with it the possibility of child sex rights. Treating young children as speaking, knowing and experiencing sexual subjects, and taking their concerns, pleasures and fears seriously, as the research on which this chapter is based sought to do, can create the space to enable young children to recognize and exercise their rights. This points clearly to the need for sexual literacy and openness in early childhood education, and for children to be treated in a rights-respecting way – respecting their rights to think about sex and sexuality, their rights to talk about sex rights and their rights to act.

References

Deacon, R., R. Morrell and J. Prinsloo (1999) 'Discipline and homophobia in South African schools: the limits of legislated transformation', in D. Epstein and J. Sears (eds), *A Dangerous Knowing: Sexual Pedagogy and Popular Culture*, London: Cassell.

Department of Health (2005) *Summary Report: National HIV and Syphilis Antenatal Sero-prevalence Survey in South Africa 2002*, Department of Health, Health Systems Research, Research Coordination and Epidemiology, Republic of South Africa.

James, A., C. Jencks and A. Prout (1998) *Theorising Childhood*, Cambridge: Polity Press.

Mitchell, C. and A. Smith (2003) 'Sick of AIDS: life, literacy and South African youth', *Culture, Health and Sexuality*, 5(6): 512–22.

O'Sullivan, L. F., A. Harrison, R. Morrell, A. Monroe-Wise and M. Kubeka (2006) 'Gender dynamics in the primary sexual relationships of young rural South African women and men', *Culture, Health and Sexuality*, 8(2): 99–113.

Phillips, H. (2004) 'HIV/AIDS in the context of South Africa's epidemic history', in D. Kauffman and D. Lindauer (eds), *Aids and South Africa: The Social Expression of a Pandemic*, Basingstoke: Palgrave Macmillan.

Prout, A. (2000) *The Body, Childhood and Society*, New York: St Martin's Press.

Renold, E. (2005) *Girls, Boys and Junior Sexualities: Exploring Children's Gender and Sexual Relations in the Primary School*, London: Routledge Falmer.

Silin, J. (1995) *Sex, Death and the Education of Children: Our Passion for Ignorance in the Age of AIDS*, New York: Teachers College Press.

UNAIDS (2005) *UNAIDS in South Africa*, <www.unaids.org> (accessed 31 March 2006).

UNICEF (2003) *Human Rights Approach and Development Programming*, Nairobi: UNICEF.

Waites, M. (2005) *The Age of Consent. Young People, Sexuality and Citizenship*, Basingstoke: Palgrave Macmillan.

Weeks, J. (2000) *Making Sexual History*, Cambridge: Polity Press.

Whiteside, A. and C. Sunter (2000) *AIDS: The Challenge for South Africa*, Cape Town: Human & Rousseau and Tafelberg.

7 | The rights of man

ALAN GREIG

This chapter explores the subject of sexual rights and the claims about such rights as they are made by and for men. It considers the different bases of these claims, which range from some men's experience of sexual oppression to other men's experience of their gender socialization. The chapter highlights the issues of power and privilege, which often lie hidden within such claims, and calls for a discourse of 'men and sexual rights' that can take account of both gender norms and sexual hierarchies. Central to this call is a conception of accountability that is at once personal and political; the political accountability of duty-bearers to promote and protect the sexual rights of all rights holders, men and women; and the personal accountability of men in relation to the ways in which their gender privilege serves to deny the sexual rights of others. My understanding of these issues springs from my work over the last twenty years on HIV/AIDS, gender and violence, mostly as an independent consultant working with non-profit organizations to support their efforts in the global South and as an activist working on issues of masculinity, violence and social justice in the USA.

Male responsibilities?

Sexual rights are a fundamental element of human rights. They encompass the right to experience a pleasurable sexuality, which is essential in and of itself and, at the same time, is a fundamental vehicle of communication and love between people. Sexual rights include the right to liberty and autonomy in the responsible exercise of sexuality. (HERA 1999)

The struggle to include sex and sexuality within the language and instruments of international human rights agreements continues to this day. Notwithstanding the universality that is, by definition, central to these agreements, the practical struggle for sexual rights has been largely fought on the terrain of gender equality. This has been a struggle for women's sexual rights in the face of the gender and sexual oppression that men perpetrate against women.

The short history of this struggle begins at the 1993 Vienna Human Rights Conference where, for the first time in the international arena, attention is given to women as subjects of human rights and women's bodies as the objects of human rights violations. This work lays important foundations for the subsequent discourses of reproductive and sexual rights that are developed at the landmark Cairo and Beijing conferences in 1994 and 1995, respectively. Not only do the declarations produced at Cairo and Beijing characterize sexual rights in terms of women's control over their sexual lives; women's rights are counterposed with men's sexual responsibilities to respect these rights.

Given this gender analysis, what can men's relationship be to sexual rights claims whose goal is to radically change social and sexual arrangements of power from which they benefit? After all, as Connell (1995) has noted: '[In a] gender order where men dominate, women cannot avoid constituting men as an interest group concerned with defence, and women as an interest group concerned with change.' What sense can it make to talk of 'men' as some kind of singular, internally coherent category when what the extremely heterogeneous group called 'men' fundamentally share in common is Connell's 'patriarchal dividend', the privilege that comes with simply being male? For, notwithstanding three or more decades of feminist struggle and women's movements, and all the gains that have been made in gender equality, it remains in so many ways a 'man's world'. Given this, what can men's interest be in the social and sexual revolution being proposed by advocates for sexual rights?

The sexual oppression of (some) men

The first answer to this question is to bring a more complex, and less heterosexist, gender analysis to bear on the issue of men's sexual rights and to recognize that some men's sexual rights have long been violated. Those men who 'betray' their gender through their 'feminine' representation and/or sexual relations with other men are especially vulnerable to such violation. This violence is used to 'police' the gender boundary between men and women and the heterosexual order that mandates sexual relations between genders and proscribes sex within genders. By punishing those who are seen as breaking the gender 'rules' of how a man is supposed to be and behave, such violence is a warning to all men about obeying these 'rules'. Research on groups of men who have sex with men (MSM) in Cambodia has found that violence is common, especially for those men with a feminine gender presentation (*sray sros*, who would be termed 'transgender' in countries of the economic North): 'Many "*sray sros*" experience discrimination in the form of verbal abuse, harassment, physical violence such as blows, kicks, sex under compulsion, and occasional cases of rape. As a result, they tend to hide their sexual orientation and practices, making it difficult to reach and educate them' (KHANA 2003). The consequence of such violence, as this quote makes clear, is that these men are driven 'underground', away from the services and information they need about sexual health and into hurried and secretive sexual behaviour that makes safer sex, not to mention loving relationships, much more difficult. The violence that targets such men is communal and institutional, as well as interpersonal. Men who have sex with other men suffer much of their violence at the hands of the police and other men in positions of authority. Human rights groups, such as Amnesty International, have received many allegations of torture and ill treatment in detention which indicate that the risk is high in police stations, particularly during the initial period of detention. Research conducted by Human Rights Watch in Bangladesh found that such violence at the hands of police and *mastans* (hired thugs used by political parties) was common:

> Numerous men who have sex with men who spoke with Human Rights Watch reported being raped, gang-raped, and beaten frequently by police and *mastans* ... Men who have sex with men also reported that they were regularly subjected to extortion by both police and *mastans* ... Men who engaged in sex work reported that police and *mastans* also extorted money from their clients. This extortion from clients can place the men selling sex in danger as well. (Human Rights Watch 2003)

Many countries maintain laws that prohibit or regulate sexual activity between consenting adults of the same sex. These are often called sodomy laws, and are still in existence in at least seventy states worldwide. Such laws range from regulation of specific sexual acts (for example, anal sex) to broad injunctions against 'antisocial' or 'immoral' behaviour. Whatever their exact content, such laws are used by the police to arrest and harass gay men, lesbians, bisexuals and transgender persons and constitute a grave violation of human rights, including the rights to privacy, to freedom from discrimination, and of expression and association. The violence of state laws and institutions is reinforced by violence at community level, ranging from discrimination to assault by peers, colleagues and family members. Those people who challenge norms of gender and sexuality through their sexual desires and practices and/or their gender 'presentation' face some of the most severe forms of social stigma and disapproval.

It is important to broaden our gender analysis, such that the violence experienced by 'queer' men can be properly understood as being based in gender. The violence that they suffer is based on their positioning within a gender order premised on the male supremacist logic that social relations are fundamentally hierarchical. This order insists not only on male–female hierarchies but also on hierarchies between men based on their gender status, that is the degree to which they conform to prevailing norms of masculinity and heterosexuality. Violence maintains the hierarchy by keeping the men 'who are not men enough' in their place.

Men's experience of sexual violence

But what about the men who appear to be, or strive to be, 'man enough'? What can be said of their sexual rights? Perhaps the most basic demand of advocates for sexual rights is that people be free to live their sexual lives without coercion. But men's experience of coercion in their sexual lives, irrespective of their sexual orientation or identity, often goes unmarked. On the basis of interviews with over eight thousand men aged eighteen or above, the US government's National Violence Against Women Survey estimated that 92,748 men were raped in 1995, in addition to the 302,091 women who were raped that year (Tjaden and Thoennes 2006). This figure must be considered an underestimate as men in penal institutions were not included in the survey, and from other data it is known that the prevalence of male rape in prison is significant, at least in the US context. Background information in the US Prison Rape Elimination Act, signed into law by President Bush in 2003, estimated that at least 13 per cent of US inmates had been sexually assaulted in prison. In its global overview of men's experience of rape, WHO makes clear that: 'Unfortunately, there are few reliable statistics on the number of boys and men raped in settings such as schools, prisons and refugee camps. Most experts believe that official statistics vastly under-represent the number of male rape victims. The evidence available suggests that males may be even less likely than female victims to report an assault to the authorities' (WHO 2002).

In addition to adult men's experience of sexual violence, boys' experience of child sexual abuse is only now beginning to receive the attention it deserves. Research in Peru found that among young men reporting a heterosexual experience, 11 per cent reported a non-consensual experience at first sex. A study of adolescents in Kenya reports that 4 per cent of boys were forced into first sex and a further 6 per cent were 'persuaded' to engage in sex against their will (Jejeebhoy and Bott 2005). A review of studies from twenty countries, including ten national representative surveys, showed rates of childhood sexual abuse of 3–29 per cent for boys (compared with 7–36 per cent for girls), with most studies reporting up to three times more sexual violence against girls than boys. In all countries, the offenders were overwhelmingly male when the victim was female (above 90 per cent), while studies varied on the sex of the offender when the victim was male (Finkelhor 1994).

Sexuality and masculinity

As the definition of sexual rights presented at the beginning of this chapter makes clear, such rights are concerned with more than freedom from sexual coercion and violence. They are about the freedom to live our sexual lives with joy, dignity and autonomy. The denial of women's ability to enjoy this freedom is usually attributed to unequal gender relations between women and men. In other words, it is men's patriarchal power which denies women their sexual rights. But where does this position men and their rights to live their sexual lives with joy, dignity and autonomy, especially those men who conform to prevailing norms of masculinity and heterosexuality? Aside from specific experiences of sexual violence, is there anything that is denying these men their sexual rights? A simplistic view of patriarchal privilege would suggest that the straightforward answer is 'no'. But recent developments in studies of men and masculinities are offering more nuanced accounts of how men with gender privilege come into and experience their sexuality. These accounts are bringing men back into gender, away from the abstraction of 'Patriarchal Man', and looking at the lived experience of real, as in actual, men. Such accounts are making clear that men's relationship to the gender socialization they receive and the gender order in which they live is both diverse and complex, complicit and contested. Sexuality is central to this relationship.

Looking at the ways in which masculinity and sexuality express each other in men's lives makes it possible to see more clearly the issues of sexual rights for men who conform to prevailing norms of masculinity and heterosexuality, and who observe the rules of the gender order. Heteronormative masculinity has been linked with a number of constraints on men's ability to experience joy, dignity, autonomy and safety in their sexual lives. These constraints include the equating of masculinity with risk-taking, which can lead men into sexual behaviour that puts at risk their sexual health. This is linked to the pressure on men to use sex to demonstrate their masculinity. The prevailing discourse on men, masculinity and HIV/AIDS has identified men's need to prove sexual potency as a key reason for their seeking multiple sexual partners and their desire to stay in control in their sexual relations with women.

The encouragement of risk and the pressure to prove sexual potency have also been linked to the sense of invulnerability promoted by heteronormative masculinity, associated with men in many societies being socialized to be self-reliant, not to show their emotions, and not to seek assistance in times of need or stress. Paradoxically, this can increase men's vulnerability to sexual ill health by encouraging the denial of risk and constraining men from exercising their sexual rights in a way that is protective of one of their most fundamental rights – the right to health.

The constraints of heteronormative masculinity are also evident in the feelings of sexual anxiety reported by young and adult men. A common finding across different sexual cultures is the anxiety young men report about becoming sexual in a context in which they are supposed to be knowledgeable and in control, but often feel neither. When asked about their concerns related to sex, both young and adult men often report being anxious about issues related to sexual performance, such as potency and penis size, at the same time as feeling unable to ask for help in dealing with these issues for fear of not being 'manly' enough.

These observations and findings on the ways in which heteronormative masculinity can constrain men in the exercise of their sexual rights have become commonplace in the burgeoning literature on men, masculinity and sexual health. My own work with men on gender, sexuality and HIV/AIDS in Zambia and South Africa, as well as my activism in the USA, bears out the central contention of this literature; namely, that if we want to engage men in work for gender equality (and thus the defence of women's sexual rights) it is critical to address the ways in which heteronormative gender constructions harm men (and may compromise their sexual rights).

But my experience also suggests that the harms of men's gender socialization, especially with regard to sex, are inseparable from the privileges of men's positioning within a patriarchal gender order. With this acknowledgement must come a willingness to be open to other readings of the connections between masculinity and sexuality. At the very least, it is useful to ask questions about the notion of risk in settings where men understand their sexuality to be a biological drive and natural necessity, which might preclude them from a sense of 'taking a risk'. Similarly, demonstrations of potency and virility may be as much about maintaining gender power as they are about demonstrating a gender identity, while men's sexual anxiety must be placed in the context of their expectation of and sense of entitlement to being in sexual control.

Conclusion

When we consider men's sexual rights in relation to the impact of male gender socialization on sexuality, we must also consider the privileges that accrue to men who conform to prevailing norms of masculinity and heterosexuality. This is not simply about balancing men's sexual rights with their responsibilities. More fundamentally, it is about asking questions about autonomy and accountability, about what it means to recognize the gender constructs that shape men's sexual attitudes and behaviours at the same time as holding men accountable for the choices and decisions that they do make within their sexual lives. If we are to avoid the trap of a gender essentialism, in which men are simply made by masculinity, it is imperative to be clear about the agency that men have, and that different men make very different choices about their sexual rights and the sexual rights of others. At the same time, it is important to refuse the abstraction of gender and sexuality from history and to recognize that the sexual lives of both women and men are now caught between the forces of social conservatism and religious fundamentalism on the one hand and, on the other, the pressures of commodification within sexual cultures under capitalism. Sexual pleasure, liberty and autonomy are too often crushed between this rock and a hard place.

The discourse of sexual rights is a powerful tool for women and men, of all genders and sexual identities, to deal with these pressures and forces. But it is a tool that people have different power to use. Men, especially men with the privilege that comes with conforming to norms of masculinity and heterosexuality, have a particular role to play in the social and sexual revolution that will secure sexual rights not simply for themselves but for all.

References

Connell, R. W. (1995) *Masculinities*, Cambridge: Polity Press.

Finkelhor, D. (1994) 'The international epidemiology of child sexual abuse', *Child Abuse and Neglect*, (18): 409–17.

HERA (Health, Empowerment, Rights and Accountability) (1999) 'Sexual rights', in *Women's Sexual and Reproductive Rights and Health: Action Sheets*, New York: HERA.

Human Rights Watch (2003) *Ravaging the Vulnerable: Abuses Against Persons at High Risk of HIV Infection in Bangladesh*, 15.6(C), New York: Human Rights Watch.

Jejeebhoy, S. J. and S. Bott (2005) 'Non-consensual sexual experiences of young people in developing countries: an overview', in S. J. Jejeebhoy, I. Shah and S. Thapa (eds), *Sex without Consent: Young People in Developing Countries*, London and New York: Zed Books.

KHANA (2003) *Out of the Shadows: Male-to-male Sexual Behaviour in Cambodia*, Phnom Penh: Khmer HIV/AIDS NGO Alliance.

Tjaden, P. and N. Thoennes (2006) *Extent, Nature, and Consequences of Rape Victimization: Findings from the National Violence Against Women Survey*, Washington, DC: National Institute of Justice.

WHO (2002) *World Report on Violence and Health*, Geneva: World Health Organization.

8 | Human rights interrupted: an illustration from India

SUMIT BAUDH

There is a wide spectrum of sexual acts, practices and identities the world over. The existing language of sexuality and human rights (as it has evolved out of judicial review in cases from outside India) is largely framed in the context of lesbian, gay, bisexual and transgender (LGBT) people. In turn, and as precedent case law, it seems to cater only to similar or analogous identities. The challenge is to make human rights accessible to all. In an identity-focused model, non-LGBT and indigenous groups that do not conform to these identities might lose out. These include, for example, the *Hijras* of South Asia, an indigenous community of transgender people comprising biological male and intersex individuals. The notion of *transgender* does not exactly apply in the case of *Hijras*, because they might view themselves as neither male nor female but a third gender. The ambiguity over their gender identity might then leave them in the lurch. For that matter, all those who do not subscribe to sexuality as an identity may find it hard to negotiate their rights. There is therefore a need to expand the human rights discourse, for it to go beyond narrow notions of identities, and to secure a firm foundation for sexual rights.

In this chapter I will use the example of the British colonial law, Section 377 of the Indian Penal Code 1860, which makes illegal what is termed 'carnal intercourse against the order of nature'.

> 377. Unnatural Offences.
> Whoever voluntarily has carnal intercourse against the order of nature with any man, woman or animal, shall be punished with imprisonment for life, or with imprisonment of either description for a term which may extend to ten years, and shall also be liable to fine. (Ranchhoddas and Thakore 2002: 1818)[1]

An assault on the personal liberty of every free Indian, Section 377 violates people's autonomy, independence, free will and sovereignty over their own bodies. It remains a valid law in India, a menace and a source of constant human rights violations. Although a plain reading of the law does not sanction any given sexual identity, homosexual or heterosexual, it effectively criminalizes all forms of consensual same-sex sexual activity.

Owing to its own lack of focus on identities, Section 377 provides an opportunity for a reassessment of the existing language of human rights in its application to sexuality and sexual rights.[2]

Section 377 and sexuality

What does Section 377 have to say about sex, sexuality or sexual orientation? Nothing. Not on the face of it. A plain reading of the law reveals little and is actually quite ambiguous. To begin with, what does 'carnal intercourse against the order of nature' mean? For ease of reference I will use the acronym CIATON.

The available case law makes frequent references to bestiality, buggery and biblical notions of the sin of Gomorrah and the sin of Sodom. That in itself is of little help. The meaning of sodomy has varied across centuries, continents and cultures.[3] Even its legal interpretation varies from one jurisdiction to another. Legal definitions of buggery and bestiality are similarly difficult to capture. There is a hint in the statutory explanation appended to Section 377. It states that 'penetration' is sufficient to constitute carnal intercourse, but does not clarify penetration *of what* and *by what*. From a reading of case law, it appears that penile penetration (of the anus or the mouth) is what is being alluded to.[4] Even penile masturbation of one person by another is considered 'penetration'.[5]

A study of Indian judgments under Section 377, a total of forty-six cases, reveals that thirty cases (65 per cent) deal with child sexual abuse by men. Of the thirty cases, twenty involve male children and ten involve female children (Narrain 2004: 55). Even in those cases that do involve consenting adults, there is no judicial discussion of the element of consent. Some men in these cases are referred to as 'habitual sodomites/catamites', but the judgments are emphatic that prior sexual history, or the fact that the accused male wore female attire, is of no relevance. Gender and sexuality have thus found little open articulation in the Indian judicial discourse. It is consistently and implicitly held that *only* penile–vaginal penetration that bears the potential of procreation conforms to the order of nature.

Consider the following two incidents, both involving heterosexual couples. In a divorce case, a woman alleged 'cruelty' caused by repeated acts of penile–anal penetration by the husband. It was held that a husband could indeed be 'guilty of sodomy on his wife if she was not a consenting party'.[6] Although it was a civil case, as opposed to a criminal prosecution under Section 377, it is a significant remark on the element of consent. Does Section 377 apply if a woman consents to 'sodomy'? The question has apparently not caught the judicial imagination. There was a public scandal in Delhi in December 2004 over an oral sex episode between a boy and a girl, both in their mid-teens. The boy recorded the act on his mobile camera-phone. Later, through the multi-media messaging service (MMS), he circulated the video clip to some of his friends. The clip eventually found its way on to the Internet, and was available for public view and purchase. There was a police investigation and the boy was arrested (The Hindu 2004). It did not catch the media's attention, or that of the police investigation, that penile–oral penetration is a form of CIATON, and that the girl was *equally* liable. Had it been a boy in place of the girl, it might have had some very different implications. They could *both* have faced prosecution under Section 377.

In January 2006, four men were arrested in Lucknow (the capital of the most heavily populated state in India, Uttar Pradesh) under Section 377. Without any instigation or complaint by a member of the public, the police traced the phone number of one of the accused on a gay website, and arranged a meeting. The police then forced him to call many of his friends, three of whom actually turned up. All four were arrested under a false accusation of having sex in public. In this sting operation, four innocent persons were thus prosecuted in an obviously fabricated case *only* because of their perceived sexual identity.[7]

As evidenced in the oral sex episode in Delhi, a consensual heterosexual act that involves penile–oral penetration is unlikely to be the subject of a prosecution under Section 377. On the other hand, the four men in Lucknow are currently facing prosecution because of their (homo)sexual identity – the underlying and unquestioned premise being that heterosexuality is 'normal' or 'natural'. Conversely, all that is outside of this heterosexuality is abnormal or unnatural. By proscribing what is unnatural, namely non-heterosexual sex, the law makes it implicitly compulsory that sexual activity be sought exclusively within the boundaries of heterosexuality – between a man and woman. Section 377 in effect imposes *compulsory* heterosexuality (Menon 2005).

Human rights arguments, generic limitations

There is a wide spectrum of gender and sexual identities in India.[8] There are 'men who have sex with men' (MSM). There are *Hijras*, who claim to be a third sex, defying a strictly dichotomous gender identity (Nanda 1990: 115). There are *Kothi* men who display feminine mannerisms, and prefer anal penetration by more masculine men. They also identify as non-English-speaking and coming from middle-, lower-income and working-class backgrounds (PUCL-K 2003: 19–21). There are LGBT, who (in India) are mostly urban, English-speaking, middle- and upper-middle-class men and women. Within the given diversity, there is one common element. They are all likely subjects of Section 377.

Laws like Section 377 have been the subject of judicial review the world over. The European Court of Human Rights declared sodomy laws as violative of the right to privacy.[9] A similar stand was later taken by the United Nations Human Rights Committee.[10] The Supreme Court of the United States has held that such a law violates the right to privacy.[11] The Constitutional Court of South Africa has held that such a law violates the right to privacy, the right to equality and also the right to human dignity.[12]

The three broad strands of legal argument that emerge out of judicial decriminalization are thus privacy, equality and human dignity.[13]

1 Under the privacy argument, everyone's choice of sexual conduct is seen as a private affair, which does not warrant undue state intervention. It is the classic argument that the state has no business to be in your bedroom.

2 Under the equality rights argument, sexual orientation is seen as an immutable status, similar to the phenomena of race or sex. For this argument it is necessary to conceptualize and articulate identities such as LGBT. A claim of equality follows between the homosexual and the heterosexual as two different classes of people.

3 Under the human dignity argument, people with non-heteronormative desires are seen as a permanent minority. This minority is understood to have a long and shared history of oppression, which in turn is seen to have brought them extreme disfavour and disrepute. As a set of people they are seen to be especially vulnerable to the violation of their right to live with human dignity.

Applying the privacy argument to challenge the penalization of CIATON, sexual acts like anal or oral sex are rightly argued to be a matter of fundamental choice – a choice exercised by individuals in the privacy of their bedrooms which the state should not interfere with. Whether people choose to insert a finger or a penis in their anus, it is none of the state's business.

The equality argument would hold the penalization as discriminatory among distinct sexual orientations. Arguably penile–vaginal penetration is considered *natural*, in turn lending substantial legitimacy to a heterosexual act. But if the heterosexual is naturally inclined to penile–vaginal penetration, the homosexual is seen to be similarly inclined to penile–anal penetration, thereby evoking a claim of equality between the respective and inherent natures of the heterosexual and the homosexual. Further, not all heterosexual activity is necessarily limited to penile–vaginal penetration. Heterosexual couples are known to engage in oral and anal sex. How can it be that oral and anal sex is fine between heterosexual couples, but not between homosexual couples? A law that penalizes homosexual acts exclusively is therefore discriminatory based on sexual orientation.

The human dignity argument rests on the vulnerability of a class or a community of people having non-heteronormative desires. Their vulnerability is in part seen to have been caused by the penalization of their sexual acts. The stigma of criminality is an affront to their right to live with human dignity.

Of the case law that contributed to the three arguments, all cases without exception arose in the context of what are called 'homosexual' or 'gay' men. The three arguments have done well in creating a language of sexual rights, but not without some generic limitations. There is a precondition of placing people into neat categories – heterosexual *or* homosexual, lesbian, gay *or* straight.

1 In the privacy argument it is implicit that most people are heterosexual; there are a *few* who are not but they should be allowed their private space.
2 The human dignity argument is founded on their seemingly cohesive minority status. It implies that heterosexuals are the majority, and that there is a neat and clearly identifiable minority that has a *shared* collective history.
3 The equality argument places a homosexual on the same footing as a heterosexual, but with the necessary comparator being the heterosexual. Again, the unmistakable premise is that if the heterosexual does something, so can the homosexual. What if the heterosexual does *not* do what the homosexual *wants* to do? Then it is not permitted. It is the heterosexual who sets the standard. The homosexual may comply with it, but is not allowed a new standard, an entirely new and different way of just being herself as she is.

Heterosexuality clearly emerges as the norm. It is this heteronormativity which remains unchallenged in the judicial human rights discourse. Far from being challenged, it is not even acknowledged. Not just that, heteronormativity is actually reinforced through the ways in which judgments (on issues of sexuality) are worded and framed.

Human rights interrupted

Sexual diversity in India poses a challenge to the identity-based model implicit in the three legal arguments. Those who do not conform to prescribed sexual orientation identities will fall beyond its purview. For example, *Hijras* could be men who cross-dress, castrated men or inter-sexed individuals. A complex indigenous identity, *Hijra* is not a sexual identity but more to do with gender, the 'third sex' as it is sometimes called, neither man nor woman. A *Hijra*'s sexual acts (for instance, with men) therefore defy understanding of both heterosexual and homosexual. Further, as a community *Hijras* have a unique and indeed much longer history and cannot be so easily clubbed together with the comparatively recent LGBT identities in India. Lastly, in some regions, the sexual activity of *Hijras* occurs in what are called *hamams* (public bathhouses). The status of *hamams* in the privacy argument, perhaps closest to that of brothels, is left in the lurch. Another difficulty with privacy is that not everyone can afford it. *Hijras* and *Kothi* men who indulge in sex work may solicit on the streets, leading to sex in public toilets or public parks. Far from their being motivated by a toilet fetish or the excitement of outdoor sex, this happens owing to a lack of available 'private' spaces. Within the strict sanitization of the privacy argument, where and how does one accommodate the realities of *Hijra* lives? Are they best ignored because of the complexity *Hijras* pose? What then of *Hijras*' sexual rights, their human rights? They are neglected, avoided or, indeed, interrupted.

The currently pending Writ Petition (of 2001, in the Delhi High Court) challenging the constitutional validity of Section 377 has emerged in the context of Section 377 being an obstruction to carrying out HIV/AIDS outreach work among MSM. It broadly relies on claims of privacy, equality and human dignity. It includes arguments to the effect that: (i) the law is 'arbitrary' in its classification of natural and unnatural sex; and (ii) it causes a serious setback to HIV/AIDS outreach work, thus violating the right to life. The Writ Petition mentions MSM, homosexual and gay men in the equality argument and in the context of HIV/AIDS outreach work. It is indeed implausible to articulate the equality argument without first setting in place a cohesive identity such as gay. Similarly, the HIV/AIDS argument must have 'high risk groups' like MSM and gay men as points of reference. There are also non-identity-focused arguments: of violation of privacy; and that the law is arbitrary in its classification of natural and unnatural.

When it comes to sexual identities, the petition is perhaps in a weak situation. Foremost, it is public interest litigation. It is not a direct claim by an affected 'real' person, but a claim by a non-governmental organiza-tion (NGO), Naz India Trust. Before it could be taken up on its merits, the Delhi High Court dismissed the case on the ground that there was no real cause of action and that the NGO had no *locus standi*. The Supreme

Court of India, however (in a later appeal), set aside the dismissal and sent it back to the High Court for its consideration. That is where it is at this stage.

More recently, on 22 November 2006, Voices Against 377, a coalition of individuals and NGOs based in Delhi, filed an intervention pleading itself as an interested party. Although it supports the main petitioner's aim (to decriminalize private and consensual same-sex sexual activity), Voices' position can be set apart in two ways. First, it brings to the court the context of same-sex-desiring people, including those who identify as LGBT, *Hijra* and *Kothi* – thus widening the set of people (identities) affected. Second, it argues that the law effectively violates the right to know and be informed of important sexuality issues. Although in some way Voices is representing the cause of affected people, it is not a real person. The personhood of a directly affected 'victim' is still missing.

Formulation of sexual identities in India is a challenge, not only in the courts. There is an emerging politics around issues of sexuality, which in some ways differs from the LGBT movement of the West. Whether it could (or indeed should) ever be the same is another matter. A prominent difference, for example, is that most of the MSM do not necessarily subscribe to 'sexual orientation' identities (Seabrook 1999: 180). One could wonder why would they not, one could lament that they should, or one could take the reality as given and accordingly address it. The legal challenge to Section 377 should therefore be grounded in the context of people to whom the pink triangle means nothing or very little. Beyond this, it would be far too speculative to comment on the outcome of the litigation. Until it is decided (hopefully favourably), the human rights of LGBT and non-LGBT people affected by Section 377 lie in a state of suspension, interruption, and uncertainty.

Ways forward

Sweden's International Policy on Sexual and Reproductive Health and Rights, February 2006, is the first of its kind and a pioneer in advocating a progressive language. In its strategic areas (for Sweden's international work), the focus on homosexual, bisexual and transgendered people begins with open acknowledgement, and indeed a critique, of heteronormativity. It goes on to develop a refreshing take on transsexual and intersexual persons, which could be useful in grappling with *Hijra* realities. Further, the policy states that LGBT

[...] definitions are not universal. LGBT persons do not always identify themselves by such labels, but use the language and identities that have emerged in the particular contexts within which they live their lives. Heed must therefore be paid to the existing conceptual nomenclature for sexual orientation and gender identities in different societies. (Ministry for Foreign Affairs 2006: 17)

This is all very good, and useful for addressing some of the concerns raised in this chapter.

The Swedish policy creates a wider canvas for articulating sexual rights. In particular, that 'all people [...] have a right to their own body and sexuality' (ibid.: 8). This is a claim most useful in the context of Section 377 in India, where the law blatantly intrudes into consenting people's liberty by telling them *what they can (or cannot) do with which part of their bodies*. There is a need for human rights language to reflect such a progressive approach, and to acknowledge and indeed promote people's autonomy, independence, free will and sovereignty over their bodies.

Decriminalization of consensual sexual acts is only one aspect; there is a need to strengthen anti-discrimination laws that protect people with alternative sexualities. In this regard the constitution of South Africa is exemplary in providing for sexual orientation as a stated ground for protection against discrimination within its Bill of Rights (Republic of South Africa 1996). While the South African constitution is very progressive and must be deemed to be a model to be followed, however, inscribing 'sexual orientation' in the legal text also runs into the problem of defining rights on the basis of identities. Sexual orientation does not cover gender identity or gender expression. It may also be the case that many people who experience same-sex sexual desires and conduct do not feel covered – on the basis of either sexual orientation or gender identity. That is why a more universal ground on which to articulate human rights and sexuality is very important.

The advances of human rights made on the basis of the right to privacy, equality or human dignity are most significant and need to be applied in more and more cases the world over. Alongside these advances, however, there is a need to expand the boundaries of our thinking. There is a need to expand the human rights discourse, for it to go beyond notions of identities, to secure a firm and a more generic principle that bolsters sexual rights. Manifestations of sexuality might depend on a range of factors: personal temperament, conservative or liberal values, a sense of propriety or impropriety, morality, and so on and so forth. Regardless of its manifestation, dormant or otherwise, sexuality remains an integral component of human experience. Aspects of human life, such as health, livelihood and shelter, are being increasingly articulated in a rights-based language. Sexuality is an undeniable strand of human experience. What, then, keeps it from having its own place, its own articulation, in the spectrum of human rights? Indeed, it should find its rightful place in the bill of rights of every constitution, of every human rights charter. Its exact content and form might still be debatable, and there is a need to start this debate.

Can a *right to sexual autonomy* be a stated human right? It would include providing legal protection to permit individuals to identify with a particular gender identity or sexual orientation. Both the private and public aspects of one's sexual and gender identity could be protected as a legitimate choice of sexual self-determination (Katyal 2002). Using sexual autonomy as a conceptual framework avoids the problems of exclusion, for example of the Indian MSM, who are often left outside categories of protection based on sexual orientation (because they might view themselves as heterosexual). This framework can also harmoniously coexist with identity-based models. It is entirely possible to have a non-discrimination clause based on sexual orientation *and* to construe the right to privacy to include aspects of a person's sexual identity (ibid.: 172–3).

Defining a right to sexual autonomy could possibly challenge Section 377, but it is purely academic at this stage. Building on it would none the less be useful for a rights-based approach to a spectrum of issues – contraception, abortion, marital rape, sex work, sexual diversity, gender identity and expression, pursuit of pleasure, etc. Each of these, and the right to sexual autonomy in particular, could well be an independent discourse. For present purposes, I will conclude by saying that laws like Section 377 that impinge upon sexual self-determination are unjust and iniquitous. The Indian CIATON offers an opportunity to question surveillance, scrutiny and subjugation of our bodies, without necessarily marking ourselves with available labels of sexual identity.

Acknowledgements

I am grateful to Professor Robert Wintemute, Professor of Human Rights Law, School of Law, King's College London, for supervising my LLM (2001/02) full unit course essay. This chapter has emerged from that. Professor Wintemute also provided me with useful comments and inputs on a draft version of this chapter. I am grateful to human rights lawyer Ms Nandita Haksar for her comments; I am also grateful to my former colleagues at the AMAN Trust, Richa Singh, with whom I had useful discussions, as well as Dilip Simeon, Amanda Shah and Juhi Tyagi, for their critical inputs on draft versions; to my activist friends Arvind Narrain and Pramada Menon for their timely and insightful comments; to Radhika

Chandiramani of the South and Southeast Asia Resource Centre on Sexuality; to the Institute of Development Studies (IDS) for giving me the opportunity to present this chapter at the workshop Realizing Sexual Rights, 28–30 September 2005, Brighton, which provided me with valuable feedback, particularly from Susan Jolly; and to the Swedish Ministry for Foreign Affairs for giving me the opportunity to present this chapter at the workshop Sexual Rights and Development, 6 April 2006, Stockholm, which provided me with valuable feedback, particularly from Sonia Corrêa and Ulrika Sundberg.

Notes

1 A general comment states that: [t]his Section is intended to punish the offence of sodomy, buggery and bestiality. The offence consists in carnal knowledge committed against the order of nature by a person with a man, or in the same unnatural manner with a woman, or by a man or woman in any manner with an animal.

A much older commentary, by Sir Hari Singh Gour, states: 'This Section punishes what is "unnatural" carnal intercourse, and which is accounted a great crime since the destruction of Sodom and Gomorrah. But in spite of the high penalties to which it is justly subject, it is a crime which seldom comes to light, though it is notoriously widespread even in high society, and it is certainly not confined to any age or nationality, though it is a crime often detected amongst school boys and prisoners' (Gour 1928: 1936).

2 My analysis is limited to consensual sexual activity between adults (ruling out rape or child abuse), and to judicial protection of human rights.

3 'In various times and places everything from the ordinary heterosexual intercourse in an atypical position to oral contact with animals' (Boswell 1980: 93).

4 'Lohana, Vasanthlal, Devchand vs State', *All India Reporter*, Gujarat, 1962, p. 252.

5 'Brother John Anthony vs The State', *Criminal Law Journal*, 1992, p. 1352.

6 'Grace Jayamani, Petitioner vs E. P. Peter, Respondent', *All India Reporter*, Karnataka, 1982, p. 46.

7 From an unpublished fact-finding report written by Elavarthi Manohar of the National Campaign on Sexuality Rights (NCSR), Tulika Srivastava of the Association for Advocacy and Legal Initiatives (AALI), Lucknow, Jashodhara Dasgupta of Sahayog, Lucknow, Maya Sharma of Parma, Baroda, Vivek Divan, a human rights lawyer from Bombay, and Arvind Narrain of the Alternative Law Forum, Bangalore. Some of the online published reports of the incident can be accessed at: <http://hrw.org/english/docs/2006/01/11/india12398.htm>, <http://www.ilga.org/news_results.asp?LanguageID=1&FileCategory=1&ZoneID=3&FileID=734>.

8 The stated diversity (of gender and sexual identities and conduct) is not exclusively specific to India. There many other examples that could be stated from other countries, such as Brazil and Indonesia.

9 'Dudgeon vs United Kingdom', Ser. A, No. 45, 1981; 'Norris vs Ireland', Ser. A, no. 142, 1988; 'Modinos vs Cyprus', Ser. A, no. 259, 1993.

10 'Toonen vs Australia' (Communication no. 488/1992), UN Doc. CCPR/C/50/488/1992, 1994.

11 'Lawrence & Garner vs State of Texas', <www.supremecourtus.

gov/opinions/02pdf/02-102.pdf>;
Also, see the decision of the Kentucky
Supreme Court in 'Commonwealth of
Kentucky vs Jeffrey Wasson', 842 SW
2d 487 (Ky 1992).

12 'National Coalition for Gay
and Lesbian Equality vs The Minister
of Justice', 1 SA 6, 1999.

13 I have borrowed the first
two from Wintemute's classification (Wintemute 1995: 17). I have
done away with Wintemute's third
classification, 'sex discrimination
argument', because none of the cases
relevant to this chapter makes any
reference to this argument. I have
replaced it with the human dignity
argument from the South African
judgment, 'National Coalition for
Gay and Lesbian Equality vs The
Minister of Justice', 1 SA 6, 1999.

References

Boswell, J. (1980) *Christianity, Social
Tolerance and Homosexuality: Gay
People in Western Europe from the
Beginning of the Christian Era to
the Fourteenth Century*, Chicago,
IL: University of Chicago Press.

Gour, H. S. (1928) *The Penal Law of
India*, 4th edn, vol. II, Calcutta:
Butterworth & Co. (India) Ltd.

Hindu, The (2004) 20 December,
<www.hindu.com/2004/12/20/
stories/2004122008600100.htm>
(accessed 9 May 2007).

Katyal, S. (2002) 'Exporting identity',
Yale Journal of Law and Feminism,
14(1): 97–176.

Menon, N. (2005) 'How natural is
normal? Feminism and compulsory heterosexuality', in A. Narrain
and G. Bhan (eds), *Because I Have
a Voice: Queer Politics in India*,
New Delhi: Yoda Press, pp. 33–9.

Ministry for Foreign Affairs (2006)
*Sweden's International Policy on
Sexual and Reproductive Health
and Rights*, Ministry for Foreign
Affairs, Stockholm, February,
<www.sweden.gov.se/content/1/
c6/06/14/89/712f7e0c.pdf>
(accessed 9 May 2007).

Nanda, S. (1990) *Neither Man nor
Woman: The Hijras of India*, Bel-
mont, CA: Wadsworth Publishing
Company.

Narrain, A. (2004) *Queer: Despised
Sexuality, Law and Social Change*,
Bangalore: Books for Change.

PUCL-K (People's Union for Civil Liberties, Karnataka) (2003) *Human
Rights Violations Against the Transgender Community: A Study of Kothi
and Hijra Sex Workers in Bangalore,
India*, Karnataka: PUCL-K.

Ranchhoddas, R. and D. K. Thakore
(2002) *The Indian Penal Code*, 29th
edn, Delhi: Wadhwa.

Republic of South Africa (1996) *Constitution of South Africa*, Section
9 (3), <www.polity.org.za/polity/
govdocs/constitution/index.html>
(accessed 9 May 2007).

Seabrook, J. (1999) *Love in a Different
Climate: Men Who Have Sex with
Men in India*, London: Verso.

Wintemute, R. (1995) *Sexual Orientation and Human Rights*, Oxford:
Clarendon Press.

TWO | **Gender and sex orders**

9 | Discrimination against lesbians in the workplace

ALEJANDRA SARDÁ

'I think this can be done, and should be done: to dignify what you are. We can't live like ostriches with our heads buried in the sand. And when you come out and say it, it disarms them.' Rosa María, interviewee from Mexico

This chapter addresses the challenges faced by lesbians in Latin America in obtaining, preserving and enjoying paid employment. It is very hard for women to enjoy their sexual beings if those same beings are the reason why they are unemployed, fear unemployment at any time or are subjected to harassment and ridicule in their workplace. The strategy that is most widely employed by lesbians to survive in the workplace is to keep silent about their sexual preferences. That silence has implications for their physical, mental and sexual health. But it is also a social problem, as it deprives society as a whole of the possibility of acknowledging and enjoying its sexual and erotic diversity. Women should not be made to choose between their sexual and gender expression and their material survival. Societies should not be deprived of any part of their richness in the name of so-called 'moral principles' that impose uniformity in the wide array of bodies, desires and expressions that humanity has been blessed with.

Drawing on a study commissioned by the Latin American programme of the International Gay and Lesbian Human Rights Commission (IG-LHRC),[1] carried out in 2004/05, this chapter applies a human rights lens to examine the situation of lesbians in the workplace in five Latin American countries, in partnership with ADEIM Simbiosis, a lesbian group in Bolivia, Criola, a black women's group in Brazil, Red Nosotras LBT, a network of lesbians, bisexual and trans women in Colombia, Cattrachas, a lesbian group in Honduras, and Artemisa, a young women's group working on sexual rights in Mexico. The study explored lesbians' exercise of the right to work (wages, working conditions, hiring and promotion practices) and the right to social security (social insurance, pensions, bereavement and sick leave). Different approaches to collecting data were used in each setting: focus groups in Bolivia and individual, in-depth interviews in Brazil, Colombia, Honduras and Mexico. We did our best to diversify as much as possible the range of women interviewed for this study. Overall, the documentation reflects the lives of lesbians who are between nineteen and fifty years of age, with thirty as the average age, ranging from working- to middle-class and primary- to university-educated. In terms of race, most respondents from Bolivia, Colombia, Honduras and Mexico self-identify as *'mestizas'*,[2] with a minority identifying as 'white'. All our respondents from Brazil were black women. We were not able to reach indigenous women who identify as lesbians, as our research was restricted to urban areas.

The research was published in book form as *Unnatural, Unsuitable, Unemployed! Lesbians and Workplace Discrimination in Bolivia, Brazil, Colombia, Honduras and Mexico*[3] in January 2006 in English, Spanish and Portuguese versions. It was launched at the Hemispheric Social Forum in Caracas and formed the basis for a series of events in Brazil, Colombia, Honduras, Bolivia and Mexico aimed at advocacy and awareness-raising among public officers, union leaders, social movements (the feminist, women's, human rights and social justice movements in particular) and – most importantly – the lesbian community itself. This chapter presents the main findings from the study and makes recommendations for advocacy and action to enhance the rights of lesbian workers in the workplace. We consider this study to be a preliminary one – its value lies in being the first on the subject and in the roads it might open for further, more in-depth studies.

Lesbians as women workers: the Latin American context

In recent decades, Latin America has seen a substantial rise in the number of women in the labour market. In a recent ILO study, Abramo and Valenzuela (2005) report a rise from 39 per cent in 1990 to 44.7 per cent in 2002, compared with a relatively stable rate of labour market participation by men, at around 74 per cent (ibid.). Unemployment is higher among women than men: between 1990 and 2004, unemployment among urban females rose from 6.5 to 13 per cent, compared to a rise from 5.3 to 9.1 per cent for men, which Abramo and Valenzuela attribute to better education, urban growth, lower fertility rates and changing cultural practices in favour of women's autonomy. The region has also seen a significant rise in female-headed households, ranging from 19 to 31 per cent (ibid.). Economic crises in the region, coupled with the implementation of neoliberal market reforms and the growth of export processing zones and the informal economy, have spurred the entry of more and more women into the labour market, closing the gap between the economic participation of poorer and better-off women. Around 50 per cent of those women who work find employment in the informal sector, where wage differentials between women and men are the highest in the world, with women earning just over half the amount earned by men (ILO 2004; Abramo and Valenzuela 2005).

There are a few key elements that contextualize the situation in which lesbians are – or try to be – part of the workforce in Latin America. In order for lesbians to be able to assert their identity, financial independence is a basic ingredient.[4] If they have no employment possibilities or their salaries are not enough for them to survive, lesbians might be forced to live with family members and submit to their lifestyles, which in many cases implies leading a double life and hiding their sexual preference. This has particularly serious effects on young lesbians, whom unemployment affects the most. The same goes for lesbians aged forty or older, for whom it is very hard to find employment and who sometimes are forced to go back to their family home (after a break-up, for instance) and to revert to 'closeted' behaviour. In certain cases – for both young and older lesbians – lack of economic possibilities might keep them from leaving a troublesome or even abusive partner. Both young and older lesbians may be required by families to play the role of care providers for sick family members, the elderly or infants, in exchange for their keep. Such unpaid work can severely restrict their choices and possibilities of employment.

For lesbians, working in the informal economy means that they find themselves sidelined from the strides certain countries – such as Brazil, Colombia and Mexico – have begun to make in terms of equal rights and non-discrimination, particularly with regard to social benefits and anti-discriminatory protection. If they work in family-owned businesses, it reinforces their dependence on their family and, if the family has a negative attitude towards their lesbianism, restricts their possibilities for sexual expression. If their work involves clandestine activities, they are exposed to all manner of abuses with no possibility to resort to whatever protections the law might provide.

Sexual rights in Latin America: the legal context

Homosexuality is not illegal in any of the countries studied. On the contrary, the legal context is very positive in the cases of Mexico, Brazil and Colombia. Since 2003, Mexico has had a Federal Law to Eliminate and Prevent Discrimination which includes 'sexual preferences' as a protected category and also prevents discrimination based on 'physical appearance, dress, speech and gesture'.[5] The text of this law is exemplary; but it is quite weak in terms of enforcement. Like many anti-discriminatory laws in the region (and elsewhere), it binds the public sector much more than private actors. The law creates a National Council that has the power to impose sanctions on public officers found guilty of discrimination, but in the case of private actors its only powers are those of mediation. Discrimination based on 'sexual orientation' is forbidden in Mexico City and three other states.[6]

In Colombia, the Constitutional Court is well known for its positive rulings against discrimination based on sexual orientation. To give only one example: in 1998, the court repealed Article 46e of Decree 2277 (1979), which forbade 'homosexuals' to practise the teaching professions.[7] In Brazil, ten states[8] (and more than 120 cities!) have made discrimination based on sexual orientation illegal. Same-sex couples can register their unions before a notary public in the state of Rio Grande do Sul, to enjoy the same rights as de facto couples. Rights to social security are granted to same-sex couples in five states.[9] Numerous rulings by the Brazilian judiciary recognize inheritance, social benefits and permanent residence rights for individuals in same-sex relationships. In 2003, the Brazil without Homophobia programme was launched as an effort to fight discrimination based on sexual orientation and gender identity at different levels. Implementation has been unequal. Some ministries (such as those of Culture and Health) have been very active while others (such as Labour) have not started to implement the programme at the time of writing.

In Bolivia, the situation is different. The General Labour Law includes 'honourability' as a requirement for employment and mandates employers to 'guarantee that morality exists among the workers'.[10] In 2004, under pressure from the Catholic Church, the executive vetoed a Sexual and Reproductive Rights Law that would have forbidden discrimination based on sexual orientation with regard to the enjoyment of those rights. Honduras is the only country in Latin America that has passed a law explicitly forbidding marriage between people of the same sex. The law was passed in October 2004, under pressure from the Bush administration and in a context of frantic activism from Christian groups with representation at the highest state levels. Legal registration of gay organizations was possible in the country only after August 2004.

Lesbians in Latin America: the struggle for visibility

In the region as a whole, but particularly in the countries studied, lesbians have played a key role in creating more visibility and recognition as citizens for themselves, gay men, trans people and – to a lesser extent as yet – bisexuals. Gay and lesbian movements started to flourish in Latin America in the late 1960s and early 1970s. It is worth noting that they were not a simple replication of the movements involved in the Stonewall riots that according to some US scholars gave birth to gay and lesbian struggles the world over. In countries like Argentina, Brazil, Colombia, Mexico or Peru, gay and lesbian struggles were born in times when 'liberation' was the key word – particularly for the young, the goal was to achieve economic, political, cultural, racial and sexual liberation. Most of the gay pioneers were communists, Trotskyites or otherwise involved in left-wing parties or even guerrilla groups. When they started to apply the principles of liberation to their own identities as gay men, they were faced with the deep machismo and homophobia that still permeate most of the Latin American left. The first gay groups created in these countries were the products of such confrontations. The first women who called themselves lesbians and started fighting for 'sexual liberation' alongside gay men or on their own were also coming from the left, but the most influential factor in their case was feminism. The first openly lesbian groups created in Mexico, Brazil and Peru in the early 1980s were lesbian-feminist groups.

Since then, in spite of military dictatorships, economic hardship, male chauvinism in the left and the trade unions, and a vigorous religious (Catholic and evangelical) right wing, lesbians (and gay men and trans people) have never looked back. On the contrary, as the years went by, they became a presence that no government wanting to call itself 'democratic' and 'modern' could afford to exclude. Today, gay men, lesbians and trans people sit as advisers in National Councils Against Discrimination in Argentina, Brazil and Mexico and at the tables where anti-discriminatory laws and policies are debated in Colombia, Guatemala, Chile and Paraguay.

Important as the legal victories and the political clout are, in our opinion the greatest achievements of lesbians (and gay men) in the region lie in the cultural sphere. Thirty years ago, most people in the region could easily claim never to have met a lesbian, or even not to know what the word meant. Even for progressive individuals, it was accepted to utter homophobic remarks. There was almost no representation of same-sex desire in the arts or the media, except for the occasional sensationalist piece. Today, hardly anyone could claim not to know what a lesbian is, when in all Latin American countries there are Pride Parades ranging in size from 1.5 million people in São Paulo to a few dozen in Panama City, but all equally visible and audible. In all Latin American countries there is at least one gay and lesbian organization that is quoted in the media, organizes cultural and political events, submits law proposals, talks to politicians and engages in open debates on TV. No progressive intellectual would want to be called 'homophobic', as the term now denotes someone who is not very educated, backward in his/her thinking, intolerant, etc. In fact, in most countries, the most recognized intellectuals, human rights activists and artists have made public statements in favour of equality for gays and lesbians on repeated occasions. Gays and lesbians (and sometimes also trans and bisexual people) are often portrayed in the arts and the media, sometimes still under a sensationalist light but more and more often as complex human beings, with love/desire stories, like anyone else.

This cultural change – which sustains and will outlive all legal achievements – is the product of the many years of tireless work undertaken by dozens of lesbians, gay men, trans and bisexual people all over the region. It has been translated into legal gains, but even more often it can be seen in other gains, less visible but sometimes even more important for those who can enjoy them: families that not only 'understand' but also celebrate their gay or lesbian children, straight friends who share confidences and parties with same-sex couples, schools where lesbian mothers or gay fathers can openly talk to teachers and other parents about their children's lives, adolescents who do not feel terrified or ashamed when the desire for someone of their same sex/gender first strikes them.

In the workplace, however, lesbians continue to face discrimination. The following sections describe the experiences of lesbian workers in Bolivia, Brazil, Colombia, Honduras and Mexico, and explore the issues that these raise for the realization of the sexual, workers' and human rights of lesbians in the workplace.

Sexual orientation and gender expression: two dimensions of discrimination against lesbians in the workplace

In the course of our research, we documented two types of discrimination that affect lesbians in the workplace. One is based on their sexual preference; the other is based on their gender expression – that is, on how they behave, appear or present themselves with regard to societal expectations of gender. Before presenting the findings of the research, it is worth clarifying the differences between 'sexual orientation' and 'gender expression'. As bases for discrimination and abuse, but also as elements for self-discovery, empowerment, organizing and advocacy, the categories sometimes overlap. But they do not necessarily do so in each and every case. And they are not automatically related: in fact, to 'look feminine' is a strategy deployed by some lesbians to avoid being spotted as such.

Sexual orientation describes whom you are attracted to – erotically and sometimes also emotionally. It could be someone of your gender, some-one of a different gender or both, at different times or simultaneously. In the case of the women studied here, they defined themselves as lesbians (women who felt erotically and emotionally attracted to other individuals who also defined themselves as women). 'Gender expression' relates to how people manifest the way in which they perceive themselves as gendered beings. An example is the way people dress, and whether it is conventionally feminine or masculine, or defies these conventions. Some of the women interviewed were 'butch' or 'masculine' in their dress codes, and for this reason faced discrimination. Women who are not lesbians but whose gender presentation does not follow the rigid lines along which femininity is expressed in Latin American societies might well be subjected to discriminatory treatment too.

The term 'sexual orientation' has a long history and has already been included in anti-discriminatory provisions all over the world. At this point, it is important to realize that the term by itself is not enough to address all the situations in which people are discriminated against and abused because of their sexuality, nor does it contain all the different identities or communities that are organizing themselves around sexual rights. Incorporating discrimination based on gender expression into policy discourses – and particularly to those related to development issues – would somehow help to diminish the dangers involved in identity politics and in attaching claims to identities, as 'gender expression' is more fluid, less determined and imperative than 'sexual orientation'. Accordingly, in the account that follows, we present findings relating to sexual preference/orientation and gender expression separately.

Discrimination based on sexual preference/orientation

The stories that our interviewees told about discrimination based on sexual preference or orientation follow a similar pattern – with a few remarkable exceptions – that goes 'from disclosure to firing'.

Disclosure In most cases, disclosure is the result of someone informing the employee's boss that she is a lesbian and that she lives with another woman, in an erotic relationship. The informant is usually another em-ployee who is competing with the lesbian worker for a promotion, or who wants to score a few points with the boss, by showing her/his loyalty to the public image of the company. In most cases, the 'discovery' results from watching what the worker does outside her job, usually by following her – or from accidentally meeting the lesbian worker with her partner in the street. In other cases, it comes as the result of a flagrant violation of privacy rights:

> In my free time I liked to coin phrases and write poems on lesbian topics. Some of my co-workers took the notebook from my till and showed it to the staff manager. (Marta, Bolivia, bookstore cashier)

In some cases, disclosure is triggered by an episode of sexual harassment.

> The administrative director stalked me all the time. One day, he heard me talking on the phone to my partner. After that, the stalking got worse because he said he wanted to 'cure me' of being a lesbian. I managed to reject him, but he went to my supervisor and told her that I was a lesbian. (Rosemary, clerk at a Holiday Inn hotel, Honduras)

> Both managers harassed me, the night manager and the day manager ... At one point, the night manager said he thought I was a lesbian and that was why I wouldn't give in to him. (Rubi, saleswoman at a department store, Mexico)

Firing/'voluntary' resignation In most cases, firing follows disclosure. In other cases, workers are subjected to mistreatment by co-workers and their bosses, in the hope that they will quit of their own accord:

> [My co-workers] started calling me '*marimacha*'[11] behind my back. A week later, the manager started calling my co-workers to ask them whether I'd ever touched them or harassed them, if I drank alcohol or smoked. (Vilma Georgina, factory worker, Honduras)

> They tagged my locker and my chair with names. I also became the target of religious and homophobic comments. (María, factory worker, Mexico)

> Even in the bathroom they had written graffiti about me being butch. My superiors have done nothing to stop the harassment; on the contrary, they contribute in some way to keep it going. (Helga, clerk at a factory, Honduras)

In most cases, firing is done swiftly and without offering further explanations. The following account is typical:

> He said I should be thankful he had not told all my colleagues that I was a lesbian, and I would be better off leaving right away and not complaining. (Marta, bookstore cashier, Bolivia)

When explanations are provided, they are usually linked to how the company would be perceived if it is known that a lesbian is working there:

> He said he wasn't doing it because he himself was homophobic but because he served the public and someone might somehow find out and he would lose his clients. (Patty, clerk at a law firm, Bolivia)

In a few cases, the 'moral' argument is explicit:

> He told me what I was doing was against all morals and that he couldn't accept my lifestyle. (Tania, secretary at a bookstore, Bolivia)

> She said my work was impeccable but working with young girls was risky in my condition. (Zeta, high-school teacher, Colombia)

> He said I will not be 'good company' for the youth in the community. (Cristina, community worker, Brazil)

Discrimination based on gender expression

Gender expression operates in a way that is different from sexual orientation. In this case, discrimination happens mostly in hiring practices: women who do not adjust to the societal ideas about feminine appearance have serious difficulties finding work – or keeping it when a change of supervisors places them before someone for whom 'good appearance' is a work requirement:

> The first thing he [her new boss] did was try to force me to either change my dress style or quit my job. Since I didn't agree to his request, I had to resign. Because of how I dress I often have trouble getting a job, since I'm not exactly the most feminine woman. (Marcela – outreach worker in a charity, Bolivia)

> I learnt the hard way that applying for a job in banks or stores was useless, since those jobs required contact with customers and they preferred women who dressed provocatively. Me, I always dress masculine. (Sonia, Honduras)

> In her report, the psychologist suggested that I be hired only under condition of 'follow-up of the teacher–student relations' as during the interview I had 'evidenced unfeminine gestures and attitudes'. (Janet, schoolteacher, Colombia)

'Survival' strategies

Most of our interviewees wanted to avoid the painful consequences of being identified as lesbians in their workplace. *Hiding* their sexual preferences seemed to be the basic strategy they employed. They did this by going out with men and letting co-workers see it; by avoiding any talk about their personal lives; by being 'very feminine' in their appearance; and by saying that they were married or in a relationship with a man, if asked. In the case of those affected by discrimination based on gender expression, 'hiding' can take the form of looking for jobs that would not bring them come into contact with the public. Sonia, from Honduras, says: 'I'm in charge of payroll at the factory, so the fact that I always dress masculine does not affect me much. The people around me have already got used to it.'

Some who feel they could not hide resort to *proving their worth* as a strategy to keep their jobs: 'I'm undeniably lesbian. I've held on to this job through a lot of effort and extra hours' (Sonia, Honduras, factory clerk). Some of those who refuse to hide resort to *looking for work in more supportive environments.* This strategy requires a certain degree of class/educational privilege, and some hard choices – as one of our interviewees said: '[In the school where I work now] they don't pay that well, but you don't have to hide who you are. I traded money for that well-being' (Zeta, Colombia). Many lesbians who work for NGOs made similar comments. Art venues and academia were also mentioned as spaces that allow more freedom.

In the case of those who have been faced with discriminatory treatment, the most usual behaviour is *to accept it silently and leave.* Reasons given by our interviewees for not reacting were not having a choice and not feeling emotionally capable of facing the process that filing a lawsuit would entail. It is worth noting here that in countries like Bolivia or Honduras – where legal protections are almost non-existent – most interviewees reacted with astonishment when asked whether they ever thought about taking action after being fired. The possibility had not even occurred to them. For Colombian, Mexican and Brazilian interviewees the issue was more that of long, uncertain and difficult legal procedures.

Successes

There are some cases in which lesbian workers have been faced with discriminatory treatment and have successfully managed to confront it and keep their jobs. Even though they are a minority, they show that possibilities exist and – what is even more important – their stories reveal the components that, if circumstances are changed, might allow others to resist as well. Unfortunately, the situation is still such that being successful requires openly lesbian workers to be exceptional, proving their 'competence' or making explicit their knowledge about their rights. In order to confront and defeat bias in the workplace, lesbians still need to have a lot of willpower and, even though it is not an 'iron rule', some degree of privilege might also help.

Two features are recurrent in these 'exceptional' stories. These are, first, the existence of *outside mechanisms for protection that women can invoke and their knowledge about them.* In Honduras, Helga – a government employee – told her manager that she would denounce him to the Human Rights Special Prosecutor if he didn't stop the co-workers who were mistreating her. In Mexico, Karina – who taught English at a private academy – invoked the city's anti-discriminatory law and her connections with Amnesty International to turn the threat of being fired (after the mother of a student had complained about her being a lesbian) into a transfer to another branch of the school. Second, the ability to build *relationships of trust and appreciation* with co-workers and bosses who are not homophobic. In Brazil, Cristina – a nurse – was denied promotion because her supervisor did not consider her capable of filling the post because she was lesbian. Her co-workers interceded and convinced the reluctant supervisor. Both Karina (see above) and Rubí – a clerk at a department store – in Mexico had female supervisors who, knowing beforehand that they were lesbians, interceded on their behalf to stop them from being fired.

Conclusions

The situation of working lesbians in Latin America calls for action. Mobilization and advocacy are needed to raise the visibility of labour rights and other social and economic rights not linked to partnership/ marriage, because by and large the discourses and strategies have concentrated more on civil and political rights and on recognition of civil unions/marriage as the only way to access social benefits. The discourse on intersectionality and the indivisibility of rights has started to permeate lesbian and gay struggles in Latin America more and more in recent years. The World and Continental Social Forums have been spaces where discussion of issues of socio-economic justice and its intersection with discrimination based on sexual preference has taken place.[12] This discourse, however, has not yet made it to the forefront of lesbian and gay activism.

Even though lesbians are the subject of this chapter, it is worth noting that trans movements have been articulating quite clearly – particularly in Argentina and Brazil, where trans movements are well organized and highly visible – that socio-economic demands are inextricable from their broader claim to citizenship (see Campuzano, this volume).

In the study it became very clear that there is a rift between lesbian, gay and women's concerns and the trade union movement that, in the region, remains largely in the hands of men, most of whom have very limited gender awareness, let alone positive attitudes towards sexual diversity. This situation has been slowly changing in recent decades, thanks to the efforts of dedicated women (some of them feminists) working from inside the trade unions. For instance, right now in Argentina the most progressive trade union – Central de Trabajadores Argentinos (CTA) – is leading the campaign for the legalization of abortion together with a wide array of feminist and women's organizations. That would have been unthinkable ten years ago and it still is an unthinkable position for the two mainstream (and much more powerful) trade unions in the country. Difficult as it might be, an alliance between women and feminists already working inside trade unions and lesbian and gay activists is of the essence if significant improvement is ever to be achieved in this field.

Last but not least, the issue of informal work is a serious problem in the region, not just for lesbians and for women, but for everybody. It is, of course, far beyond the scope of this chapter to deal with this issue in the depth it deserves, or suggest approaches or solutions to it. But we would like to propose that this is an issue that could help bring together a broad alliance of civil society groups in order to consider and propose solutions. And, if advocated by lesbian and gay groups, such an alliance could contribute to enhancing their status as meaningful civil society actors. More research is required, spanning not only a range of countries, but a much broader and diverse universe covering the various sectors of the labour market (formal and informal), and exploring intersections between sexual preference, race/ethnicity and age. This sort of research is of fundamental importance for the drafting and design of public laws and policies that contribute to guaranteeing lesbian populations – in all their diversity – the full exercise of their rights in the workplace.

The existence of anti-discriminatory protections is important. But in order to be effective, they must be followed by intensive social debate and awareness-raising. Thus, we consider it important to support advocacy efforts towards such legislation in the countries where it does not yet exist. Adding the category of 'gender expression' to current and future legislation, as well as educating activists, the media, public officers and the community as a whole about what it means, is important because 'sexual orientation' in itself does not cover many of the situations in which people are discriminated against. Also in terms of legal advocacy, campaigns are needed for provisions that would eliminate age require-ments for jobs, as well as for definitions of 'good appearance' that clearly prevent it from becoming synonymous with racist and ageist definitions of 'beauty'. Once again, we are aware that law in itself is not an answer to bias, but it provides a platform from which to engage in long-term efforts to change societal perceptions.

Efforts have been made in some countries, notably Brazil and Colombia, to work with the unions on anti-discrimination initiatives. Such efforts are of key importance and must be fully supported and expanded. It would also be productive to support initiatives towards making the links between sexual preferences/orientation, gender expression and economic discrimination in other inter-movements work (with social justice, feminist, women's, indigenous peoples, black and youth movements). Attractive, well-designed and targeted campaigns for raising public awareness on this issue are a necessity. It would be advisable to avoid victimization and favour approaches that highlight how non-discrimination and diversity contribute to enrich the life of communities.

Finally, we would like to suggest that external funding agencies supporting programmes and organizations in the region should also play a role in affirming the rights of workers in the organizations with which they work. This can be done, for instance, by explicitly encouraging their counterparts to include the amounts required for retirement and other social benefits in their budgets, and promoting among them awareness of their role as employers and the need to perform that role in a manner consistent with fundamental human rights principles.

Notes

1 IGLHRC is a non-governmental, non-profit organization with offices in New York and Buenos Aires, founded in 1990. IGLHRC's mission is to secure the full enjoyment of the human rights of all people and communities subject to discrimination or abuse on the basis of sexual orientation or expression, gender identity or expression, and/or HIV status. IGLHRC effects this mission through advocacy, documentation, coalition-building, public education and technical assistance.

2 'Mestizas/os' – those of mixed Spanish and indigenous descent constitute the majority of the population in those countries, and are well represented in the middle and working classes.

3 In Spanish, the report is called *La invisibilidad garantizaba el puchero* and in Portuguese *A invisibilidade é o ganha-pão*.

4 This statement does not imply that, in order to be a lesbian, one must break all ties to one's family and community. Growing acceptance of lesbian and gay children is a fact in most Latin American societies – in urban areas but also, increasingly, in rural areas as well. But even under the best conditions, financial independence helps all women (lesbians included) to feel more empowered and to build more equal relationships with their families and communities.

5 *Ley Federal para Prevenir y Eliminar la Discriminación, Artículo* 4.

6 Nuevo León (since 2004), Chipas (2003) and Aguascalientes (2003).

7 *Corte Constitucional de Colombia, sentencia* C-491/98.

8 Alagoas, Bahia, Federal District, Mato Grosso, Minas Gerais, São Paulo, Sergipe, Rio de Janeiro, Rio Grande do Sul and Santa Catarina.

9 Bahia, Goiás, Paraíba, Paraná and Roraima.

10 *Ley General de Trabajo, Artículo 65: 'La vacancia producida en cualquier cargo será provista con el empleado u obrero inmediatamente inferior siempre que reúna honorabilidad, competencia y antigüedad en el servicio'. Artículo 67: 'El patrono está obligado a adoptar todas las precauciones necesarias para la vida, salud y moralidad de sus trabajadores'.*

11 Tomboy, bull-dyke.

12 For more details, see in particular the work done by Dialogo Sur-Sur LGBT <www.movimientos.org>.

References

Abramo, L. and M. E. Valenzuela, (2005) 'Women's labour force participation rates in Latin America', *International Labour Review*, Special issue on 'Women's Labour Force Participation', 144(4), Geneva: International Labour Office.

ADEIM-Simbiosis, Artemisa, Cattrachas, Criola, IGLHRC, Red Nosotras LBT (2006) *Unnatural, Unsuitable, Unemployed! Lesbians and Workplace Discrimination in Bolivia, Brazil, Colombia, Honduras and Mexico*, ADEIM-Simbiosis, Bolivia, Artemisa, Mexico, Cattrachas, Honduras, Criola, Brazil, IGLHRC, New York, and Red Nosotras LBT, Colombia.

ILO (International Labour Organization) (2004) *Panorama laboral*, Lima (the full document can be consulted, in Spanish, at <www.oit.org.pe>).

10 | Ruling masculinities in post-apartheid South Africa[1]

KOPANO RATELE

Jacob Zuma and 'a better life for all'

It may well be that the High Court of South Africa will return a verdict of not guilty at the end of the corruption trial of former Deputy President Jacob Gedleyihlekisa Zuma, due to take place from July 2007. Mr Zuma may yet reach the heights of South African political life, as he himself has suggested. Perhaps, too, he will prove to be the one to lead the country to the promised 'better life for all'.

'A better life for all' is a slogan of the former national movement and current ruling party in South Africa, the African National Congress, which at worst is employed with ever more frequency during election periods, and at best is meant to epitomize the centrality and serious-ness of development in the party's policies. In its manifesto for the first inclusive democratic national elections the ANC, as an example, main-tained: 'South Africa's first democratic elections are about our common yearning for freedom, peace and a better life for all. They are about a past of oppression and despair and a future of hope and democracy' (ANC 1994). Ten years on, during the last national elections in 2004, in his party presidential message, Thabo Mbeki would say: 'Our First Ten Years of Freedom have been ten years of growing unity in action; ten years of peace and stability; ten years of increasingly making resources in the hands of the state available to uplift disadvantaged South Africans; ten years of expanding opportunities to build a better life for all' (ibid.). And in a speech given at the congress of the National Union of Mineworkers, the deputy president of the party, Zuma, asked: 'Can we strengthen this alliance on the same principles that it was founded and ensure that it takes our struggle forward as we try to build a better life for all and to reverse the legacy of apartheid and of poverty?' (Zuma 2006).

Promises of 'a better life for all' notwithstanding, should Zuma become president of the country there is cause for suspecting that he will be hard put to inspire hope or confidence in sections of the population of South Africa. This lack of belief in the possibility of 'a better life' that might be brought to fruition by Zuma is, however, not only because of a second case, in which the sixty-four-year-old man stood accused of raping a thirty-one-year-old family friend and national liberation struggle comrade, who even during her gruelling cross-examination in court referred to him as *umalume* (uncle). Nevertheless, the theatre around that particular case, including the intimidation of the plaintiff by the declared supporters of Zuma, is among the reasons for the wariness (see Hlongwa and Msomi 2006, Ndebele 2006, Zulu and Msomi 2006). About the public spectacle and theatrics that transfixed a nation, Njabulo Ndebele wrote:

> At issue here are webs of social and political relationships that may bedevil professional conduct. It is how Zuma resolves such conflicting loyalties that may explain his apparent disregard for the broad public in his dramatic appearances before his supporters immediately after two recent court appearances on the rape charges. He just seems unaware of the rest of us. His single-minded focus is his political home: the ANC and the 'broad alliance'.
>
> ... In this battle the rest of us are an anonymous mass, despite strong notions of public morality in this country. It is the force of this morality that has many of us wanting to see even faint signs of pain on the face of a public figure facing a charge of rape.
>
> ... The conflicting loyalties to family and to a constitutional public result in a psychological blind spot in which the public is invoked only to embarrass opponents, not because it is itself seen as aggrieved. The ability to see the public as aggrieved would almost certainly have resulted in different strategies and tactics. Instead, this blind spot, accentuated by the personal nightmare of his fall from grace, has distorted Zuma's judgment. (2006: 19)

The political drama around the case, and the aggressive tactics pursued by the defendant's side and supporters in that case notwithstanding, there was no saying at any point that the High Court would not acquit Zuma on this charge. On Monday, 8 May 2006, Zuma was found not guilty by Judge Willem van der Merwe at the Johannesburg High Court. It has to be stated at the outset that South African criminal law and the acquittal of Zuma are not the main concerns of this chapter (for a discussion of these matters, see, for example, Govender 2006). What is of concern is the public psycho-political theatre.

A range of moments from the rape trial of Zuma are available from which we can approach this concern and draw the links to sexualities and a ruling masculinity. These moments include the fact that Zuma, who was at one time tasked with leading the anti-HIV and AIDS campaign, knowingly had unprotected coitus with a woman he knew to be HIV positive; that he stated in court that he went ahead and had sex anyway even though no condoms were available because in his culture a man could be accused of rape for leaving a woman sexually aroused; and that he testified that he had taken a shower after the incident because he believed a shower would reduce the risk of infection (see News24. com 2006).

Given the import of the idea of 'a better life for all', however, and with the intention of thinking of development beyond political sloganeering and electioneering, at the same time as assessing the events that continue to take place around Zuma in particular and other African political leaders more generally, what is called for is considered reflection on the question of the use of politics for human betterment. I wish to look, though not always directly, at this question of a better life for all as it relates to sexual and gender life. In this reflection, research from pro-feminist studies of men and masculinity will be drawn on, with the arguments informed by insights from discourse analysis.

In this chapter, it is therefore not the rape trial of Zuma, or even his corruption trial, but rather a less publicized moment to which I would like to draw attention – in order to think about the interconnections between sexualities, masculine power and the notion of 'a better life'. It is at this moment, concerning a matter that could never be brought before a court of law, that Zuma's discursive political and psychological practices reveal themselves as unable to inspire confidence in some sections of South African society. Here Charmaine Pereira's argument concerning how power relations and status shield the sexual improprieties of the powerful is applicable (2006).

'Wrong' sex, the Bill of Rights and discursive political acts

The moment in question came in the form of a question about cunnilingus/fellatio. The question was put to Zuma as the then deputy president during a debate in the national parliament of South Africa. At issue was whether or not oral sex is, in a manner of speaking, 'right'.

Zuma's answer during a debate was that oral sex is wrong, unnatural. He also said it was a subject he was not prepared to talk about. Of some significance is the fact that at the time he uttered these words, Zuma was featuring in a national media campaign to encourage people to talk openly about sexuality as part of the larger project to stem the spread of HIV/AIDS. His exact words were:

> I can't answer on wrong things that people do that are unnatural. I can't talk about that. ... I don't know really whether I should have an opinion on some of the things ... because I don't understand what do they mean

123

[*sic*]. We are talking about education about sex, not other things that are not sex. I wouldn't be able to have an opinion on that one. (Maclennan 2002; also see Mail & Guardian online 2002a, 2002b)

Since forty years of discourse studies have taught us the productivity of discourse and the immanence of sexual and gender power in talk and text, I feel no urgent need to rehearse their assumptions and findings. To fully appreciate the impact of this particular utterance, Zuma's words should be juxtaposed against the Bill of Rights of South Africa. In contrast to Zuma's expressed sentiments, then, the Bill of Rights makes it very clear that the state may not unfairly discriminate, directly or indirectly, against anyone on the grounds of belief, culture, language, birth, gender, sex and sexual orientation. Why, then, was the second-most powerful political actor in government contradicting the spirit, if not the letter, of a developing constitutional and human rights culture? While for some a contradiction like this one was hardly surprising, something we have come to expect from African politicians, for others, beyond crying out for vigorous challenge, it holds some instructive lessons.

Zuma's constitution-contradicting discursive move means, first, that serious contemplation of the meaning of 'a better life' suggests that those concerned with development ought to simultaneously appreciate the need to strengthen human rights generally and not forget sexual rights specifically. Second, the ANC's deputy president's words suggest that there is a need not to relax vigilance on issues of sexual and gender equality, particularly when dealing with what are at first glance non-sexual matters – for instance, poverty, income-generation projects, displacement or famine. This latter political lesson derives also from nearly forty years of feminist thinking and activity around the politics of sex.

What the former deputy president of the country and former chair of the South African National Aids Council did in the response under discussion was to constitute a psychology, politics and culture that are unsupportive of sexual practices other than those acceptable to what can be called a historically ruling masculinity. Research shows that the ruling masculinity in South Africa, as in other parts of the world, has as some of its constituent elements assertive heterosexuality, control of economic decisions within (and outside) the home, political authority and cultural ascendancy (see, for example, Mares 1999). This is reflected in the words of several of the subjects in Mankayi's study of male soldiers:

Daniel: [Men] want a lot of it. For a man sex ... generally [is about] the more, the better. If we had our own way, we'd just like to have sex with a woman. Then two or more nights later ... have sex with another woman.

Tulani: We go to girls having this mind and we tell our minds, if she can arrive here on the base, I will kiss her, have sex with her.

Mtobeli: You see a woman ... you start having feelings for a woman. Even if you know that you have your own partner ... I think it's something natural ... I think it's natural.

Jeff: She might have a great butt, she might have a great pair of breasts, but she's got it and you've noticed it ... compliment her. She's got it, why not ... if it attracts your eye, it's like a good painting, it's there, I mean, and if that feeling of yours become way stronger then, ja, it does. (2005)

Similar connections between ruling masculinity and heterosexuality are revealed by a study examining talk by professional men on the meanings they attach to their gendered and racial identities. For example, one of the men, Ricky, said:

And then, no, as to promiscuity, it's a no-no, see. You can't go on and be promiscuous, while saying you have a thing with me as a girl. But at the same time, me, I do accept that you must understand, if you do catch me, that I'm promiscuous, say no, it's a man's thing, see [translation from is'camtho, one of the hybrid street languages spoken in South Africa]. (Ratele 2001)

In a recent study on masculinity focusing on boys from several high schools around the Western Cape, similar thinking was evident. First, in response to the question 'What is a man?', some of the boys answered that a man is 'always considered ... the head of the household while women are subordinate to men. Therefore a woman is not allowed to [be equal to] her husband when it comes to household decision-making'. In regard to the question of sexuality, a boy said 'the problem with abstinence is that you might go crazy, if you are a man' (Ratele et al. forthcoming). From discussion on gay and lesbian identities in that study, it was also clear that 'a real man' does not behave in ways that are 'unmanly' and does not have sex with another man. As a boy in one group said, 'like some gays you can't even tell that they're gay ... among themselves they don't parade around with it. I don't mind if they're like that, but I mean if they walk around going like "hello doll" and that little kiss thingy ... ' (he doesn't need to finish his idea); and another boy in another school, in reference to men looking after children, said, 'when you look after a child, you also have to put on an apron which makes you look like a moffie' (ibid.).

Because of his political power, however, Zuma was doing more than merely telling us the truth about his psyche and own self. Because of his cultural authority (inferred from his positioning as an older, relatively well-off Zulu man with authority), he was doing more than simply articulating a certain political discourse, one among many. Because of his social position, he also drew a bold line between South African citizens who view him as the embodiment of the true masculine, and others whose practices do not accord with those which he suggests are 'naturally' right.

Over and above his claims about the truth of social (as opposed to self-) identity, beyond his culture-authorizing articulation, and past his boundary-drawing game, Zuma chose to speak against the rights of equality, privacy and sexual orientation contained in the constitution he had sworn to uphold. Equally baffling, he also effectively discouraged open discussion of these 'other things that are not sex'. This was baffling because Zuma and other political and social celebrities, as key actors in a national campaign to curb the spread of HIV/AIDS, were supposed to encourage open talk of sexuality; yet here he decided to go against one of the strategies thought to be most important in the campaign.

What this speech act demonstrates, therefore, is that even when legal and constitutional battles have been won, there is a real risk of residual aversion (even prospects of backlash) to the rights of sexual minorities on the part of those who are charged with guarding those rights. When Zuma said he 'can't answer on wrong things that people do that are unnatural', as a powerfully positioned figure within government, he compromised the sexual choices and happiness of individual men and women and subjects of the state he served, and which has declared its duty to protect certain basic rights.

Furthermore, if, in a place such as South Africa, where the rights to equality and sexual orientation are part of the foundational law, a politician demonstrates that we cannot trust even those entrusted with defending these rights (a constitution he swore to protect), society must be defended (see Foucault 2003). It is not, however, the 'people who do wrong things ... that are unnatural' against whom society must be defended. Newly democratic societies are in need of defending from those who have more power – those who might believe 'they are above or outside of the law'. Thus, one way to defend society is for policies and projects that speak of 'a better life' to also give due consideration to the right to a better sexual and gender life in addition to a better economic life.

Given this discursive move by Zuma, it is of interest that he was at one point married to four women. But the fact of Zuma's polygamous status is pointed out here to illuminate the connections and contradictions among sexualities, sexual rights, development and masculinities.

Zuma's marital history is common knowledge. And it should be made clear at once that South African law permits polygamous marriages – embodied in the Recognition of Customary Marriages Act, No. 120 of 1998 (Republic of South Africa 1998). During the same year that this legislation was enacted, the South African Demographic and Health Survey (1998) reported that between one in six and one in five of thirty- to forty-nine-year-old married women were married to a man with more than one wife. This act might be considered progressive, given the culturally racist legal history of South Africa, as it gives some legal standing to African women in particular.

That the practice of polygamy was until not too long ago treated as inferior to 'white heterosexual marriages' and governed by administrative laws exclusively for blacks[2] highlights a striking ignorance on the part of anyone who parses oral sex as unnatural of problems faced by others for practices formerly marginalized under apartheid law. At the same time, even though polygamous marriages are now equal to other forms of legal marriages, it can be argued that they are potentially inimical to the freedoms and advancement of women, as well as presenting a challenge to gender equity. It should also be noted that Article 6 of the Protocol to the African Charter on Human and Peoples' Rights on the Rights of Women in Africa encourages 'monogamy … as the preferred form of marriage' (African Commission on Human and Peoples' Rights 2003). Where polygamy exists, however, the protocol seeks to promote and protect the rights of women, and calls for both women and men to be regarded as equal partners in marriage. The protocol is silent on alternative non-heterosexual lives and relationships, as is the African Charter.

Here, then, is another lesson: irrespective of the cultural status of a practice, when looking at a traditional practice (such as polygamy) development thinkers and critical citizens must strive to relate it to enlarging choices. It is no coincidence that polygamy most often occurs in rural, underdeveloped areas, and that it usually takes place between a socially powerful man and women who by definition have very little social power. The majority of women in polygamous unions in South Africa, for instance, have little or no education and are between the ages of forty and forty-four (in other words, their opportunities to improve their status are decreasing). It must be added that education, including sexuality, gender and human rights education, remains one of the major arenas of intervention for the empowerment of girls and women, just as it is important for national development; yet this is the arena where economic chances and the available choices regarding one's body are starkly limited.

The organization of sexual life and the role of ruling masculinity

Having deployed masculinity to explain Zuma's discursive practice, it is important to make some remarks about this concept, especially the idea of ruling masculinity. Once again, I wish to demonstrate how ruling masculinity is linked to sexuality and to human and sexual rights. A ruling masculinity is powerfully capable of organizing ideas on sexuality and human rights. The same association holds between masculinity and development: the notion of masculinity can and does shape ideas on development.

Masculinity has achieved an enviable standing among social scientific concepts, attaining, indeed, disciplinary status. Even among those who do not directly study men and masculinity, the construct has been deployed in attempts to explain varied conditions, characterizations and conventions: from social and family relations in rural spaces to urban life, risk-taking and mining, and from violence and national liberation struggles to international politics and culture (see, for example, Ouzgane and Morrell 2005; Reid and Walker 2005). In brief, masculinity has reconfigured judgements on relations within the world of males, the world between men and women and children, and the world per se.

This fetishizing of the concept of masculinity has its downside, however. In particular, one notes the lack of precision in use and the loose conception by many of those who employ it. It is therefore useful to indicate that there are different – and not necessarily helpful – understandings of the idea and place of masculinity in analysing social, political and economic worlds (for example, Clare 2000; Dobson 2002; Meintjies 1991). It should be noted that it is not only masculinist thinking on gender relations which is troubled by lack of a clear definition of masculinity. Development scholars and practitioners also need to concern themselves with the definitional aspects of the concept – as indeed scholars of masculinity have done for some time.

One outcome of the debate on the concept of masculinity and its utility is the importance that some thinkers have accorded to talking about men's social and material practices and relations – 'what men do or think or feel' (Hearn 1996: 214). Ruling masculinity indicates a design of practices, relations and supportive cognitive and affective discourses that seek to have us believe in the naturalness of men's power over women, other men and children. Another outcome of the debate is a preference for using the term 'masculinities', rather than the singular form. In tandem with this thinking is the contention that masculinity is not one single thing, that there are a variety of masculinities, a position favoured by the fact that masculinities intersect with and co-produce one another according to poverty, wealth and inequality, with ethnicity and sexualities, with race, space in a country and location on the globe. I am thus distinguishing between what might be called sympathetic and critical conceptions of masculinity. Indeed, the notion of hegemonic masculinity bolsters these arguments, embracing the same network of practices, embodiment, relationality and action, of plurality, intersections and location (see Carrigan et al. 1985, Connell 1983; Connell et al. 1982; Kessler et al. 1982).

Prompted by such loose deployment of masculinity as an explanatory framework, as well as some insightful criticisms of the concept of hege-monic masculinity, Connell and Messerschmidt (2005) recently revisited the latter. In the same way that ruling masculinity is employed here, these authors stress that hegemonic masculinity is intended to convey something more than simply a focus on men's biologies. Hegemonic masculinity is not an identity, not a set of role expectations, and not only about practices. Masculinities in general and dominant ones specifically are fundamentally about discursive material power, as well as resistance practices that shape relations males have in and to the world. These rela-tions cover those arrangements males and females have with respect to institutions, structures, laws and policies over and above males' relations to their own bodies, bodies of other males and female bodies.

Ruling heterosexual masculinity's relation to 'a better life' in post-apartheid South Africa

The itinerary of a man's practices and the idea of heterosexual mas-culinity might overlap one another at a particular moment, but more often than not they tend to veer away from each other. Males are usually in pursuit of, or negotiating with or for, a minority, trying to radically change the ruling masculinity. Men are not naturally heterosexual and 'masculine'. This is supported on the one hand by the fact that there are (for the purpose of pleasure, among other reasons) men who dress up in women's clothes, men who enjoy sex with men, men who have sex with men and women, women who prefer women sexually, and women who have sex with both women and men. In addition, this observation is strengthened by the fact that Zuma is not the only African nor African government incumbent nor politician in the world whose discursive or material practices around sexual life deserve close attention. This points to the continuing dominance of a certain configuration of being sexual – being a woman or being a man.

Heterosexual masculinity is not only about what a male says or does about sex, but equally about the techniques of power. And so politicians in Latvia, Poland, Uganda, the United States, Zimbabwe, China and India, as some of many examples (see Human Rights Watch 2004, 2005a, 2005b), have either inveighed against 'unnatural vices' (Epprecht 1998) or have gone along with discrimination against sexualities and sexual relations other than heterosexual ones. In these cases, the fist of the ruling heterosexual masculinity emerges to crush those men and women whose practices are regarded as queer. For example, in 2005 the Latvian president, Vaira Vike-Freiberga, signed into law a constitutional amendment defining marriage as the union of a man and a woman. A similar constitutional amendment (stating that 'marriage is lawful only if entered into between a man and a woman', and that 'it is unlawful for same-sex couples to marry') was approved by the Ugandan parliament, with the law proscribing same-sex marriage signed by President Yoweri Museveni – who has pronounced against homosexuality on several occasions. Since 1990, the maximum penalty for the offence of 'carnal knowledge against the order of nature' has been life imprisonment, with a maximum of seven years' imprisonment for 'attempts' at homosexual activity (see Human Rights Watch 2005b).

It needs to be spelled out that even in these cases of sexual discrimination, where a form of masculinity, supported by political power, aggressively reasserts its ascendancy over other forms, the undeniable fact is that gay masculinities exist, as do women who do not desire men sexually. It is the challenge posed by this reality which sends rulers (ruling masculinity) into a rage. This, contradictorily, is an indication of the resistance practices in different locales which subsequently shape the relations that ruling males (those with more power) have with other males, with females and with the social and material world.

National, social and cultural development: sexual war zones

Zuma's utterance in Parliament imperilled anyone – male or female, heterosexual or queer – whose sexual repertoires go beyond penetrative heterosex, just as many women and men are failed by the notion of 'a better life' for all if this remains deaf and blind to the significance of sexuality, and sexual rights in particular, to their personal freedom, development and happiness. Hence, as needful of attention as the practices of powerful figures are the omissions to be found in governmental, regional and continental development policies (as much in their languages as their aims). Whereas a framework such as the New Partnership for Africa's Development (2001) has as one of its objectives accelerating the empowerment of women and thus reducing poverty, the lack of attention to sexuality is disturbing, especially where scholarship and activism in the arena of sexuality have shown that it implicates and is implicated in politics, economics and society (Tamale 2006). Surely this reticence and blindness are as intolerable and dangerous as the trafficking in girls and women, female genital cutting, sexual slavery, the use of rape as a weapon of war, and forced pregnancy and marriage that continue apace throughout the continent (and indeed the globe): crimes and violations that go to the heart of the social, economic and political power of men over children and women. Surely it must be clear that gender- and sexually based violence is an outrage against the rights to the bodily integrity and life of women and sexual minorities, just as it violates and denies choice and desire (Jolly and Cornwall 2004). Considerations of sexual rights cannot be divorced from the struggles for equality, justice and democracy (see, for instance, Petchesky 2001). A development policy that remains quiet on the subject of sexual rights is likely to compromise its stated aims – including those of eradicating poverty, creating sustainable growth, and fully and beneficially integrating into the global economy.

The examples of sexual discrimination referred to earlier further illustrate the way that the development of nations or cultures is imagined, arranged and regulated. Part of the regulating imagination is the need to 'protect' the nation or culture from 'wrongdoers', 'abnormalities' and 'perversion'. It is clear, however, that nations, societies and cultures are continually contested and contesting – just as sexual conduct and relations are not 'natural' entities, so masculinities and sexual identities and rights are fields of power. A point that needs to be emphasized is how sexuality is a site of this imagination and contestation, the ground whereon a nation or culture fashions and reforms itself, develops or stunts the whole or parts of the whole, moves forward or regresses.

Worded differently, if the former deputy president of South Africa had spoken only for himself, if he was merely constituting a psycho-moral self and universe in which he as a private citizen opposed others whose practices he has a right to believe are immoral and unnatural, there would perhaps be less of a problem. But it must now be obvious, from his case and other such instances around the world, that there is a seething struggle going on. Difference, and dissidence from ruling masculinity, can be literally deadly. Recent news stories from South Africa, such as the one about the battering and murder of nineteen-year-old Zoliswa Nkonyana by a mob of males for the 'crime' of being a lesbian, attest to the intensity and seriousness of this struggle (Huisman 2006; see also Orford 2006). More significantly, it must now be keenly appreciated that around the world there is an ascendant heterosexual masculine culture, which is not afraid to get violent, and which is centrally embedded in national and state arrangements of power. All these cases are to be read as striking associations of sexuality and masculinity on one side (often riddled with paradox), and nation, society or culture on the other side; and it must be noted that there is a mutually formative configuration between these various elements.

Thus, when an individual occupies a privileged political and social position, his or her speech acts have a denunciatory capacity that works to inhibit the rights and choices of those against whom the words are directed. These 'othered' people in this particular case include those who have non-coital sex, including lesbians and young people trying to avoid pregnancy and sexually transmitted infections (STIs). But they extend to include those who do not always prefer heterosexual penile–vaginal intercourse (a preference that is being presumed and naturalized here), including bisexuals, gays and transgender persons.

Ruling men with political, economic, social or cultural power who repudiate in public oral and other 'wrong' sexual practices silence other men and women with less political voice, less education and less cultural and economic power. In societies and cultures where women and men are unequal, the sexual rights, choices, desires and pleasure of women and marginal men are likely to be curtailed by the words of such powerful men.

Conclusion

Among other things, this chapter has shown how events around Zuma are symptomatic and instructive of how the idea of 'a better life' is deeply troubled by sexual politics, gendered power and cultural hegemonies. Following Charmaine Pereira's recent contribution on *zina* in *Feminist Africa* (2006), this chapter has tried to show that power both defines and shields the transgressions of those who wield authority in society, sexuality being as much a matter of political and religious sanction as it is a private affair. The events around Zuma have here been held up for scrutiny to reveal that 'a good life' holds different meanings for African women as opposed to men, for queers as opposed to non-queers, for *iziduna* (headmen) as opposed to commoners, and for '100% Zulu-boys' (a slogan incribed on the T-shirts of Zuma supporters at his rape trial) (see, for example, Moya 2006) as opposed to somehow less than fully fledged Zulu boys and Zulu girls.

Notes

1 An earlier version of this chapter was published in *Feminist Africa*, 6: 48–64. It is reproduced here with the journal's kind permission.

2 I wish to thank Raymond Suttner for clarifying this point for me, as well as for reading and commenting on the chapter. I also wish to thank Helen Moffett and the anonymous reviewers who commented on the chapter.

References

African Commission on Human and Peoples' Rights (2003) 'Protocol to the African Charter on Human and Peoples' Rights on the Rights of Women in Africa', Adopted by the 2nd Ordinary Session of the Assembly of the Union, Maputo, 11 July.

ANC (African National Congress) (1994) '1994 election manifesto of the African National Congress', <www.anc.org.za/ancdocs/policy/manifesto.html> (accessed 14 May 2007).

— (2004) 'Manifesto 2004: a people's contract to create work and fight poverty', <www.anc.org.za/elections/2004/manifesto-f.htm> (accessed 14 May 2007).

Carrigan, T., R. W. Connell and J. Lee (1985) 'Toward a new sociology of masculinity', *Theory and Society*, 14: 551–604.

Clare, A. (2000) *On Men: Masculinities in Crisis*, London: Chatto & Windus.

Connell, R. W. (1983) *Which Way is Up? Essays on Sex, Class and Culture*, Sydney: Allen and Unwin.

Connell, R. W. and J. W. Messerschmidt (2005) 'Hegemonic masculinity: rethinking the concept', *Gender and Society*, 19(6): 829–59.

Connell, R. W., D. J. Ashenden, S. Kessler and G. W. Dowsett (1982) *Making the Difference: Schools, Families and Social Division*, Sydney: Allen and Unwin.

Dobson, J. (2002) *Bringing Up Boys: Practical Advice and Encouragement for Those Shaping the Next Generation of Men*, Vereeniging: Christian Art Publishers.

Epprecht, M. (1998) 'The "unsaying" of indigenous homosexualities in Zimbabwe: mapping a blindspot in an African masculinity', *Journal of Southern African Studies*, Special issue on Masculinities in Southern Africa, 246: 631–51.

Foucault, M. (2003) *Society Must be Defended: Lectures at the College de France, 1975–1976*, New York: Picador.

Govender, P. (2006) 'You have struck a woman, you have struck a rock', Mail & Guardian Online, 17 March, <www.mg.co.za> (accessed 14 May 2007).

Hearn, J. (1996) 'Is masculinity dead? A critique of the concept of masculinity/masculinities', in M. Mac an Ghaill (ed.), *Understanding Masculinities: Social Relations and Cultural Arenas*, Milton Keynes: Open University Press.

Hlongwa, W. and S. Msomi (2006) 'Zuma accuser's home looted', *City Press*, 5 March.

Huisman, B. (2006) 'Teen beaten to death for being a lesbian', *Sunday Times*, 19 February.

Human Rights Watch (2004) *In a Time of Torture: The Assault on Justice in Egypt's Crackdown on Homosexual Conduct*, New York: Human Rights Watch.

— (2005a) 'China: police shut down gay, lesbian event: government persecutes civil society groups that address HIV/AIDS', <http://hrw.org/> (accessed 14 May 2007).

— (2005b) 'Uganda: same-sex marriage ban deepens repression: in Uganda, colonial-era sodomy law already mandates life in prison', <http://hrw.org/> (accessed 14 May 2007).

Jolly, S. and A. Cornwall (2004) 'The power of pleasure', <www.ids.ac.uk/ids/news/Archive%202004/powerpleasure.html> (accessed 14 May 2007).

Kessler, S. J., D. J. Ashenden, R. W. Connell and G. W. Dowsett (1982) Ockers and Disco-maniacs, Sydney: Inner City Education Centre.

Maclennan, B. (2002) 'Zuma says he's not prepared to talk about oral sex', The Herald, 13 June, <www.theherald.co.za/herald/2002/06/13/news/n09_13062002.htm> (accessed 14 May 2007).

Mail & Guardian Online (2002a) 'Looking a gift blow in the mouth', 28 June, <www.mg.co.za> (accessed 14 May 2007).

— (2002b) 'Oral sex can save South Africans from Aids', 14 June, <www.mg.co.za> (accessed 14 May 2007).

Mankayi, N. (2005) 'Constructions of masculinity, sexuality and risky sexual practices of male soldiers', Unpublished PhD dissertation, Stellenbosch University.

Mares, T. (1999) The Quest for Maleness, Cape Town: Lionheart Publishing.

Meintjies, F. (1991) 'Men, feminism and masculinity', Agenda, 11: 11–14.

Moya, F. (2006) '100% Zuluboy', Mail & Guardian Online, 6 April, <www.mg.co.za> (accessed 14 May 2007).

Ndebele, N. (2006) 'Why Zuma's bravado is brutalising the public', Sunday Times, 5 March.

New Partnership for Africa's Development (2001) 'New Partnership for Africa's Development, 2001 framework document', <www.nepad.org/2005/files/home.php> (accessed 14 May 2007).

News24.com. (2006) 'Zuma tells of sex – the Zuma files: special report', <www.news24.com/News24/South_Africa/Zuma/0,,2-7-1840_1910081,00.html> (accessed 14 May 2007).

Orford, M. (2006) 'The deadly cost of breaking the silence', Feminist Africa, 6: 77–82.

Ouzgane, L. and R. Morrell (eds) (2005) African Masculinities: Men in Africa from the Late Nineteenth Century to the Present, New York and Scottsville: Palgrave Macmillan and University of Natal Press.

Pereira, C. (2006) 'Zina and transgressive heterosexuality in northern Nigeria', Feminist Africa, 5: 52–79.

Petchesky, R. P. (2001) 'Sexual rights: inventing a concept, mapping an international practice', in M. Blasius (ed.), Sexual Identities: Queer Politics, Princeton, NJ: Princeton University Press.

Ratele, K. (2001) 'Between ouens: everyday makings of masculinity', in R. Morrell (ed.), Changing Men in Southern Africa, London/Scottsville: Zed/University of Natal Press.

Ratele, R., E. Fouten, T. Shefer, A. Strebel, N. J. Shabalala and R. Buikema (forthcoming) 'Moffies, jocks and cool guys: boys' accounts of masculinity and their resistance in context', in T. Shefer, K. Ratele, A. Strebel, N. J. Shabalala and R. Buikema (eds), From Boys to Men: Masculinity and Risk.

Reid, G. and L. Walker (eds) (2005) Men Behaving Differently: South African Men since 1994, Cape Town: Double Storey.

Republic of South Africa (1998) Recognition of Customary Marriages Act, No. 120 of 1998, Pretoria: Republic of South Africa.

Tamale, S. (2006) 'Eroticism, sensuality and "women's secrets" among the Baganda: a critical analysis', *Feminist Africa*, 5: 9–36.

Zulu, M. and S. Msomi (2006) 'Break-in at Zuma's accuser', *City Press*, 11 December.

Zuma, J. (2006) Address delivered by the Deputy President, Jacob Zuma, at the National Union of Mineworkers National Congress, 24 May, <www.anc.org.za/ancdocs/history/zuma/2006/jz0524.html> (accessed 14 May 2007).

11 | Gender, identity and *travesti* rights in Peru

GIUSEPPE CAMPUZANO

Colonial ordinances and assumptions

'If any Indian male dresses in female Indian clothes or any Indian female in male Indian clothes, the ... Mayor should arrest them. The first time they should be given one hundred lashes and have their hair cut in public. The second time they should be tied for six hours to a pole at the market in full view of all. The third time they should be sent to the sheriff of the valley or to the Mayor of the Villa de Santiago de Miraflores, to have justice done to them in conformity with the law.' Gregorio Gonzales de Cuenca, *Ordenanzas de los Indios* (Ordinances of the Indians), 1556

This ordinance, passed 450 years ago by the Spanish colonial government, was the first legal proscription of *travestism* in Peru. Its origins lie in the Bible: 'The woman shall not wear that which pertaineth unto a man, neither shall a man put on a woman's garment ...' (Deuteronomy, 22:5), and 'Doth not even nature itself teach you, that, if a man have long hair, it is a shame unto him? But if a woman have long hair, it is a glory to her: for her hair is given to her for a covering' (1 Corinthians, 12:14–15).[1] Bonnie and Vern Bullough observe that since 'simulated sex-change was often a part of the fertility cults of the time, the biblical writers were probably much more hostile to cross-dressing at this time than were later commentators' (Bullough and Bullough 1993: 40). They underestimated later levels of hostility.

Nearly five hundred years ago, the Spanish colonizers came to Latin America to assume control of the Inca Empire (*c.* AD 1538). Their desire for the rumoured unlimited gold was a large part of the reason for their subjugation of the continent, along with the prestige of empire and a cheap labour force. Judge Gonzales de Cuenca presented the *Ordenanzas de los Indios* as the genesis of a new order. This departed from the *encomienda* system, where indigenous localities were assigned to settlers to manage, and moved to the *reductions* system, where indigenous localities were converted to Christianity and then returned to their former Indian administrators. The Crown expected to recuperate the control of production by integrating Indian administrators into the colonial scheme of power. This new organization also claimed, at least on paper, to pre-serve parts of native cultures. The requirement of Christian conversion and the prioritization of production implied the opposite, and led to suppression of some indigenous identities.

Travestis, a term that has survived into contemporary times and is used in Latin America to describe those who cross genders, sex and dress, came from one of these suppressed identities. The very concept of *travesti*, literally meaning cross-dressing, was born out of the colonizers' fixation with gender binaries, including the imperative to dress according to one's place within a rigid gender dichotomy, in which there were two clearly defined sexes and two genders premised on these sexes.[2] Pre-Hispanic gender was read through this lens; *travestism* became, within this schema, dressing across the binary.

While *travesti* was originally a pejorative adjective, it has been re-worked into a political noun by Argentinean and Peruvian *travesti* activists, renaming the 'duality as power', which androgyny and her-maphroditism meant in ancient cultures of both East and West. In this chapter, I trace the pre-Hispanic history of *travestis* in Peru. I explore what recovering the valorization given to the role of the *travesti* in indigenous culture has to offer the struggles of *travestis* for rights and recognition in contemporary Peru.

The pre-Hispanic gender continuum and colonial reaction

In pre-Hispanic times, gender was not limited to masculine or femi-nine. Principles of non-binary thinking remain apparent in the design of the traditional Andean woven *Aymara* bag, which is formed through repeated paired bands of different colours in such a way that each has its pair on the opposite half of the bag (Cereceda 1986). The total number of bands is always odd so one of them always remains without a pair, acting as the central axis (*Chhima*), separator as well as nexus of these two halves. This concept of 'one amongst paired things but without a pair' (*Chhullu*) can be used to reinterpret the persons depicted below by Spanish chroniclers throughout colonial America:

> ... generally among the Andean and Yungas, the demon has placed this vice beneath a sort of sanctity, so that every temple or major worshipping place has a man or two, or more, depending on the idol, who dress as women ever since they were children, and talk as such, imitating women in their manners, dress and everything else. On holidays and religious festivals, the masters and nobles have carnal and indecent intercourse with these people. This I know because I have punished two of them: one

of them an Indian of the Andes, in a temple that they call Guaca, from the province of Conchucos, border of the city of Huanuco; the other one was from the province of Chincha. I talked to them about this wicked thing they committed, and aggravating the indecency of this sin, they answered that it was not their fault, because ever since their childhood they have been put there by their chiefs for this wicked and abominable vice, and to be priests and guard the temples of their idols. (Pedro Cieza de León 1553, *La Crónica del Perú* [The Chronicles of Peru, author's translation])

For the Catholic colonialists, there was no place for alternative gender roles. But why should those who took on such roles have provoked such hatred, condemnation and punishment as described above? To illuminate this question, I turn to Murray Davis.

[A]nything that undermines confidence in the scheme of classification on which people base their lives sickens them as though the very ground on which they stood precipitously dropped away. The vertigo produced by the loss of cognitive orientation is similar to that produced by the loss of physical orientation ... People will regard any phenomenon that produces this disorientation as 'disgusting' or 'dirty'. To be so regarded, however, the phenomenon must threaten to destroy not only one of their fundamental cognitive categories but their whole cognitive system. (Davis 1983, cited in Bornstein 1994: 72)

The practices of these 'priests' were so at odds with the Spanish colonial theocentric and phallocentric view that the Spaniards could rationalize that they were saving natives even while they were exploiting them and obliterating elements of their culture. Colonial ordinances ordered the 'Indians', categorizing and counting them: a powerful tool to enforce the docility and utility of Indian bodies.

Controlling bodies

A pre-Hispanic print (Figure 11.1), agreed by several anthropologists to be depicting a religious event, shows winged men preparing and offering a brew to a copulating couple, one superhuman and one 'bi-gender', while gods and humans watch and wait, eating human meat as part of the ritual. The travestied body appears to mediate between the natural and supernatural worlds.

Let us now move to contemporary Peru, where in some parts of the Andes *travestis* perform ancestral harvest rituals – now portrayed as 'dance exhibitions', which continue to play an important social role

FIGURE 11.1 Drawing by Christopher B. Donnan (Moche Archive, UCLA) from the original Moche culture *huaco* (pottery)

within communities. They have exchanged *calientito* (an Andean alcoholic beverage) for beer, and low heels for transparent platform shoes, as they successfully transform their ritual into a technical dance show. It is instructive to note that this happens in places where development has not been wholly successful. This does not mean that development constitutes destruction, nor that these societies have remained 'pure'. What I am suggesting is that perhaps the diminished impact of development has permitted the building of a bridge, maybe not too solid or formulated, but enough to allow inclusion through a correlation between two cultures, past and present.

In post-colonial times *travesti* has been interpreted through the identities of 'LGBT' (lesbian, gay, bisexual and transgender). The inclusion of *travesti* within these normative sexual identities shows how alternative genders have become categorized through the lens of sexuality as a result of a lack of historical perspective. The association of *travesti* with sexual – rather than alternative gender – identities has led to them being subject to discrimination and attack on the basis of their assumed sexuality. A report by the Citizens Commission on Human Rights notes that the Peruvian Túpac Amaru Revolutionary Movement (MRTA) 'tended to view gay men and lesbians as "anti-revolutionary" or as "products of bourgeois decadence" and therefore as a threat to the leftist political project' (ICCHRLA 1996: 19). Chauvin (1991) reports that in 1990 and 1991, more than forty *travestis* were killed in Lima, Peru, by right-wing groups known as '*mata cabros*' or 'kill faggots'. By these means, the Peruvian Truth and Reconciliation Commission's final report records that the MRTA 'aimed to legitimate themselves before the population, encouraging the social preconceptions against homosexuality' (IFCVR 2003: 433).

We see here the results of a tragic misunderstanding: in their revolt against post-colonial sexual freedoms, the anti-colonialists inscribed further the ideology of the colonialists. Here we see biblical ideology being reinforced by the (atheist) extreme left wing. Sexual activists and researchers perpetuate this worsening situation by working within a colonial framework, instead of building development upon pre-colonial discourse.

Gender lost its breadth, depth and elasticity during the colonial exchange of beliefs and ideologies. These have not been recouped in post-colonial times. The Peruvian *travesti*, however, remains as the hinge between pairs, previously connecting the pre-Hispanic worlds of gods and humans and the living and dead, and now linking past to present. *Travestis* persist in performing mediating roles within society, then as shamans and now as beauticians or witches, therapists who listen and transform – by injecting liquid silicon into the bodies of their peers.[3] This contemporary scene powerfully resembles that portrayed in the Moche pottery portrayed above: a group of *travesti* friends warming up with some alcoholic beverage, offered by the 'patient', chatting about and planning the septic procedure (without anaesthetic) to be realized – which would realize them. The exploration of the self, with its postmodern shifts, remains intact. *Travestis* connect the different sides of beings: spiritual and material, reality and dream. They and their roles have not disappeared. They have mutated.[4]

The twenty-first-century *travesti*

Modern legal battles around transgender identity recognition are subject to and reproduce gender normativity. Even the most progressive, as in Belgium, Germany, the UK and Spain, fail to validate ambiguous gendered self-expression. While people in these countries have won certain rights to change sex, they do not yet have any rights to choose either to stay at an in-between state or to transit back and forth. Concepts like 'gender dysphoria' or 'gender identity disorder' are used to justify transsexual operations and legal recognition of changed sex. These concepts, however, are in themselves anchored to gender normativity, denying intersexualism and occasional *travestism*. In this context of gender normativity, some *travestis* have adopted 'hysterical' practices pursuing an idealized femininity. These are outlined below.

Body transformation Many of my *travesti* colleagues and friends inject liquid silicon into their bodies to increase voluptuousness of chest, hips and buttocks, in spite of the potential for disfigurement and threats to health (e.g. substance migration around the body, tumours, necrosis, infection, pulmonary embolism or death). This 'decision' has many facets. The *travesti* majority is poor, and thus excluded from other, more expensive options for bodily transformation, since health policies define these procedures as 'cosmetic', although they are essential to their psychological well-being. *Travestis* also seek alternative services – shamans, beauticians, automedication – since they do not trust the health services. These factors, combined with a lack of knowledge and low self-esteem, result in a complex route back to liquid silicon as the only way to meet their goal. Cosmetic surgery implants and automedicated ingestion of hormones, although perhaps initially 'successful', can also fail in the medium or longer term owing to side effects or changes in aesthetic trends.

One friend, Carla, for example, had injected liquid silicon into her forehead, cheeks, chest, hips and buttocks to achieve the desired voluptuousness. After emigrating to Europe and earning enough money, her aesthetic and procedure perceptions changed. She decided to go for silicone implants. The surgeon told her that in order to proceed, they would have to remove all the liquid silicon, including from those parts of the body to where it had migrated. Carla decided to go ahead with this painful procedure, which has now left large scars. When I asked her whether she was satisfied with the results, she answered affirmatively. Might she have pursued different aims or used different methods without normative pressures?

Choice of 'macho' partners and violent relationships I met Rosa when we were teenagers. Some years later I ran into her at a club and asked where she had disappeared to. She answered that she now has a violent and controlling partner who does not allow her to leave home, and that she was out partying only because he was away on a work trip. After some time I met her again. She told me everything was better, that things changed since they started 'modern' (exchanging active and passive roles) sex, and the beatings, verbal violence and isolation had stopped. Gender-busting practices have liberated both partners.

Denial of their sexually active role *Travestis* commonly admit to taking only a passive role with their sexual partners, and may ridicule those who do otherwise. When I met Gata at a discotheque, we quickly started talking about men and sex. Later a common friend told me that Gata had a female partner and two children and that she does sex work as the breadwinner for her family. I asked our common friend why Gata had not told me. The friend explained that other *travestis* tease Gata about it, to which she objects violently. Gata had somehow developed two genders, one for her social scene and work, and one for her family life.

Denial of the 'former' male When he decided to dress as a woman, Jana tore up any family photographs of herself where she appeared as a man, and asked her mother to give away all her men's clothes to the church. At the same time, he gave up work as a teacher of religion and she became a hairdresser. Some days later she bumped into 'himself' at home; her mother had disobeyed, giving her past clothes to her brother. Today Jana is a *travesti* activist with a master's degree in gender studies. When watching a family video, she came across a strange man on the screen; suddenly she realized that man was herself. When prompted to explain what she experienced when facing up to 'himself' again, she could not describe the feeling. A sort of pity, maybe embarrassment, maybe nostalgia, filled her face: 'It seems that man should have happened a long time ago.'

The worst of both gender roles *Travestis* have inherited the worst of both gender roles. When a *travesti* is beaten, she is perceived as male enough for policemen, or anyone, to freely hit him. In relationships it depends. Sometimes masculinity prevails, when it comes to working to maintain the family and/or partner. Sometimes femininity prevails, as *travestis* are subjects of violence and victimization by the same family circle. Suddenly, once again, masculinity takes over when the law arbitrates. In the labour market, discrimination means that sex work is almost the only available option.

This wrong time/place situation has deepened for contemporary *travestis* with the incongruity between their practices of a sensuality that defies gender boundaries, and a discourse of binary genders as the cornerstone of identity construction. Through their journey, from dresses to bodies, *travestis* have turned the 'hystericization of the woman's body' – which Foucault described in an early draft of his *Histoire de la Sexualité* (Foucault 1979) – into an essence, and appropriated it within their own discourse; transmuting the violence outside and taking it inside their minds and bodies.

It is not simply a matter of assigning *travestis* a unique gender or sexuality, nor taking for granted their homosexuality or their desire to become a genital woman.[5] *Travestis* need freeing from normative pressures, to enable them to actualize their own self-expression. Far from being unreflexive products of culture, *travestis* undergo critical processes of self-examination, which might usefully be deployed in a wider context.

Post-feminist transgender? Where is the post-feminist transgender? When did vestments as symbols of power, the androgynous as double synonym of perfection, get lost? How did the enriching multiple points of view (before: a female within a male body; after: a male within a female body) as a major advantage become denied? The effort to reclaim *travesti* subjectivity has ramifications that also affect women. The challenge to *travesti* exclusion is not enough by itself. It needs to be paralleled by studies of the subjectivities of pre-Hispanic Peruvian women, to challenge the stereotypes that exclude and oppress them.[6] The demand from *travestis* that they be recognized and empowered as the women they visibly are challenges the stereotype that the poverty and powerlessness of Peruvian women are natural, and can be allowed to remain. Thus the demand for *travesti* rights is inextricably bound up with the aims of the feminist movement to emancipate women, of all kinds, everywhere.

Reflections

> The master's tools will never dismantle the master's house. They may allow us temporarily to beat him at his own game, but they will never enable us to bring about genuine change. (Lorde 1984: 112)

For Peru's *travestis* the struggle for rights and for recognition can be fortified if only we could reclaim our history. Revisiting pre-Hispanic traditions that show the existence of in-between genders reveals how we have been forced to fit colonial gender binaries. Peruvian *travestis* are not alone: indigenous transgender identities existed across cultures, space and time the world over, suppressed and reviled by colonial Christianities. Reclaiming our history calls for us not only to reconstitute the inclusive culture of the past, but to reclaim *travesti* identities in all their variety. We need to enquire into *travesti* pasts in all regions of our country to affirm *travestis* in the present and build respect for contemporary *travestis'* desires and needs, whether as consumers, religious people, sex workers, bisexuals, parents or women. As this chapter suggests, and as activities such as the Travesti Museum of Peru – a travelling exhibition celebrating pre-Hispanic and contemporary *travesti* culture – demonstrate, art's political dimension can be used to powerful effect in this struggle.

Maybe it is time for a new challenge to the structure of 'the Master's House', which, as Afro-American lesbian Audre Lorde noted, cannot be dismantled using the master's tools. *Travestis* are indeed objects of gender. But they are also subjects, capable of gender self-determination, as many feminists in the 1960s demanded. It is time to listen to the wide range of critical intersex and transgender narratives and learn from their problematization of conventional gender thinking, and from their experiences. To do this, we need to work with women's movements to move beyond the limiting dichotomies that constrain us all. Applying the principle of gender relativity would result in a healthier and wiser development, one in which people can claim their rights to combine genders, to transit and to choose.

Notes

1 King James authorized translation.

2 Much feminist work has problematized gender binaries (see, for example, Butler 1990). There is also voluminous research on alternative transgender formulations in the anthropological and historical studies of spiritual traditions, strongly reinforcing the view of gender as a continuum (see, for example, Eliade 1964; Bullough and Bullough 1993; Conner et al. 1997; and Herdt 1996). Only the Judaeo/Christian/Muslim complex of faiths insists on this particular juxtaposition of binary sexes and genders.

3 Examples like this have been held by legal and health authorities to be unethical/criminal, but this is not dissimilar to reaction to anti-abortion policies and the lack of gender opportunities and a society willing to find a culprit other that itself.

4 On this point, the literary metaphor of Latin America as a *travesti* is useful; *travestism* becomes a historical, not metaphorical, model for the cultural development of any colonized territories such as the Americas.

5 Sex work is an ideal metaphor when working on this issue; gender and eroticism not as desires but rather as results of the sex market and gender labels.

6 The investigation 'Divine and Human' undertaken by Marisa

Villavicencio and exhibited in 2004 in Peru, Mexico, and the USA recontextualizes women's roles in former Peruvian societies.

References

Arboleda, M. (1981) 'Representaciones artísticas de actividades homoeróticas en la cerámica Moche' [Artistic representations of homoerotic activities in Moche pottery], *Boletín de Lima*, pp. 16–18.

Bornstein, K. (1994) *Gender Outlaw; On Men, Women, and the Rest of Us*, New York: Vintage.

Bullough, B. and V. Bullough (1993) *Cross Dressing, Sex, and Gender*, Philadelphia: University of Pennsylvania Press.

Butler, J. (1990) *Gender Trouble, Feminism and the Subversion of Identity*, London: Routledge.

Cereceda, V. (1986) 'The semiology of Andean textiles: the Talegas of Isluga', in J. V. Murra, N. Wachtel and J. Revel (eds), *Anthropological History of Andean Polities*, Cambridge: Cambridge University Press, pp. 149–73.

Chauvin, L. (1991) 'Struggling in Peru: a steady diet of oppression fails to extinguish the gay and lesbian movement in Peru', *Gay Community News*, 8, March, pp. 18–24.

Conner, R. P., D. Sparks, M. Sparks and G. Anzaldua (1997) *Cassells*

Encyclopedia of Queer Myth, Symbol and Spirit: Gay, Lesbian, Bisexual and Transgender Lore, London: Cassells.

Davis, M. S. (1983) *Smut: Erotic Reality/Obscene Ideology*, Chicago, IL: University of Chicago Press.

Eliade, M. (1964) *Shamanism, Archaic Techniques of Ecstasy*, New York: Bollingen Foundation.

Foucault, M. (1979) *The History of Sexuality*, part 1, Harmondsworth: Penguin.

Gonzales de Cuenca, G. (1556) *Ordenanzas de los Indios* [Ordinances of the Indians], Archivo General de Indias, Patronato 189, r. 11.

Herdt, G. (ed.) (1996) *Third Sex, Third Gender; Beyond Sexual Dimorphism in Culture and History*, New York: Zone Books.

ICCHRLA (1996) 'Violence unveiled: repression against lesbians and homosexuals in Latin America', *ICCHRLA Special Bulletin*, Toronto: Inter-Church Committee on Human Rights in Latin America.

IFCVR (2003) *Informe final de la Comisión de la Verdad y Reconciliación* [Truth and Reconciliation Commission Final Report], Lima: IFCVR.

Lorde, A. (1984), 'The master's tools will never dismantle the master's house', in A. Lorde (ed.), *Sister Outsider: Essays and Speeches*, Freedom, CA: Crossing Press.

12 | Small powers, little choice: reproductive and sexual rights in slums in Bangladesh

SABINA FAIZ RASHID

What do we mean when we speak of the reproductive and sexual rights of women, particularly in the context of extreme poverty and rapid social and economic change? This chapter explores this question through an examination of the evolving factors that shape young women's reproductive and sexual health experiences. It is based on ethnographic fieldwork in an urban slum in Dhaka with married adolescent girls aged fifteen to nineteen, their families and community members.[1]

Young Bangladeshi women's lives are changing. Financial constraints compel many young women to work in garment factories to earn a living, which exposes them to men in the public domain and the work environment. At the same time, shifts are taking place from traditional arranged marriages to 'love marriages'. While on the one hand young women have greater mobility and freedom to choose their own partners, on the other hand the urban environment has resulted in greater social and marital insecurity. Paradoxically, married adolescent women, in the face of these insecurities, often rely on their sexuality as an economic resource, to hold on to spouses or to attract potential suitors. My research uncovered a 'hidden world', some married adolescent women speaking frankly about their love affairs, their sexual experiences with their husbands and their thoughts and feelings about their sexual needs and desires. Slum conditions and poverty, however, also mean that the lived experiences of engaging in sexual relations with their spouses are fraught with contradictions, as some women tolerate bad marriages and forced sex, which place them at risk of adverse reproductive experiences.

Background

Structural and social inequalities, a harsh political economy and indifference on the part of the state have made the urban poor in Bangladesh a marginalized group. There is little known about the combined effects of macropolitical and economic conditions and social and cultural factors on women's reproductive health experiences and their lives. Informed by critical medical anthropology, this chapter illustrates how the reproductive and sexual lives of young women in an urban slum are embedded in the social, political and economic structures of their lives.

The rapid entry of rural poor families into Dhaka has led to a swift increase in urban population growth, slum settlements and worsening poverty. A total of 40–70 per cent of urban population growth is now attributed to rural–urban migration (Wood 1998; World Bank and Bangladesh Centre for Advanced Studies 1998; Islam et al. 1997). Almost 60 per cent of the urban poor live in extreme poverty, and the remainder in 'hard-core' poverty, in which families survive on a monthly household income (1995) of only US$44 (Wood 1998; Perry 2000). Urban slum dwellers constituted 30 per cent of the total 14 million population of Dhaka in 2002.

Migrants are unable to find affordable housing, and live in insecure tenure arrangements, setting up or renting small rooms with mud floors and bamboo or tin/polythene roofs, in settlements built on vacant or disused land on the margins of the city, never knowing when their slum will be demolished, leaving them homeless (Islam 1996). Phulbari, where this study was carried out, is typical. It has a high proportion of squatter households, with most of the poor resettled here after being forcibly evicted in 1975 from different parts of the city (Afsar 2000). The alleyways are tiny and congested; the rooms are dark and damp and have no fans. Most of the drains overflow with water, sewage and excrement, particularly during the rainy season. Married adolescent women are particularly vulnerable in this slum environment.

Love affairs and changing marriage practices

Marriage is socially, culturally and religiously approved of in Bangladesh. A woman's only source of approved status is through marriage and motherhood. Therefore, marriage is a turning point in a young woman's life – a major rite of passage, on which her future and fortune depend (Rozario 1992; White 1992). Literature is sparse on marriage practices and adolescent women's experiences of married life: their sexual negotiating abilities, levels of autonomy, decision-making opportunities and communication with husbands. The few studies that exist provide useful insights into the underlying values and norms of society, which shape gender relations and female status, but present a fairly homogeneous and unchanging picture of adolescent women's lives (Rozario 1992; Khan et al. 2002; Aziz and Maloney 1985).

Despite the maintenance of many of the traditional norms, such as marriages arranged by family members, it appears that there are changes occurring in the urban slums. While seventy-two young women had arranged marriages, eighty-one admitted to having a love/elopement marriage, without parental permission. Such marriages are spoken of as '*prem*', and in many cases the couple may run off and get married without parental permission or in some cases someone – an aunt or family friend – may assist them in getting married. In most cases, the family eventually accepts them. Observations reveal that poverty pushes parents increasingly to rely on unmarried daughters to work outside the home to earn an income, and some parents are unable or do not want daughters to marry immediately. For unmarried adolescent women, meeting potential partners is made easier in urban areas as there are more opportunities to interact with unrelated men, a finding supported elsewhere (Naved et al. 1997). A number of adolescent women shared experiences of actively initiating relationships and pursuing men, with some young women resorting to manipulation, while others spoke of exchanging notes and sharing kisses. Although no one admitted to premarital sex, gossip and speculation circulated about particular young couples who were rumoured to have had premarital sex. Friends of young couples provide alibis and help them find places to meet in private. One resident in Section 1 of the slum was known to rent out her room to drug users and young couples. As Amin et al. (1997) note, traditional values relating to marriage and sexuality influence young women: men sometimes use the promise of marriage to persuade young girls to have sex or to date.

Bulu, a married seventeen-year-old, like some other young women interviewed, took the initiative with her second husband when they were dating. She said, 'Five days after he first gave me the flower, I gave him a red stone ring. I said, "Let's see your hand." He gave me his hand and I put the ring on his hand. He said, "Why did you give me this? I should be giving you the ring instead!"' According to Farida, a married eighteen-year-old, her sister-in-law, Dilu, manipulated her brother into a relationship and marriage:

> Everyone knows that Dilu manipulated my brother into marrying her. She is very clever ... she made up her mind that she would marry my brother. She even threatened suicide if she was not allowed to marry him. My brother did not want to marry her. She said to the elders, 'I am pregnant with his child. If he does not marry me I will commit suicide' ... but on her wedding night she started menstruating!

In some cases, boys belonging to local gangs in the slum were hired by adolescent women to 'set up' young men in a compromising situation, so they would be forced to marry the girl. Mahmuda, an unmarried fourteen-year-old, was desperately in love with Jamal. She explained, 'Selim [the gang leader] said to me, "Give me Taka 1,000 [approx US$15] and I can make Jamal marry you. You let us know when you meet him next time and we will pretend to catch you in a room together alone and then he will be forced to marry you."' She declined because she believed coerced marriages in such circumstances did not last very long.

Listening to adolescent women's narratives, a divergence appears between traditional gender ideologies and the new social situation young women find themselves in, where romances happen, hearts are broken, young women actively court males, even deceive them, and a few admit to having sexual relations. The case of Dilu is a telling example: she was strong willed and very independent minded, and rather than passively accepting rejection, she was adamant to marry the young man. The interesting thing here was that she did not lose face for admitting to being pregnant; rather the man whose family lived in the slum stood to lose face in the community if he did not do the right thing by marrying her. An important factor may have been that Dilu was the daughter of a relatively wealthy landlord in Phulbari. Her father was richer and more powerful than her in-laws' family, who were poorer landlords.

Cases like this indicate that, like men, young women are able to exert power and influence over poorer men, if they have access to valued resources, in this case class, status and economic wealth. This highlights the significance of these factors in understanding power relations and the level of manoeuvrability they can afford young women. Very few women are in Dilu's situation, however. More often, social and economic insecurity in the slum lead to tense and short-lived marital relationships, leaving young women even more vulnerable.

Instability of marriages

Marital instability was a widespread concern among the women in the slum and poverty, unpaid dowry demands, unemployment and drug use were all blamed as contributory factors. Of the 153 young women taking part in this study, seventeen were already separated or had been abandoned by their husbands. In addition, among the fifty who had in-depth interviews, seven young women revealed that they had been previously married and that this was their second marriage. Of this group of seven, four were sharing their husbands with a co-wife. Further probing found that the other three suspected their husbands had another woman or co-wife. Those who were deserted by their husbands found that working conditions, low wages and social and economic discrimination in the slum and among the workforce made them worse off than before, a finding supported elsewhere (Jesmin and Salway 2000). Young women

149

spoke of the physical insecurity of living alone and the need for a male protector, be it a father, brother, son or fictive 'uncle'.

The few studies available suggest that social fragmentation and the heterogeneity of the urban population heighten marital instability. Moreover, love marriages increasingly concern only the couple rather than other family members, so the wider family and relatives are less likely to intervene when problems set in. As most families in the slums tend to be more nuclear oriented, support from the larger extended family tends to be absent, a finding supported elsewhere (Salway et al. 2003). One study found that since slums are relatively anonymous, it is easier for men as well as for women to hide their marital history, relocate and remarry without anyone knowing, so they are less likely to face sanctions (Jesmin and Salway 2000). While the traditional framework of arranged marriages imposes a number of restrictions on young women, love marriages in urban areas offer them greater choice and freedom; but ironically less security and certainty.

While most adolescent women claimed to be currently married, in reality not all of their husbands were regular residents in their households, nor made household contributions. Adolescent women chose to remain with their 'partially absent' husbands rather than be completely alone, and were willing to tolerate their husband's second marriages, because the trade-off was at least continued social acceptance and physical and economic security. An adolescent woman with a young child explained:

> If one's husband is not there, then what work will I do? How will I look after my child and bring him up? If one does not have a husband then one is always in tension – what will happen to me? Will someone harm me? My husband gives me Taka 40 [$US 1.00] to do shopping, if I didn't have a husband I would have to manage with very little. Will I go to the streets to find work?

Nasima, like many married adolescent women, was saddled with a young child and with limited job prospects. She preferred to tolerate her husband's second wife, rather than try to manage on her own. Some adolescent women expressed feelings of affection for their spouses, and remained emotionally wounded by their husband's infidelities and re-marriages. Most of the young women were also pragmatic about their reasons for not leaving their husbands. A common statement by young women was: 'Is it so easy to leave the husband? Can I just leave him? How many times will a girl get married in her life? What if the second husband is worse than this one?'

For women, job opportunities in the cities are few and remain in a narrow range of occupations: in garment factories, as domestic servants, or in brick-breaking work, which is common among older women and is extremely low-status and low-paid work.[2] Two of the abandoned young women interviewed turned to sex work to manage their households. In the first case, the woman's family knew about her occupation and accepted it as she contributed generously to the household income. In the second case, the young woman was living alone and had no family in the slum. Eventually, once her occupation became known, she had to leave the slum after being sexually harassed by leaders. It is difficult to assess the extent of these kinds of situations because of the sensitivity of the topic, but they are probably not uncommon. Finally, unlike adolescent men, young women cannot work without fear of rape and harassment in and outside the slum. Being married and the presence of a husband or other male guardian usually entails some degree of protection from male strangers.

The discussions below will clearly illustrate how all these factors compel young women to tolerate difficult marriages, which do result in adverse reproductive health experiences and behaviour.

Sexuality and desires

Some of the married adolescent women spoke frankly about their love affairs and their sexual experiences with their husbands. Surprisingly, some of them also shared their thoughts and feelings about their sexual needs and desires. Stories of first sexual experiences were not so positive, and young women shared the trauma of not knowing what to expect but realizing that they were expected to be willing and compliant.

The first time A young woman shared her first experience of sexual inter-course with her husband:

> When we had sex the first night I was fast asleep. He put his hands on my chest. My breasts were so small then – like little seeds. I woke up when he pinched my breasts. I asked him, 'What are you doing? Why are you touching me like that?' He said to me, 'Don't tell anyone this. If you do then this is shame. You can't tell anyone this. If you do people will make fun of you.' Then he put his hands on me and kissed me. He kept kissing me. I was so confused and I didn't know what to think – all sorts of things were going through my head. Is this what husbands and wives do? I was so young – I don't think I really understood. I was very scared, though. He said to me, 'This is what a wife has to give her husband and if she doesn't then a husband can go elsewhere for it.' He came on top of

me and tried to enter me. I screamed out in pain and tried to push him off me. He put his hands over my mouth and forcefully entered me. It was so painful. He said to me, 'You have to give it to me!' My vagina was completely swollen. I couldn't walk for eight days. My back hurt and I was really upset. I cried ...

This was fairly typical of many of the stories I heard from young women regarding their first sexual encounter. There were also, however, a few stories of caring and thoughtful husbands who wanted to make the first time special. An older adolescent woman recalled:

My husband came up to me and said, 'You must come to my room tonight' ... I was sleeping with my mother-in-law and then he came into my room and picked me up and took me to his room. I was scared ... my heart was beating loudly. Then when I came to the room I saw that he had put biscuits, sweets and a glass of water and a jug with water for me ... I felt less scared then ... he slowly explained to me what he was going to do and we chatted for some time before we had sex.

Wanting sex In the conversations with married adolescent women, it also became apparent that sex with one's husband improves considerably over time. Some of the adolescent women spoke of enjoying sex, and even initiating the sexual encounter to meet their needs. One young woman explained, 'I really like it when he puts himself [his penis] inside me, that is the most enjoyable part of it ... ' Another woman shared her feelings:

When I want it I turn over to face him and that is how he knows that I want to have sex with him, or I will put the baby on one side of the bed and he knows that I want to have sex with him. I also put my hands on his back or legs and he turns around and smiles and says, 'What's up?' My husband has never said no. He can't have enough of it frankly. When he wants me he will tell me, 'Today I have work with you' and I pretend not to understand and smile and say, 'What work?' Sometimes we even have sex on the floor next to the bed.

When asked if she gets embarrassed because of a lack of privacy (she has some holes in her newspaper/cardboard walls), the woman looks amazed and retorts, 'Why should I be embarrassed? I am having sex with my husband and not with anyone else.'

A young woman described how she and her husband had sex frequently, even indulging in the afternoons when he came home for lunch, but she felt harassed by the community. She was upset because some of the neighbours made rude comments about them and tried to spy on their activities. 'These people in the slum are bad, they try and look through the holes in our walls [cardboard walls] and make comments behind our backs ...'

Interestingly, a few adolescent women also spoke candidly about 'unsatisfying sex' and 'husbands who could not or would not' have sex as often as they wanted to. Some of them reported, 'I am left unsatisfied ... he is too quick and I don't feel much'; 'he can't do anything and we rarely ever have sex'; and 'he never wants to touch me and does not even come near me any more ...' One young woman complained:

> He has sex with me once in three months. He has no desire. He comes to lie down and all he does is read and then he turns over and goes to sleep. He never says anything. I don't understand why he is doing this. Can you tell me why this is happening?

Another young woman justified her husband's behaviour and stated:

> We have sex maybe once a month. Sex is good for the body – the *mon* (heart) remains happy and the body feels lighter ... otherwise there is also build-up of needs in the body. Women don't lose their strength as they don't have to be as active as the man. For men this is bad, as they get older they become weak and there is pressure on their bodies when they have sex.

These young women admitted that they did not share their thoughts with anyone. Women in general mentioned that it was socially unacceptable to show one's desires and they were often reluctant to express their feelings to their husbands. An adolescent girl explained, 'There are many women who are ashamed to show their desire – a woman may not want to tell her husband. Others will insinuate that their husbands cannot satisfy them, hence they desire sex all the time. So this is *lajja* [shame]!' In the context of Bangladesh, where women are expected to be sexually passive and men 'have uncontrollable urges', these women will be looked upon suspiciously and husbands may fear their infidelity. Observations in the slum found that men monitored their wives' movements closely and they were chastised for being out of the home too frequently.

He wants sex all the time and I can't say no! Discussions revealed that many women associate the onset of abnormal discharge and other gynaecological problems with early marriage, becoming sexually active at a young age and having sex frequently with demanding husbands, who refuse to back down. Young women revealed that forced sex is a

153

common occurrence within married life.[3] Rosina, who was fourteen years old and had a love marriage, and whom I had become quite close to during fieldwork, confided that her husband would often get 'high on drugs and come home and demand rough sex', which was uncomfortable and painful and resulted in her suffering from episodes of itching and discharge. She said:

> He does not listen to me at all and even if I say no, he just does not listen.
> My body aches after the sex. He is very forceful and does not want to take
> no for an answer. He just grabs me and pushes me down. I don't scream
> out of shame. My mother-in-law sleeps next door to us. If I ask him
> later on why did you do this to me, he hugs me and holds me close and
> says, 'Look, I won't ever do this again to you,' but then again when he is
> high on drugs he does it again. After one incident, I was in pain, and he
> warmed up water and brought it for me to wash myself.

Married adolescent women perceive any kind of discharge as extremely worrying and remain anxious about the perceived effects of weakness and loss of calcium and more serious consequences such as boils and cancer in the uterus, which is believed to lead to infertility. While frequent sex was blamed as a cause of discharge, discomfort and itching, adolescent women were reluctant to reject their husbands' advances, fearing that they would go elsewhere to meet their needs. More often, women are trying to please their husbands, an accepted notion that women must be sexually available (see also Stark 1993; Khan et al. 2002). This highlights the role of gender and sexuality structures in promoting the vulnerability of young women.

Sexually transmitted illnesses and inability to negotiate As discussed earlier, the need to hold on to one's husband is extremely important. Some of the married adolescent women admitted to overlooking their husbands' behaviour and tolerating extramarital relationships and co-wives, in exchange for security and respectability. Some of the young women also recognize their husbands' sexual relations with co-wives and other women as risk factors for the onset of severe abnormal discharge and other 'bad' illnesses. Discussions on sexual health are whispered: stigma surrounding sex-related disease is one reason for this silence. But the silence is also a form of denial: a way of coping with the reality of living with unfaithful husbands, and being unable to change their social and material conditions.

Ten married adolescent women told us that their husbands were suffering from discharge, boils and sores on the penis and itching. Only one adolescent woman spoke of suffering from a sexually transmitted infection ('bad discharge'). Joshna, recently abandoned by her husband, who had left her with a sexual illness, said:

> I didn't know he was sick. We had sex as normal and then after a few weeks, one day he had sores all over his penis and even on his balls. It itched like crazy. And pus and watery stuff came out. Soon after, I was suffering from severe smelly discharge and itching and I went and saw this woman doctor with my mother for treatment. I didn't want to go to the local clinic in the slum, as they will only talk.

Rumours were rife in the slum that after Joshna's husband had abandoned her, she was having sexual relations with a well-known drug dealer in the slum, who paid her expenses and took care of her. Towards the end of my fieldwork I heard that he had married her. She became his third wife.

Joshna is unusual, as most women are reluctant to share their own experiences of suffering from sexually transmitted illnesses. Conversations reveal that women appear to have a network of close family and friends whom they can turn to for support, but the fear always remains of slander by other women in the slum. This is the most common reason given for keeping silent about such illnesses:

> Apa [sister], you must be careful what you share with whom, because once a fight breaks out they will shout out all your secrets to the world. If people hear that I have discharge problems then they will say I have a bad character. If I tell someone else then that woman will tell someone else. Then they will discuss among themselves, 'Look, this is what she talks about. She has no shame. She must have been up to no good.' Then there is all this bad talk.

Having a sexually transmitted infection (STI) is associated with promiscuity and reflects negatively on the person. In Bangladesh, family planning has traditionally been separated from other services, including treatment of STIs, which has influenced its acceptability in the community, but contributed to the stigmatization of sexual health. Public health messages regarding STIs aimed at sex workers have meant that they are perceived as the main vectors of disease. Thus, condom use continues to be associated with promiscuity and something husbands and wives do not need to do.

The norm is that men are expected to be unfaithful and by nature 'have uncontrollable urges', and young women are expected to be loyal and faithful. Thus there exists the sexual double standard which permits

155

polygamy for men, while women's sexuality is controlled. The reality is sometimes different: slum women alluded to other young women who were abandoned or in polygamous marriages, who slept with other men in exchange for food, cash and other rewards. Although some of the married adolescent women are aware that condoms are an effective barrier to STIs, the reality of their lives makes it difficult for them to demand condom use. A wife insisting on condom use may imply that she was unfaithful while he was away or that she does not trust her husband. It is not uncommon for older men married to younger second wives to become jealous and suspect their wife's fidelity. As Sobo points out in her study of inner-city US women, cultural ideals dictate that a healthy relationship (marriage) 'involves a healthy disease free partner'. She argues that the use of condoms indicates that the partners are not sexually exclusive and signals a lack of mutual trust. Thus in some ways, condom use denotes a failed relationship, and inversely unsafe sex implies a close relationship (Sobo 1997). These understandings make the awareness of and acceptability of condom use difficult to negotiate in the slum context.

In addition, most men were averse to using condoms. Only four out of 153 adolescent women's husbands took responsibility for fertility control and agreed to wear condoms during sex, and even these four used them inconsistently.[4] Condom use in this case was seen as something related to fertility control rather than for safe sex. Practical constraints make condom use hard for young couples sharing living space no bigger than 25 square feet with other family members. One young woman explained, 'We are poor. We all stay in the same room. You have the luxury of having separate rooms. We all stay in the one room – mother, brother, daughter, son and husband. So when my husband and I want to do it [sex], it is very quick ... and the main thing on my mind is that no one sees us!'

Poverty, sociocultural ideals and gender relations make it hard to ask for condoms, and young women do not want to alienate their husbands by insisting. The marital bed is a place where a woman's status as a desired wife (and therefore her security) is acknowledged. By sleeping with his wife a husband communicates to her that she is secure within the household and his choice of sexual partner is an acknowledgement of her value. The needs of affection, acceptance and pleasure may also be met here (Stark 1993: 44). In the absence of material resources, a young woman's sexuality is what she can offer and manipulate to hold on to her husband's (or other men's) affections, although young women do recognize that the trade-off is a risky reproductive experience. One health consequence of untreated STIs is increased susceptibility to HIV infections. A 1996 study of 542 men and 993 women in five Dhaka slums recorded levels of current syphilis at 11.5 per cent for men and 5.4 per cent for women, and of hepatitis B at 5.8 and 2.9 per cent respectively, while gonorrhoea and chlamydia were below 1 per cent for both sexes (Sabin et al. 1997).

Sexuality and power

While reproductive health is a concern for young women, their narratives also reveal worries about their long-term desirability and sexuality in their married lives. A few adolescent women frankly shared their anxieties about having 'loose vaginas' from too much sex and from bearing children, and their husbands rejecting them later for younger females. A young woman explained:

> A man wants good *mal* [tight vagina], and if you have sex too much then the place becomes too big. My thing [vagina] is OK ... it is just right. Men don't have similar problems as they have more power ... their bodies are not affected ... but if a woman's thing [vagina] becomes big, then men don't find enjoyment! That is why these men marry so many times.

There are arguments and fights related to suspicion and jealousy, with women often accusing each other of seducing their husbands. There were always stories of women who flirted with other men, and of those who had betrayed their neighbours, friends and even sisters in eloping with their partners. Older as well as adolescent married women worried often that their husbands would leave them for younger women. A married adolescent woman, Roshonara, nineteen years old, explained, 'All men are dogs, they are all the same. Wherever they see a young *kochi* girl they go running.'

Some studies expect that a woman's autonomy and decision-making vary with age and position in the family, and generally that prestige and influence increase as a woman becomes older (Stark 1993: 110). Observations in the slum indicate, however, that paradoxically young women, because of their youth, are also advantaged, as they are able to manipulate their only assets, their bodies, to gain power. Shehnaz is fifteen years old, married and shares her husband, who is forty years old, with an older co-wife; she explains why she has the upper hand in her marriage:

> My husband is older than me. His first wife has big saggy breasts and because she is older he does not like her any more [sexually] and that is why he has married again. It does not matter that I am his second wife, I have much more pull over him and he has more affection for me. She has

no strength. He can never ever say no to me! He gives me two-thirds of his income but he gives her so much less.

In the context of poverty and competition for men, young women can mark their superiority over older women through their youth, and their attractiveness (sexuality) becomes an important source of power.

Conclusion

Poor married adolescent women experience contradictory roles in the local systems of power in which their lives are embedded. Without economic independence and social autonomy, many engage in painful sex, as well as risky sexual relations. While gender relations are open to negotiation, they are still shaped by structural and social factors outside their control. Some young women may fall in love and 'elope'. A small number talk of desiring, initiating and enjoying sex with their husbands. But overwhelmingly young women behave pragmatically. This may result in greater risk to their bodies and reproductive health, but it is in exchange for security. These decisions are taken as survival strategies, but they may eventually become 'death strategies' for young women (Schoepf 1998: 107, cited in Lock and Kaufert 1998).

Poor married adolescent women construct a 'political economy of the body' in their reproductive and sexual health negotiations, often at a cost to their bodies and health (Petchesky 2001). The reproductive experiences and behaviour of the urban adolescent women in this study bring into relief issues of political economy, the structural roots of poverty, power and powerlessness, social hierarchies of age, gender and class, and cultural practices. For poor adolescent women, reproductive and sexual health cannot be separated from the social, political and economic conditions of everyday life. So what do reproductive and sexual rights mean for married adolescent women living in urban slums in Dhaka city? They mean something quite different to what is normally implied in sexual rights discussion: they mean something to forfeit in exchange for tenuous rights to security; they mean a short-lived power – mediated by men – over other equally poor but older women. But they very rarely mean having control over one's sexual experiences or being able to act responsibly in the interests of one's sexual health.

Acknowledgements

This study (Project A 15054) was supported financially by the Special Programme of Research, Development and Research Training in Human Reproduction, World Health Organization, Geneva. I would like to thank all the married adolescent girls and their families for their time, kindness and patience. I am grateful to Nipu Sharmeen, research assistant, for her valuable assistance during fieldwork. Some sections of this paper have been published in *Plainspeak* (Issue 1, 2007) and are reproduced here with permission.

Notes

1 The fieldwork on which this chapter is based was carried out from December 2001 to January 2003 and involved 153 married adolescent girls, aged fifteen to nineteen, including fifty in-depth interviews, eight case studies, and observations and discussions with family and community members.

2 Women are excluded from a range of jobs open to men. These include: the transport sector (rickshaw-pulling, baby-taxi-driving, etc.), most skilled craftwork (carpet work, mosaic work) and the majority of the service industry and retail sector jobs (shops, restaurants, hotels, grocery stores, hairdressers), and working in certain markets that involve movement at night (Salway et al. 2003).

3 Khan et al. (2002) also found that forced sex is a relatively common phenomenon within married life. Out of their fifty-four informants, thirty-two reported experiencing forced sex on a regular basis.

4 Khan et al. (2002) found that with contraceptive use, particularly condom use, it was the husbands who made the final decision on whether to use it or not.

References

Afsar, R. (2000) *Rural–Urban Migration in Bangladesh. Causes, Consequences and Challenges*, Dhaka: University Press Limited.

Amin, S., I. Diamond, R. T. Naved and M. Newby (1997) 'Transition to adulthood for working girls: the case of Bangladeshi garment workers', Unpublished paper from 'Adolescence and Marriage among Female Garment Workers of Dhaka', Population Council Workshop 1997, Dhaka: BIDS (Bangladesh Institute of Development Studies).

Aziz, K. M. A. and C. Maloney (1985) *Life Stages, Gender and Fertility in Bangladesh*, Dhaka: ICDDR.

Islam, N. (1996) *The Urban Poor in Bangladesh*, Dhaka: Centre for Urban Studies.

Islam, N., N. Huda, F. B. Narayan and P. B. Rana (eds) (1997) *Addressing the Urban Poverty Agenda in Bangladesh: Critical Issues and the 1995 Survey Findings*, Dhaka: University Press Limited (for the Asian Development Bank).

Jesmin, S. and S. Salway (2000) 'Policy arena. Marriage among the urban poor of Dhaka: instability and uncertainty', *Journal of International Development*, 12: 698–705.

Khan, M. E., J. W. Townsend and S. D'Costa (2002) 'Behind closed doors: a qualitative study of sexual behaviour of married women in Bangladesh', *Culture, Health and Sexuality*, 4(2): 237–56.

Lock, M. and P. A. Kaufert (1998) 'Introduction', in M. Lock and P. A. Kaufert (eds), *Pragmatic Women and Body Politics*, Cambridge: Cambridge University Press, pp. 1–28.

Naved, T. R., M. Newby, S. Amin and I. Diamond (1997) 'Female labor migration and its implications for marriage and childbearing in Bangladesh', Unpublished paper from 'Adolescence and Marriage among Female Garment Workers of Dhaka', Population Council Workshop 1997, Dhaka: BIDS (Bangladesh Institute of Development Studies).

Perry, H. (2000) *Health for All in Bangladesh. Lessons in Primary Health Care for the Twenty-First Century*, Dhaka: University Press Limited.

Petchesky, R. P. (2001) 'Re-theorizing reproductive health and rights in the light of feminist cross-cultural research', in C. M. Obermeyer (ed.), *Cultural Perspectives on Reproductive Health*, Oxford: Oxford University Press, pp. 277–300.

Rozario, S. (1992) *Purity and Communal Boundaries. Women and Social Change in a Bangladeshi Village*, Sydney: Allen & Unwin.

Sabin, K., M. Rahman, S. Hawkes, K. Ahsan, L. Begum, S. El Arifeen and A. H. Baqui (1997) 'A cross-sectional study on the prevalence of sexually transmitted infections among Dhaka slum dwellers', in S. Hawkes et al. (eds), *Programme and Abstracts 1997*, ASCON VI, 6th Annual Scientific Conference, Dhaka: ICDDR.

Salway, S., S. Rahman and S. Jesmin (2003) 'A profile of women's work participation among the urban poor of Dhaka', *World Development*, 31(5): 881–901.

Schoepf, B. G. (1998) 'Inscribing the body politic: women and AIDS in Africa', in M. Lock and P. A. Kaufert (eds), *Pragmatic Women and Body Politics*, Cambridge: Cambridge University Press.

Sobo, E. J. (1997) 'Love, jealousy, and unsafe sex among inner-city women', in M. Singer (ed.), *The Political Economy of AIDS*, New York: Baywood Publishing Company, Inc., pp. 75–103.

Stark, N. N. (1993) 'Gender and therapy management: reproductive decision making in rural Bangladesh', Unpublished PhD thesis, Southern Methodist University, USA

White, S. C. (1992) *Arguing with the Crocodile. Gender and Class in Bangladesh*, Dhaka: University Press.

Wood, G. (1998) 'Desperately seeking security in Dhaka slums', *Discourse. Journal of Policy Studies*, 2(2): 77–87, Dhaka: Proshika.

World Bank and Bangladesh Centre for Advanced Studies (1998) *Bangladesh 2020: A Long-run Perspective Study*, Dhaka: University Press.

13 | Social and political inclusion of sex workers as a preventive measure against trafficking: Serbian experiences

JELENA DJORDJEVIC

'When I have been chased to be beaten up they were nowhere to find to defend me, but when they need to arrest me they are always there.'
A sex worker from Belgrade

Sex workers in Serbia are an overlooked and vulnerable group. Owing to the illegality of the sale of sexual services and attitudes towards those who sell sex as deviants or 'bad' persons (Pattanaik 2002), Serbian sex workers are vulnerable to violence, exploitation and trafficking, as well as HIV/AIDS, STIs and other health risks. This chapter argues that in order to prevent trafficking of this group, as well as other forms of exploitation and abuse, the rights of people working as sex workers must be ensured. Most of the discussions on which this chapter is based derive from the outreach programme for sex workers of the Anti Trafficking Centre (ATC), an organization that I co-founded. The chapter focuses in particular on the situation of street prostitutes in Belgrade.

Corrêa and Jolly (this volume) argue that the key issue when it comes to sex workers is not determining to what extent sex workers originally chose their profession, but rather what they want now. In the Serbian context, I will argue in this chapter that this means listening to the demands of sex workers and sex workers' organizations, challenging stigma around sex work, and addressing the repressive frameworks and attitudes that pervade state institutions, including those of the police. By supporting sex workers to build their skills, we are enabling them to protect themselves against exploitation and demand their rights – as well as to decide whether to remain in sex work or not.

The unacknowledged vulnerability of sex workers to trafficking

According to Limanowska's (2005) report, 'The trafficking of human beings in south-eastern Europe' (SEE), information from many SEE countries about the functioning of the internal prostitution market leads to the conclusion that the chain of trafficking in sex workers often starts within local markets. People who organize prostitution locally sell the women who work for them and move them from place to place, ultimately selling some of them abroad. Data from the 'Regional Clearing Point's second annual report on victims of trafficking in south-eastern Europe' (Surtees 2005) suggest that Serbian victims of trafficking are increasingly being exploited in street prostitution. Evidence from work with Serbian sex workers involved in street prostitution, gathered by the Anti Trafficking Centre, suggests that the vulnerability of these sex workers to trafficking, disease and violence is exacerbated by the illegality of their work and by the marginalization faced by undocumented sex workers from minority ethnic groups such as the Roma. Of particular concern are the levels of violence and abuse that sex workers suffer at the hands of the police, which is a direct consequence of the fact that Serbian law criminalizes the sale of sex. While the popular image of the trafficking victim is of an innocent girl who is lured into the sex industry against her will, this chapter shows that those who already work within the sex industry are as vulnerable to trafficking and exploitation. It suggests that solutions lie not in treating sex workers as a problem but in involving them in coming up with solutions that can reduce their vulnerability and realize their rights.

For years Serbia has been described as a transit country in trafficking for sexual exploitation. In the last two years, however, Serbia has been recognized as a source and destination, as well as transit country. Serbia ratified the UN Convention against Transnational Organized Crime and its supplementing protocols and is a signatory of all regional protocols and declarations developed under the leadership of the Stability Pact Trafficking Task Force for South Eastern Europe. The continued failure of Serbia to cooperate with the International Criminal Tribunal for the former Yugoslavia in extraditing war criminals, as well as the failure of the country to meet the minimum political and economic requirements necessary to enter EU accession negotiations, makes EU membership a distant dream for Serbia (Lindstrom 2006).

Serbia is confronted with a myriad of political and economic problems, including high unemployment rates, social dislocation and corruption, as well as the hard legacy of war, especially with regard to the impunity of people implicated in war crimes and cooperation with war crime investigations (ibid.). The role of the welfare state has changed significantly over the years, and it is now unable to assist its citizens. Non-governmental organizations (NGOs) have taken over the role of the state in social care, and deal with issues such as violence against women, child abuse, trafficking and many other social problems. The very fact that the Serbian state is not dealing with war crimes and the protection of essential human rights, that people in Serbia suffer from police torture in prisons, that violence against women is not taken seriously and offenders are not punished, is some indication of the challenge in this context of encouraging the state to deal with the question of protecting sex workers against trafficking, violence and exploitation. While combating trafficking is as high on the agenda of international organizations working in Serbia as it is for local NGOs, a combination of lack of state capacity and lack of political will mean that the traffic in women persists; and sex workers remain among the most vulnerable.

Combating trafficking in Serbia: narratives, policies and actors

Anti-trafficking policy-making in the Balkans would not exist without the involvement of the various international organizations and transnational actors who placed trafficking high on the political agenda and produced policies to combat it. As acknowledged by Lindstrom (ibid.), however, anti-trafficking policy-making can not be strictly understood as a 'top down' process as there are many other actors who are involved in the policy-making with diverse levels of influence over what will be taken as the dominant approach to trafficking. This section introduces some of these actors and contrasts the different approaches they have taken to address the issue of trafficking.

Trafficking: positions and policies Serbia is designated in the Strategy for Combating Trafficking in Human Beings of the Republic of Serbia for 2005–08 primarily as a transit point and destination for the citizens of Romania, Bulgaria, Ukraine and Moldova trafficked towards western Europe and the UN-administered province of Kosovo. The Strategy also suggests that Serbia has become a country of origin with a number of Serbian nationals (women) trafficked abroad to Bosnia, Kosovo, Italy, Montenegro and Romania, as well as internally within Serbia. The Strategy recommends the establishment of a National Team for Combating Trafficking, comprising a working group consisting of local institutions, NGOs and international organizations, dealing with prevention, victim assistance, protection, law enforcement and trafficking in children. The Strategy placed the Ministry of the Interior in charge of appointing the National Coordinator to oversee and coordinate all activities related to anti-trafficking work, resulting in the appointment of a high-ranking police officer to this position.

Trafficking is represented in the Strategy as a problem of organized crime. This gives rise to an approach that puts the emphasis on criminal law and the criminal justice system and aims to introduce more stringent criminal legislation and heavier punishments for offenders. It also aims at improving international police cooperation and developing other measures that help in prosecuting the offenders. Combating trafficking under this approach, as Wijers and van Doorninck (2002) argue, becomes equated with combating organized crime, subordinating the interests of women to those of the state in dealing with organized crime. Within such an approach 'trafficked' persons are often exposed to secondary victimization, as they are treated as 'disposable' witnesses serving the interests of law enforcement (ibid.).

It is not surprising that a law-enforcement-centred approach has gained such power in the country, as it used the definition of trafficking developed within the UN Protocol to Prevent, Suppress and Punish Trafficking in Persons, Especially Women and Children, as a basis for developing policies to prevent trafficking, protect victims and prosecute offenders. The definition of trafficking used in the Protocol was framed by concerns about transnational organized crime, not about the protection and promotion of the rights of migrants or sex workers (O'Connell Davidson 2003; Ditmore, this volume); the Protocol is itself a supplement to the UN Convention on Organized Crime. The role of the Stability Pact Task Force, through its group on Trafficking in Human Beings, formed to deal with the humanitarian crisis in the region in 1999, was also significant in putting pressure on and giving incentives to Serbia in eliminating a problem that keeps economically and politically unstable countries (read migrant- and crime-exporting states) from its long-awaited 'Euro-Atlantic integration' through strengthening law enforcement measures.

The organized crime-centred approach is not the only approach which can be extracted from a careful reading of the Strategy. Focusing on the human rights of the victims of trafficking is presented as a priority, and as something that can go hand in hand with combating organized crime and strengthening law enforcement mechanisms. Viewing trafficking as a human rights issue is the main approach taken by NGOs, which have had a significant influence on the state in Serbia. This approach talks primarily of women and girls trafficked for the purpose of sexual exploitation.

Within the human rights approach to trafficking, there are two different schools of thought. Neo-abolitionist feminists led by the Coalition Against Trafficking in Women (CATW) define prostitution as a violation of women's human rights that is equal to slavery: it becomes something that can never be consented to, or chosen as a profession (Doezema 2005). CATW lobby for measures to make prostitution illegal and suppress the general market for prostitution by legal penalties against clients, brothel owners and other 'third parties' (O'Connell Davidson 2003; Doezema 2005). This approach is criticized by organizations such as the Global Alliance Against Trafficking in Women (GAATW), whose vision on trafficking is inspired by the global sex worker rights movement. According to them, trafficking is characterized by the use of force during the migration process and/or consequent labour or service (Doezema 2005). GAATW emphasizes that it is not the work as such which violates women's human rights, but conditions of deceit, abuse, violence, debt bondage, blackmail and deprivation of freedom of movement – be it in relation to sexual labour, domestic labour or in other sectors.

GAATW, together with sex workers' rights organizations, criticizes the neo-abolitionist feminist approach towards trafficking, arguing that it stigmatizes women working in the sex industry by reducing their status to that of either 'victims' or 'deviants' and thus denies them a legitimate place in the public debate on the issues of interest to them. Of primary concern is the extent to which the neo-abolitionist approach calls for repressive measures against sex workers rather than against 'traffickers'. This, sex worker rights advocates point out, simply makes sex workers' lives more dangerous. Yet Doezema (ibid.) argues that GAATW, too, fails to address some of the issues at stake for the sex workers' rights movement: their use of a distinction between 'voluntary' and 'forced' prostitution leaves the rights of the 'willing' prostitute out of the discussion (ibid.: 31). The trafficking discourse used by women's organizations relies on the idea that deceit was used to get women to leave home. There is now, however, a significant body of research which indicates that a large number of migrant women who work in the sex industry did know that their work would have a sexual component, if not constituting prostitution itself (Agustín 2005).[1]

Running through accounts of women's migration under 'presumed' trafficking is the assumption that prostitution cannot ever be something that women actively choose to do to earn a living; or indeed that migrant women can be independent agents who decide to use commercial sex for instrumental ends (Agustín 2005). A third approach to trafficking focuses on illegal migration (Lindstom 2006), an approach that is closely associated with the International Organization for Migration (IOM), an organization particularly known for its work in providing direct assistance to trafficked persons through its return and reintegration programme (ibid.; SIDA 2003; IOM 2005). One of the shortcomings of treating migrant sex workers in this way is that they become stigmatized as a result, and their possibilities are restricted. The first evaluation of IOM's counter-trafficking programme in Serbia looked at IOM's return programme for foreign victims of trafficking. Evaluators agreed that a programme that asks its beneficiaries to sign a voluntary return document in a foreign language, carry an 'IOM bag' as a recognition mark, or which gives $US150 as a 'reinstallation grant' to beneficiaries upon their return is not an empowering programme (SIDA 2003).

These three approaches to trafficking – treating it as organized crime, as a human rights issue and in terms of illegal migration – come together in the policy of another influential actor involved in anti-trafficking work in the Balkans, the European Union. Given that EU membership is the top priority for all governments in the region and that the EU is the largest donor, it can exert a great deal of direction over policy agendas (Lindstrom 2006). Looking at the European Parliament's 2001 Comprehensive European Strategy on Trafficking in Women, which was entitled 'The misery behind the fantasy: from poverty to sex slavery', Lindstrom argues that the EU frames the issue of trafficking as a matter of organized crime, prostitution, migration and human rights, as well as EU enlargement. This, she continues, is especially reflected in the multiple strategies proposed in the report to combat the problem: strengthening and coordinating law enforcement capacities at a region-wide level; tightening external borders and visa controls; supporting human rights groups in exposing the issue; providing humanitarian, legal and social assistance to victims of trafficking; and, finally, improving the social and economic conditions of women within and beyond the EU border. Most initiatives that the EU has supported to date, however, Lindstrom comments, have focused on enhancing the law enforcement capacity to enforce border controls and fight organized crime.

Anti-trafficking efforts in the Balkans A number of NGOs have been active in anti-trafficking efforts in the Balkans in recent years, supported by funding from international organizations keen to use them as a bridge into building government capacity. The first response from NGOs in the Balkans to trafficking came from women's organizations working in the area of violence against women and those running shelters for battered women (Limanowska 2005). In the course of their work they responded to the need to support trafficked persons and started developing programmes. It was women's NGOs, argues Limanowska, which first warned both international agencies and government about trafficking; and it was through trafficking that these organizations first began to talk with the government about violence against women. Owing to pressure applied by international organizations advocating that state actors recognize women's NGOs as equal partners in counter-trafficking work, violence against women became a topic discussed between state institutions and women's organizations for the first time.

The relationship between women's organizations and the state is a recent partnership, formed at the instigation of international organizations; it is one that has been highly contested from the very beginning. During the war as well as in post-conflict restructuring, women's organizations had always stood in opposition to the government. There was a justifiable scepticism among them about the government committing to work on human rights violations, while at the same time many of those involved in war crimes were 'enjoying' impunity in Serbia, many of them continuing to work within state institutions (Djordjevic 2005; Limanowska 2005). In addition, many activists had direct experience of state-sponsored police brutality. To give an example, I was once speaking at a press conference on trafficking when one of the police officers approached me and said: 'I would like to apologize to you.' 'Why?' I asked. 'In the last years I have been ordered to beat you and those similar to you [members of women's NGOs] on the streets while you were protesting. But now,' he said, 'in the same way as I was ordered before, I am ordered to cooperate with you.' This was an important signal for me, indicating that it will take a long time before Serbia disconnects with its difficult past and the former regime. But this apology also made me wonder to what extent this 'cooperation' is about meeting the need to show the international community that human rights are being respected, rather than arising out of a genuine recognition that the state has a duty to protect them.

As an activist within the feminist movement, I have had the opportunity to participate in various women's groups mobilizing around trafficking. In the course of that work I have become highly critical of the activities of the majority of women's organizations working on trafficking. Women's organizations working on trafficking started 'cooperating' (I use this term loosely) with state institutions at the insistence of international organizations. Through engaging with anti-trafficking initiatives, women's organizations believed they could address violence against women and prostitution. Their approach to trafficking 'closed the door' against exploring who else, beyond 'vulnerable' women, might experience exploitation in the process of migration. It represented all migrant women as passive and ignorant (Agustín 2005) and represented their experience of migration as dehumanizing, 'ugly' and purely exploitative. All migrant sex workers came to be represented as victims of trafficking.

Once designated (or presumed) to be 'victims' of 'trafficking', women become passive objects of interventions on their behalf by NGOs, government and international organizations. Stories of horrific abuse that some women encountered in the process of migration were often used in Serbia in calling for state intervention (see Doezema 2005). However 'true' these accounts might be for some women, research has shown that not all women (if any) fit into the category used in these kinds of narratives. Yet it was exactly this narrow understanding of trafficking which brought state institutions on board. Governments, in the same way as women's organizations, saw that they could address some of their concerns about social change through trafficking (ibid.). It was not long before NGOs lost control over the development of policies (if they ever had it) and some even became complicit in the government's efforts to restrict the migration of women and to 'police' prostitutes.

In conclusion, vast networks of women's organizations and international organizations, transnational actors as well as local governments have been directly involved in anti-trafficking policy-making in Serbia. And yet, different actors have highlighted different approaches to trafficking, depending on what they saw as the problem needing to be solved. It is because trafficking in women is related to so many areas and the interests of so many actors that measures developed to address it need to be carefully questioned to find out whose 'problems' and interests the above-mentioned strategies actually serve (Wijers and van Doorninck 2002).

Supporting street sex workers in Serbia Three years ago the Anti Trafficking Centre (ATC) and Jazas – Yugoslav Association against HIV/AIDS – came together to initiate a support programme for sex workers in Serbia. Women and transgender persons in the sex industry in Serbia are constantly attacked and insulted by clients, passers-by or the police. Unfortunately, existing shelters for battered women and survivors of trafficking run by women's organizations are still not receptive to women and transgender persons (self-identifying as women) who work in the sex industry. Some NGOs offer help, mostly in the form of legal assistance. The support programme was set up primarily as an HIV-prevention intervention, offering support to women, men and transgender persons offering sexual services on the streets through its outreach programme, as well as through its mobile team unit. The outreach programme consists of two persons visiting certain areas in Belgrade where street prostitution takes place. Members of the outreach team distribute condoms and lubricants to sex workers on the spot. The organized mobile unit has a gynaecologist, a psychotherapist, a psychiatrist and a general practice doctor, and visits various areas in towns once a week. There, sex workers can get tested for HIV/AIDS and can receive counselling on HIV/AIDS and sexually transmitted infections. If needed, they receive treatment for such infections. ATC activists have broadened the remit of the programme, referring people to contacts within the state institutions and certain NGOs.

As the first organization working in Serbia to offer a support programme for this group, ATC outreach volunteers experienced a lot of mistrust from sex workers at the outset. This is understandable given the existing level of discrimination and violence against those who work in the sex industry. Only after some months did those who worked in street prostitution become more open to talking about their experiences and asking for support. At first, the assistance offered through the outreach programme consisted of giving out free condoms and lubricants, organizing gynaecological testing on the spot, and providing professional psychological support through the once- or twice-weekly visits of the mobile unit. Very soon, however, our services had to expand to address the level of violence that we were confronted with, as well as the diverse needs of the group we were assisting. We became a referral agency. Since women had previously experienced a high level of discrimination from various agencies, both governmental and non-governmental, we found that unless outreach workers escorted them to the desired institution they would not go to ask for assistance. Building a network of sensitized professionals to whom we can refer women and who can respond to the needs of the person referred without imposing a particular interpretation of their experience became one of our key challenges.

Punishment rather than protection

The health services offered by the mobile unit proved to be insufficient to meet women's health needs. To access state healthcare, sex workers need to have registration cards. The majority of those who work on the streets, however, are from the Roma ethnic community, the most socially disenfranchised community in Serbia. Many Roma people are not registered with the state. This prevents them from receiving health insurance and protection. The story told to us by Kristina, a Roma transgender person, illustrates just how difficult being an undocumented worker is in this context; and demonstrates, at the same time, some of the factors that can trigger sex worker migration.

Kristina is a Romany transgender person, aged thirty-five. She grew up in Belgrade with two brothers. She had to hide her identity or they would have killed her. She was married and tried to act as a man for the sake of her daughter, who is now fourteen, but the marriage failed. All (male to female) transgender persons she knew were prostitutes, and she found this was the only solution for her as well. She started when she was thirty, never working for the benefit of somebody else, and keeping all her money for herself. Kristina had worked as a cleaning lady before and no one could tell she was a man, but identity papers later made this a problem. She asked for public welfare at the social care institution but was refused. She believes the reason was because she is Romany and transgender.

More than once Kristina expected police help, but it has never happened. Once she was assaulted by a group of young guys on the spot where she works. She reported it to a police patrol near by, but they responded that it was her own fault. In addition, the police were humiliating her, beating her up, taking money and condoms, and asking for free sexual services. She was arrested many times, every time in an extremely violent manner. She would come out of prison and two days later she would be imprisoned again. In jail transgender persons are usually put together with men and often become victims of sexual assault. The police are aware of that, but never do anything. On one occasion her hair was cut in prison, against her will. If she became a rape or robbery victim, she wouldn't report it to the police. She would deal with it, as she did before, by herself or with help from her friends. Kristina is looking at possibilities to go abroad to work.

As Kristina's story suggests, services such as those provided by the mobile unit can make a valuable contribution to sex workers' well-being in a situation where so many sex workers are excluded from state health services. Yet these services do not address the violence that women and transgender persons experience on a daily basis, and the outreach programme addresses it only on an ad hoc basis. The focus of both the outreach programme and the mobile unit was on HIV/AIDS and STI prevention; neither was able to deal adequately with the issues that underlie why women put their health and security at risk. And that bottom line is this: owing to the illegality of sex work, women, men and transgender persons offering sexual services are forced to work in insecure conditions. When they become victims of violence they do not appeal to the police for fear they will get arrested.

As I noted earlier, Serbian NGOs are trying to fill the gap of state social services by assisting socially disenfranchised groups. But sex workers are rarely beneficiaries of the services offered by civil society sectors, unless they match the stereotype of the innocent and naïve woman unwillingly forced into prostitution. While this picture evokes compassion, the picture of those who have worked before as prostitutes and want to continue, or who stand up for themselves, usually evokes hostility (Wijers

1998: 77). Common public opinion, often shared by policy-makers and service providers, is that once a woman is a prostitute she loses her rights and is no longer entitled to protection. As one police officer crudely commented: 'Prostitutes do not get raped' – meaning that standards applied to 'good' women do not apply to prostitutes and so those who get raped while working as prostitutes should expect this as part of the job. In this situation, it is the prostitute who is blamed for her immoral behaviour; any abuse she experiences is perceived to be a consequence of her work (Pheterson 1996). Every woman, Pheterson (ibid.) argues, who transgresses discriminatory gender codes, in particular those against female economic and sexual autonomy, is subjected to social and legal punishment rather than social and legal protection. It is not only those who work in the sex industry who lose out. In many cases, owing to discrimination, lack of financial resources and official documents (IDs), their children cannot enrol in school. Supporting the integration of these women and their families into society is an ongoing battle.

State (police) violence is what prevails

Besides the lack of social support for women working in street prostitution, violence on the part of the police is something that women often speak about. In a recent incident, one of the women we are in contact with was stopped by a police officer on the street. After asking for her ID and learning that she had just come out of custody, the police officer asked her for free sexual services, promising to let her go after that, i.e. not to take her back into custody. When the woman refused, he started to beat her severely on the head. We were called to support her filing charges for assault. Unfortunately, colleagues of the above-mentioned police officer were sent to the scene to file the report. Once they that realized the woman was known to the police for working as a prostitute, they took her into custody without acknowledging the assault. Similar situations of violence against women working in street prostitution are numerous and involve different levels of brutality. As Sanja's story shows, personal connections with the police often provide the only bulwark of protection against the violence that most sex workers suffer at the hands of the police.

Sanja was born in 1978. She is Serbian and lives in Belgrade. Her parents are dead. She has been a sex worker for five years. She married young, aged sixteen or seventeen, and did not complete her education. She lived with her husband for a while and gave birth to a daughter. Soon after, he started to drink and to psychologically and physically abuse her. Sanja decided to leave and went to her parents with the daughter. Her parents supported her financially. She had a friend (a girl) who was often giving her money and buying her things for the baby. Sanja was suspicious about the source of the money, and her friend confessed that she had been working in an escort agency. She offered Sanja a job at the agency as a secretary. Sanja agreed. At first she worked as a secretary and earned 10 per cent of the income from scheduled business. On one occasion, a client asked her for a sexual service. She agreed. This is when she started to sell sex. She became involved with the owner of the escort agency. He controlled her and forbade her to do sex work. When she left him, he was furious and called his friends' agencies to instruct them not to give her work. Then she heard about a place by the railway station and started working on the streets. Sanja said it is safer to work in an agency since there is security there. Also it is more discreet than on the street. Her family has no knowledge of her work. Six months ago Sanja ended a relationship with a policeman which had lasted three years. He abused her psychologically, and was extremely jealous and possessive.

While the relationship lasted she was not arrested. A few times she was taken in by the police, but her lover would come and release her. He promised to marry her and find her a better job, but nothing happened. When she left him, he kept calling for six months, begging and even threatening her. Sanja does not go out often; she has regular customers and goes out to work when called. She does not want to stay in the sex business – she would like to work in a boutique, or complete a course to be a hairdresser. Sanja has a medical care booklet, which means she has access to public health institutions. Her daughter goes to school, and Sanja says she is treated well. Sanja has been imprisoned twice for prostitution. She was just standing in the street and was taken to prison. The police patrol wrote up a statement claiming she had been caught in the act, and tried to force her to sign it. She refused. In court, however, it was explained to her that since she was registered as a sex worker, she would always be arrested if found at a hot spot.

Women tell us that they spend so much time in jail that they need to work even more to pay off their bail and compensate for time when they could not earn money. They are constantly exposed to police brutality and blackmail. And even though for some groups, such as transgender people, work in prostitution might be their only possibility of earning money, the police prevent it. They often take advantage of their position to cooperate with pimps and to make profits from the local prostitution market. In this respect it is no wonder that the police are reluctant to address the issue of violence against prostitutes and internal trafficking.

ATC's aim is to create a safe space where women working at various levels of the sex industry can come for support, which can be a beginning for building a collective voice. But this is impossible in the current context, where any such gathering is potentially problematic and could endanger us as well as the women we are assisting. This is because we could be charged with organizing prostitution. Even carrying a condom and lubricant is used as evidence against prostitutes, 'proving' that prostitution took place. There have been numerous incidents when outreach workers have been harassed and questioned by the police for carrying condoms and standing in 'prostitution zones'. In this respect we have had to adjust our working practices. We want to be able to respond to the urgent needs of women working under the repression of the police and experiencing discrimination from the state institutions that are responsible for protecting them as their citizens. Owing to a restrictive legal framework, however, what we can actually do is limited. Despite that we find different mechanisms to deal with this challenge. For example, outreach workers talk to women in the streets about their needs, about protection and self-organizing. Small workshops on various topics are carried out in cafés next to places where sex workers stand on the streets.

Migration: a non-solution

Like Kristina, some women who work in street prostitution within Serbia are looking for ways to migrate abroad, where they believe they will have more rights and will be able to work freely in the sex industry. Experience from organizations across Europe, however, suggests that women migrating for prostitution represent the most vulnerable group among prostitutes in the respective country, and many end up being trafficked.

In the majority of EU countries, sex work is not covered by labour legislation. Where it is, as in Germany and the Netherlands, different regulations apply to EU and non-EU citizens (Andrijasevic 2006); the legalization of prostitution in these countries has widened the gap between EU and non-EU prostitutes. This, Andrijasevic argues, has resulted in an enhanced dependency on third parties in arranging work and accommodation, greater vulnerability to exploitation, enforced mobility from one location to another and heightened social isolation.

The dually marginalized position in which women find themselves, being in the position of a prostitute and that of an undocumented migrant, renders them highly vulnerable to multiple forms of oppression and exploitation (Lazaridis 2002). Disadvantaged by illegal status, migrant sex workers are unable to exercise their rights. The Transnational AIDS/ STD Prevention among Migrant Prostitutes in Europe Project (TAMPEP 2001) position paper on migration and sex work argues, however, that their immigration status should not automatically deny them the human rights of access to health and social care: migrant sex workers should be offered realistic options that support them in achieving a safe environment free from fear, further abuse and exploitation. As Pattanaik puts it:

> ... the social and political inclusion of migrant sex workers is an important preventive measure against trafficking in women; a prerequisite of the social inclusion of migrant sex workers, including transgender sex workers, is the recognition and implementation of their human rights as women, as migrant women and as sex workers. (Pattanaik 2002: 227)

Many women consider migrating in the hope of finding better working conditions. As migrants, however, sex workers are even more vulnerable. The immigration regime combined with the absence of labour standards in the sex sector leaves many in a position where they have little choice but to accept extremely poor working conditions and highly exploitative employment relations (IUSW 2006). In their countries of origin, as in the example of Serbia, prostitutes are often denied basic rights, held in contempt, isolated, marginalized and sometimes criminalized (Wijers 1998: 72). As migrants, in addition to all this, they are at risk of deportation, imprisonment, harassment and abuse owing to their immigration status.

As the case of Serbia shows, whether they work locally or migrate, this group remains in need of real protection. They need power to participate in policies that determine their lives (Miller 2004). Yet, Miller continues, their claims as citizens disappear in the current stories of trafficking, which retain strong traces of the anti-vice and social purity movement. The sensationalist focus of current anti-trafficking reports masks the absence of concrete steps to create conditions for sexual and economic rights for women, men and transgender persons. And, as Miller points out, without the ability to intervene against state practices and interests that could generate unsafe migration, we are left helping those same states that regulate the movement of already constrained people. That is why there is a need to strengthen the rights of those involved as female migrants and as female migrant sex workers (Wijers 1998: 78). As Wijers argues, all strategies must be based on the recognition of women's right to self-determination, non-stigmatization and non-victimization.

Conclusion

As a feminist and anti-trafficking activist working from a rights-based perspective, I am concerned about the lack of will on the part of the state and non-state actors to engage, without moralizing, with the women, men and transgender people who work as street sex workers. Sex workers come to their attention only when they migrate for sex work and become 'victims' of trafficking. By failing to engage directly with sex workers and to work with them to determine what would enable them to address their needs and realize their rights, institutions and non-governmental organizations perpetuate the 'whore stigma'[2] and further endanger the lives of those working in prostitution.

Whether they migrate or not, sex workers have human rights. But their rights are constantly being denied. What is needed is the creation of safe spaces where the voices of the sex workers and their diverse experiences can be heard. Only then, by working together, can we start to challenge the stigma, violence and discrimination experienced by sex workers, and to demand social inclusion and recognition as well as implementation of their human rights. Non-judgemental and non-moralistic health and social care support services for sex workers are badly needed. Sex workers should be involved as partners in designing these services so that they respond to their realities and needs. Furthermore, forums for discussion should be encouraged, tackling all the issues that come up with regard to sex work – which, in the Serbian context, include repressive legislation, health and social services access, stigma, discrimination, trafficking and violence. Basing interventions on evidence rather than assumptions calls for research that would provide us with a deeper understanding of what makes prostitutes vulnerable to abuse and exploitation (including trafficking) and how they can be prevented. Public officials, civil society representatives, healthcare professionals and all those who are in contact with sex workers need to be more sensitive towards the human rights of these women, men and transgender persons and address the failure of public and private institutions to protect their rights.

Experience on the ground demonstrates that if we want to be serious about human rights, then ideological and moral arguments about trafficking and sex work must be challenged. Rather than developing policies that give power to the police, the protection and promotion of the basic rights of sex workers, particularly migrant sex workers, should be assured as an important measure against exploitation, trafficking and abuse. It has become clear to me, after several years of working with street sex workers in Serbia, that one of the most immediate steps that could be taken to reduce the risk of trafficking and HIV infection and deal effectively with the vulnerability of sex workers to violence is a change in the law. But in order to bring about this change, we need to deepen our contacts with the sex workers in Belgrade as well as in other towns in Serbia and enable them to engage directly in shaping policies and laws that can improve their lives. Sex workers are part of the solution, rather than part of the problem. It is where sex workers themselves have organized that they have been able to advance their rights throughout the world. It is time for the organizing of sex workers to happen in Serbia.

Notes

1 See, for example, Andrijasevic 2003, 2004; Agustín 2005, 2006; Cabiria 2004; Kempadoo and Doezema 1998.

2 The 'whore stigma', as Pheterson argues, is a ready instrument of sexist attack against women deemed too autonomous, such as women who speak out against men who abuse them, visible lesbians, demonstrators for abortion rights, women resisters against dictatorial regimes, streetwalking prostitutes, unveiled women, etc. As such, the 'whore stigma' can be used against any woman who serves to challenge male entitlement (1996: 12).

References

Agustín, A. (2005) 'Migrants in the mistress's house: other voices in the "trafficking" debate', *Social Politics*, 12(1): 96–117.
— (2006) 'The disappearing of a migration category: migrants who sell sex', *Journal of Ethnic and Migration Studies*, 32(1): 29–47.
Andrijasevic, R. (2003) 'The difference borders make: (il)legality, migration and trafficking in Italy among Eastern European women in prostitution', in S. Ahmed, C. Castaneda, A. Fortier and M. Sheller (eds), *Uprootings/ Regrounding: Questions of Home and Migration*, Oxford: Berg.
— (2004) 'Trafficking in women and the politics of mobility in Europe', PhD thesis, Women's Studies Department, Utrecht University.
— (2006) 'Eastern European prostitutes in western Europe since the 1980s', in K. J. Bade, P. C. Emmer, L. Lucassen and J. Oltmer (eds), *Enzyklopaedie Migration in Europa. Vom 17. Jahrhundert bis zur Gegenwart*, Schoeningh: Wilhelm Fink Verlag.
Cabiria (2004) *Women and Migration in Europe – Strategies and Empowerment*, Lyons: Le Dragon Lune Editions.
Djordjevic, J. (2005) 'Countering trafficking in women: lessons on maximizing effectiveness – the case of Serbia and Montenegro', Paper delivered at Catalyst 2005, conference held at Essex University.
Doezema, H. J. (2005) 'Sex slaves and discourse masters: the historical construction of "trafficking in women"', DPhil thesis, Institute of Development Studies, University of Sussex.
IOM (International Organization for Migration) (2005) 'Final report on IOM's counter trafficking activities funded by USAID Serbia, Belgrade', <www.iom.int> (accessed 20 August 2006).
IUSW (International Union of Sex Workers) (2006) 'Response to "Tackling human trafficking: consultation on proposals for a UK action plan"', London: IUSW.
Kempadoo, K. and J. Doezema (eds) (1998) *Global Sex Workers: Rights,*

Resistance and Redefinition, New York: Routledge.

Lazaridis, G. (2002) *Trafficking and Prostitution – the Growing Exploitation of Migrant Women in Greece*, 9(2), London, Thousand Oaks, CA, and New Delhi: Sage Publications.

Limanowska, B. (2005) 'The trafficking of human beings in southeastern Europe (SEE)', Sarajevo: UNICEF, UNOHCHR and ODIHR.

Lindstrom, N. (2006) 'Transnational responses to human trafficking: the politics of anti-trafficking in the Balkans', New York: The New School, <www.maxwell.syr.edu/moynihan/programs/ces/pcconfpdfs/Lindstrom.pdf> (accessed 10 May 2006).

Miller, A. (2004) 'The dilemmas of contemporary anti-trafficking work', RightsNewsOnline, 26(1), <www.columbia.edu/cu/humanrights/publications/rn/rn_2004_11.htm> (accessed 1 May 2005).

O'Connell Davidson, J. (2003) 'The trouble with trafficking', Paper for the Launch Workshop of the Network for European Women's Rights, Centre for the Study of Global Ethics, University of Birmingham.

Pattanaik, B. (2002) 'Conclusion – where do we go from here?', in S. Thorbek and B. Pattanaik (eds), *Transnational Prostitution – Changing Global Patterns*, London/New York: Zed Books.

Pheterson, G. (1996) *The Prostitution Prism*, Amsterdam: Amsterdam University Press.

SIDA (2003) 'IOM regional counter trafficking programme in the western Balkans', Stockholm: Edita.

Surtees, R. (2005) 'Regional clearing point's second annual report on victims of trafficking in southeastern Europe', Serbia and Montenegro: IOM and RCP.

TAMPEP (2001) 'Transnational AIDS/STD Prevention among Migrant Prostitutes in Europe Project – TAMPEP position paper on migration and sex work', Amsterdam: TAMPEP.

Wijers, M. (1998) 'Women, labour and migration – the position of trafficked women and strategies for support', in K. Kempadoo and J. Doezema (eds), *Global Sex Workers: Rights, Resistance and Redefinition*, New York: Routledge.

Wijers, M. and M. van Doorninck (2002) 'Only rights can stop wrongs: a critical assessment of anti-trafficking strategies', <www.nswp.org> (accessed 20 August 2006).

THREE | **Changing mindsets**

14 | Confronting our prejudices: women's movement experiences in Bangladesh

SHIREEN HUQ

The acceptance of sex workers' groups in national networks of women's organizations is a milestone in the history of the women's movement in Bangladesh. This chapter explores the lessons learnt by Bangladeshi women's organizations through their involvement in a campaign to support the rights of sex workers, and their struggles to defend themselves against illegal eviction threats from brothels. It suggests that these struggles gave a new – and more public – meaning to discussions on sexuality and sexual rights that had been taking place within the women's movement. The chapter focuses on the experiences of Naripokkho, a countrywide women's organization, and the lessons that this organization learnt through engagement in the struggle for sex workers' rights in Bangladesh.

Putting sexual freedom on the agenda

Naripokkho's engagement in discussions on sexuality was rooted in the experiential sharing of women's life stories that characterized the early stages of the organization's agenda-building. These stories drew out how the experience of being a woman is inevitably marked with the painful reality of women's bodies being at the centre of much of the ill treatment, denial and deprivation they suffer at the hands of their family members, strangers, institutions and policies alike. Sociocultural norms dictate what women should or should not do with their bodies. The stories depicted the many social rules restricting women's *cholaphera* (physical movement), i.e. when, where and how far they can venture out of their homes and what constitutes a legitimate reason to do so; what parts of their bodies they have to cover and how; how they have to carry themselves when in the gaze of 'undesirable others' ranging from brothers-in-law to the general public; when they can have sexual relations and with whom; whether they can insist on sexual pleasure for themselves or not; when and how often they can complain of ill health; whether they can seek healthcare, and where, when and from whom; and so on – these are all centred around women's bodies in one way or another.

The agenda that grew out of the countless testimonies of what these restrictions meant in terms not only of women's physical well-being but also of their sense of self-worth, personal freedom and happiness was one focused on interrogating every sociocultural practice that imposed such restrictions and rules, and resisting them in every way possible. What implications did they have for women's rights and freedoms? How could the rights agenda then leave out issues of sexual freedom, as it tended to do?

Putting issues of sexual freedom on to the rights agenda was a difficult task, not least because we were surrounded by conservative social mores, but more so because the usually progressive political discourses around us reflected a similar conservatism in respect of sexuality and imposed a sense of propriety totally out of sync with their otherwise radical political stance. Our attempts to redefine the rights agenda by incorporating sexual freedom met with hostility. We were ostracized for taking things too far. It was bad enough that our discussion on equality did not stop at wages and franchise but went on to talk about the right to love and pleasure. To then raise the question of sexual freedom was definitely stepping beyond the boundaries of a 'legitimate' rights discourse.

We continued our discussions, albeit within the walls of our meeting rooms. The first discussion we had on women loving women, '*narir proti narir preeti*', was received with surprising 'compassion'. We tested the waters in public in 1994 when we proposed our slogan '*Shorir amaar, shidhanto amaar*' (my body, my decision) for adoption by the International Women's Day Committee as the theme for celebrations that year. The adoption of the slogan meant that it was echoed in over a dozen places in the country where the committee members had organized events; press releases had gone out to every major newspaper; and over thirty thousand leaflets had been distributed. The backlash was instantaneous – what did we mean by *Shorir amaar, shidhanto amaar*? Were we by any chance talking of sexual freedom? Were we seeking licence for promiscuity? Some of our sisters in the International Women's Day Committee also began to have second thoughts. The slogan was too controversial.

Making alliances, becoming *attiyo*

Sex workers, and their mobilizations against evictions, helped us work out these knotty politics around sexuality. The town of Narayanganj, 11 miles outside the capital, Dhaka, is a commercial township that developed around an inland river port, and houses the largest cluster of brothels in Bangladesh. In 1991, at the height of eviction threats by self-appointed guardians of Narayanganj, the women in the Tanbazaar brothels issued a press statement making a public appeal for support. The statement read, 'We are women, we work for our living, and we are citizens of this country. Our rights as women, as workers and as citizens deserve the same respect and protection as any other citizen.' This created the basis for a new solidarity between sections of the 'mainstream' women's movement and sex workers' struggles.

Naripokkho's association with sex workers began when the Kandupatti brothel in Dhaka was closed down in 1997. This led to the formation of Ulka, the first sex workers' organization in Bangladesh. In 1999, the government turned its attention to forcefully evicting those living and working in the Narayanganj brothels. At the break of dawn, without warning or notice, truckloads of police descended on the nearly two thousand women who worked in the brothels and lived there with their children. Many were forcibly taken to government-run 'vagrant homes', where they were confined, but most managed to escape.

Upon receiving news of the Tanbazaar eviction, Ulka members rushed to the Naripokkho office. The office was immediately transformed into an impromptu shelter with over forty women sleeping there, and a few more in our homes. We were at the centre of a full-scale agitation. There was an unprecedented response to our call for action. Some eighty-four women's and human rights organizations and development NGOs representing a wide spectrum of views on social change came together to form *Shonghoti* (solidarity), an alliance in support of the rights of sex workers. For the next five weeks or so, it turned into a twenty-four-hour operation. We were together, strategizing, mobilizing, facing journalists, holding street protests, demonstrating in front of different government offices, including that of the Inspector General of Police, meeting UN officials and handing over a formal communication to the High Commissioner for Human Rights, and in between sitting around drinking tea, listening to the many untold stories of personal struggles and sharing jokes. We had become *attiyo* (related). Our political alliances had grown into our relationships. Not only did our own acquaintance with the reality of sex work deepen, but the links between the many different realities of women in and out of sex work became evident. We also received notice from our landlady to vacate the premises. Some of our new-found sisters reassured us that as soon as they could get back to business, they could raise enough money for us to buy our own premises!

Going public

The response to this agitation by the media was unprecedented. The story stayed on the front page of major newspapers for almost a month. Finally, we had an opportunity to go public with our agenda on sexual freedom! Sexuality, reproduction, health, violence, all centred on women's bodies – and that is what we had in common with women in sex work. We had to be strategic, however, in terms of how we were going to present to the media and the public the issue of our solidarity with the women in sex work. Are you supporting prostitution? The question was shot at us by journalists and by fellow travellers in the women's movement. What the broad alliance composed of an otherwise disparate range of organizations had in common was outrage, not theoretical positions on sex work and prostitution. The government had acted in an arbitrary and inhumane manner, throwing hundreds of women and children into a precarious situation. This could not go unchallenged. That was our joint position.

Many of the organizations had no idea of the heated debates on sexual exploitation and sex work that had come to preoccupy sections of the women's movement. Is 'sex work' work? This was a potentially divisive question. We chose to sidestep it for the time being, because having these organizations with us gave us much-needed political leverage and protection. We could not afford to lose them. Instead, we talked about the rights of the *women* in sex work. We put forward what had drawn us in the first instance to identify with sex workers.

The extensive media coverage brought to public attention the sex workers' realities and their demands. Putting up front what is generally considered morally reprehensible stirred the fear of what an uncontrolled, undemarcated arena of sex work may do to the social fabric. Society was better off having these women confined in brothels. Now they were everywhere. The shift in terminology used by the print media was particularly noticeable as '*jouna kormi*' (sex worker) came to replace '*potita*' (prostitute, but literally meaning 'the fallen one'). This change in terminology actually meant that we had changed the terms of the debate so that women in prostitution could no longer be seen as objects of pity or of moral opprobrium. By renaming prostitution as sex work, women engaged in the trade could be addressed as workers who were socially acceptable rights holders.

Reframing sex work

Sex work in Bangladesh has been understood in ways that display some ambivalence. On the one hand, it is seen primarily as a function of poverty, thus evoking the standard welfare response that women need to be saved and rehabilitated into respectable marriages and occupations. On the other hand, sex work is also perceived as protecting 'good' women from sexual harassment or incursions because this army of 'bad' women provide a release for 'natural' male sexual urges. Sex workers are seen to provide a 'safety-valve' function in society. Sex work also occupies an ambivalent position in our legal framework, where soliciting and pimping are considered criminal offences, but sex work within brothels by adult women is not considered illegal. This ambivalence provided a rationale for a successful legal case against the eviction to be launched, and a landmark ruling in 1999 pronounced the eviction illegal, implicitly recognizing sex work within brothels as legal.

The success of our movement for sex workers' rights is surprising when seen in the context of the predominantly moral view of sex work and of the issue of sexuality as a whole. Even in 'progressive' political and social discourse women are placed within certain conventional frameworks within which they are expected to conduct their struggles. The struggle for sex workers' rights has the potential to overturn these established norms and conventions and redefine the boundaries of women's activism and the meaning of rights work. The campaign in their support in 1990s Bangladesh not only mobilized a whole new constituency of women for our movement, it also challenged our own concepts, views and attitudes. Our campaign questioned these 'rehabilitation' prescriptions and instead raised an agenda of 'social acceptance' involving recognizing sex work as a legitimate occupation and accepting sex workers in our midst – in our movements, in our workplaces and in our homes.

One of the groups that came forward during this campaign was a group of *Hijras* (inter-sex persons), whose main livelihood is usually sex work. This committed us to a new relationship and added a whole other dimension to our sexual rights campaign. It challenged our own adoption of the standard sex/gender concepts as fixed categories, and forced us to redefine our notion of what makes a woman. The application by inter-sex groups for membership of the national network of women's organizations started for us a process of revisiting the biology versus social construction framework that had thus far informed our thinking on gender and social change.

Reflections

Over the many cups of tea that we drank together in the Naripokkho office, we compared our lives with that of our guest sex workers, as they did theirs with ours.

> 'We wish we could send our children to good schools, like you do.'
> 'Do you enjoy the sex you have with your customers?'
> 'Do you enjoy the sex you have with your husbands? How often do you have sex?'

'Once a week, maybe once a month, once in several months ...'

What we learnt from such discussions and from our relationships with these women was that our lives are not necessarily better than the lives of sex workers, and neither are they so different. Although we might negotiate our lives in different ways, we all live within the same frame of social rules regulating our sexualities and our movements. Whether we are sex workers, wives, activists or all of these, women's bodies are the site of struggles around sexuality, reproduction, health and violence. Sex workers and *Hijras* now play an active part in Naripokkho. Members of the sex workers' organization Ulka have been elected to key positions in Doorbar, the national network of women's organizations covered by Naripokkho. And the *Hijra* organization 'Bondhon' was formally accepted into the network of women's organizations in 2003. Together we continue the struggle for sexual freedom when and where possible.

15 | Sexuality education as a human right: lessons from Nigeria

ADENIKE O. ESIET

Learning about sexuality

Learning about sexuality is a lifelong process. Messages about sexuality are communicated directly or indirectly through everyday interactions and experiences and exposure to a wide variety of sources and influences. In general, however, when the term sexuality education is used, it usually refers to a consciously planned and usually formal process of teaching about sex as a biological process. Its goals are to prepare young people for puberty and prevent unwanted pregnancies and STIs. Unfortunately, it rarely addresses the psychosocial and cultural aspects, how our sexuality affects and is affected by others, a recognition of our rights and the rights of others or even guidance on how to build mutually equitable and satisfying relationships. Providing sexuality education in ways that make the connections between rights, sexuality and development requires new approaches that cover all aspects of being a sexual and gendered person, and includes the biological, psychological, social, economical and cultural dimensions of sexuality.

The approach to sexuality education taken in this chapter emphasizes a broad approach to sexuality, focusing on the whole person and presenting sexuality as a natural and positive part of life. It is structured to address the three learning domains – cognitive, affective and behavioural – and to explore values and develop social skills, with the goal of promoting sexual health (Irvin 2006). This chapter focuses on engaging young people in learning about sexuality in Nigeria, with particular reference to those who can be reached through the formal education system as the most cost-effective mechanism for achieving universal access.

Sexuality education, human rights and development

The right to experience sexuality in health and safety is widely recognized as a fundamental human right. Access to sexuality education is recognized as a human right in a wide variety of international documents, both as a right unto itself and as related to other rights. Failure to ensure access to sexuality education violates such widely recognized rights as the right to the highest attainable standard of health and the freedom of access to information (Brocato 2005). These rights are enshrined in numerous international agreements including the African Charter on Human and Peoples' Rights (Banjul Charter), the International Covenant on Civil and Political Rights (ICCPR), the International Covenant on Economic, Social and Cultural Rights (ICESCR), the Convention on the Elimination of All Forms of Discrimination Against Women (CEDAW), and the International Conference on Population and Development Programme of Action (ICPD POA).

The ICPD POA, which addresses the sexual and reproductive rights of all people, specifically recognizes the peculiar needs of adolescents. The ICPD POA explicitly supports sexuality education: 'information and services should be made available to adolescents to help them understand their sexuality and protect themselves from unwanted pregnancies, sexually transmitted diseases, and subsequent infertility. This should be combined with the education of young men to respect women's self-determination and to share responsibility with women in matters of sexuality and reproduction' (ICPD 1994). Out of the recognition of the need for young people's access to information and services, the 179 countries that signed the ICPD POA explicitly agreed that 'countries must ensure that the programmes and attitudes of healthcare providers do not restrict the access of adolescents to appropriate services and the information they need, including on sexually transmitted diseases and sexual abuse ... ' (ICPD POA, Para 7.45).

Other conferences and agreements that have affirmed the needs of young people and their right to information, counselling and other high-quality sexual and reproductive health services include the Beijing Platform for Action, the UN World Programme of Action for Youth to the Year 2000 and Beyond, the 2001 UN General Assembly Special Session on HIV/AIDS. In March 2005, when governments convened in New York for the ten-year review of implementation of the Platform for Action agreed by the 1995 Fourth World Conference on Women (FWCW) in Beijing, they unanimously recommitted themselves to implementing both the Beijing Declaration and the Platform for Action, and also recognized the critical connection between these documents and the Millennium Development Goals (MDGs).

The eight MDGs – which range from halving extreme poverty to halting the spread of HIV/AIDS and providing universal primary education, all by the target date of 2015 – form a blueprint agreed to by the world's countries and leading development institutions. The MDGs are commonly accepted as a framework for measuring development progress and as a tool to help governments and advocates mobilize resources and implement programmes that ensure sustainable and equitable development worldwide.

Even though universal access to sexual and reproductive health services (including information) is not explicitly acknowledged as a critical component necessary for achieving all these goals, investing in sexual and reproductive health, including access to sexuality education, is inextricably linked with their achievement. This point is lucidly made in SIECUS's *Making the Connection* newsletter entitled 'The underlying Millennium Development Goal: universal access to reproductive health services' (SIECUS 2004). According to the report:

> Some of the MDGs, such as ending HIV/AIDS, obviously cannot be accomplished without addressing SRHR [sexual and reproductive health rights], yet the evidence also shows that all of the MDGs are advanced when all people have access to sexuality education, family planning, and other reproductive health services. For example, targets under MDG 5 call for a three-quarters reduction of the 1990 maternal mortality ratio by 2015; reducing early pregnancy and empowering women to space their pregnancies are necessary components of improving maternal mortality. (SIECUS 2004: 6a)

Likewise, eradicating extreme poverty and hunger (MDG 1) also relies on universal access to reproductive health services. According to a report by the Global Health Council, 'poor reproductive health among youth is a poverty issue. Low levels of youth reproductive health can and do negatively impact economic development' (Global Health Council and the William and Flora Hewlett Foundation 2004). The report goes on to explain:

> ... early pregnancy contributes to intergenerational transmission of poverty through a variety of pathways. Pregnant girls may be expelled from school, either by law or from the failure of schools to enforce the rights of girls. Without education or employable skills, unmarried pregnant girls are often poorly prepared to take on the responsibilities of childrearing and face diminishing prospects for income generation. In fact, access to education (MDG 2), the empowerment of young women and girls (MDG 3), and the eradication of poverty (MDG 1) are all interrelated.

The Millennium Development Project (MDP), an independent advisory body commissioned by the UN Secretary-General to advise the UN on strategies for achieving the MDGs, released a report described by experts as the 'cost-effective blueprint for achieving Millennium Development Goals by 2015' (UNDP 2005). The report recognizes 'sexual and reproductive health' as a key element in 'adequate human capital' for 'the means to a productive life' and that core rights include 'equal rights, including reproductive rights, for women and girls'. Also, at the macro level, ensuring SRHR correlates with positive population trends that create 'an opportunity to escape poverty traps and to accelerate economic and social development' (ibid.).

In recognition of the inextricable linkage between access to sexual and reproductive health information and services and the attainment of development goals, a few countries have taken up the challenge of addressing young people's sexual and reproductive health in line with the priorities agreed in the ICPD, Cairo, and FWCW, Beijing, documents. In Africa, the devastating effect of the HIV/AIDS epidemic on the youth population has more than anything else forced governments to take action on providing access to information and services, including Uganda, Tanzania, Zambia, South Africa and more recently Nigeria. Although these initiatives shine a ray of hope, substantial challenges still remain – poor-quality, underfunded, unevenly implemented and piecemeal programming characterizes the landscape. In fact, it has become increasingly challenging to advocate and initiate comprehensive programmes for young people in the current moral environment, where significant funding is becoming available for the institutionalization of abstinence-only programmes. A recent comparison of PEPFAR funding versus population funding in twelve PEPFAR focus countries in financial year 2006 shows that PEPFAR dwarfs the resources available to family planning and other related reproductive health/population funding (Advocates for Youth n.d.). Meanwhile these programmes ignore the science concerning effective HIV prevention for young people. Preventing young people from learning that condoms are highly effective in preventing HIV creates a culture of fear around condoms, among other things. This poor state of affairs leads one to ask, if in fact sexual and reproductive health information/services are so interconnected with achieving development goals, how ready is the development community to ensure universal access to sexuality education for young people? And what kind of sexuality education?

Prospects and challenges: lessons from Nigeria

Profile of young people's sexual and reproductive health in Nigeria More than one-fifth of Nigeria's population – 26 million young people – are now aged between ten and nineteen, and like many of their contemporaries in the developing world, they face serious threats to their sexual and reproductive well-being.

More than half of all new HIV infections occur in people under the age of twenty-five, with girls disproportionately affected. Young girls aged fifteen to nineteen are five to six times more likely to be HIV positive compared to boys the same age (Kolo 2002).

Many girls are still betrothed in their teens and about 50 per cent of girls are already married by the age of twenty (Guttmacher 2004), although there are significant regional differences in this trend, with women in southern Nigeria marrying at older ages and more able to exercise autonomy in their choice of partners. Besides violating the rights of young women, early marriage has serious health and socio-economic consequences.

Fifty-four per cent of females have given birth to a child by the age of twenty (IWHC 2006), although significant regional differences also apply. Meanwhile evidence on the ground shows that teenage mothers are twice as likely as older women to die of pregnancy-related causes and the children are more likely to die in infancy.

Hospital-based studies conducted in the 1990s in Nigeria showed that adolescents make up a disproportionately high proportion of women treated for abortion complications, between 61 and 75 per cent (Adetori et al. 1999; Adewole 1992; Okonofua 1996). A large proportion of those who become teenage mothers are also not physically, emotionally or economically prepared to care for their children and their life options are curtailed.

Young people are considered asexual: the hypocritical tabooing of young people's sexuality is a prevalent norm. Despite the fact that age at marriage is rising as opportunities for schooling expand for girls and boys, many adults refuse to acknowledge that young people are sexual beings and cannot come to terms with the compelling realities of human desire, physical attraction and sexual pleasure for adolescents.

Progress in a complex and difficult setting In Nigeria, as in many countries, open dialogue on sexuality is taboo. This is more so as a result of the multiple ethnic groups that make up the country. Also, there are many religious persuasions with Islam and Christianity being the leading two. With the advent of democracy after 29 May 1999, some northern state governments decided to enforce the *shar'ia* legal code in their states, which has contributed to increasing fundamentalism and conservatism. Of great significance too is the current PEPFAR initiative of US president George W. Bush, which supports abstinence-only sexuality education. These factors have set the stage for the federal-government-led legislative effort to ban same-sex marriages/relationships in the country.

Defying this difficult climate and direct attacks from conservative elements and fundamentalist groups, civil society organizations led by Action Health Incorporated (AHI), with support from a handful of private foundations, mounted sustained advocacy that resulted in the federal government's approval for the integration of sexuality education into the school curriculum in 1999 (AHI 2002). The quest for young people's access to sexuality education in Nigeria took a turn after AHI's participation at the MacArthur Foundation-convened meeting in Cuernavaca, Mexico, at which the SIECUS sexuality guidelines were presented. Thereafter, AHI decided to galvanize a groundswell of actors to advocate for comprehensive sexuality education in Nigeria and led the process that culminated in the development and release of the 'Guidelines for Comprehensive Sexuality Education in Nigeria' in October 1996. The guidelines, subscribed to by over eighty national organizations, became a major advocacy tool which AHI subsequently used to persuade the Federal Ministry of Education (FME) to sponsor a joint memo to Nigeria's National Council on Education (NCE) in March 1999. This joint memo got the Council to approve the integration of sexuality education into the school curriculum, following which AHI worked with the FME and the Nigerian Educational Research and Development Council (NERDC) to develop and secure approval for the 'National Sexuality Education Curriculum for Primary, Secondary and Tertiary Levels' in 2001. A major setback was witnessed in 2002, when an influential regional newspaper attacked the curriculum and created widespread reaction to its implementation. With formidable collective advocacy led by FME, AHI and other civil society organizations, however, the curriculum survived, but with the proviso that it change its name and drop some topics from the primary and junior secondary levels of the curriculum.

Today, Nigeria has the 'National Family Life and HIV/AIDS Education' curriculum approved for implementation in all states of the federation. This national policy change was a major feat, and NGO and government stakeholders have been working to translate this policy into programmes with funding allocations from government and support from development agencies. Over half of the thirty-six states in the country have commenced implementation of this curriculum, with Lagos State being the first to launch full-scale implementation from 2003.

The Family Life and HIV Education (FLHE) curriculum The FLHE curriculum seeks to foster the acquisition of factual information, formation of positive attitudes, beliefs and values, as well as development of skills to cope with the biological, psychological, sociocultural and spiritual aspects of human sexuality.

The objectives of the curriculum are to ensure the promotion of preventive education by providing learners with opportunities:

- to develop a positive and factual view of self;
- to acquire the information and skills needed to take care of health, including preventing HIV/AIDS;
- to respect and value themselves and others; and
- to acquire the skills needed to make healthy decisions about sexual health and behaviour.

The curriculum is structured in such a way that it provides a framework for the acquisition of knowledge of self and family living from childhood to adulthood. Over thirty topics, including anatomy and physiology of the human reproductive system, puberty, body image, love, friendship, values, self-esteem, negotiation, STIs/HIV, abstinence, contraception, sexual abuse, gender roles, sexuality and diversity, sexuality and religion and sexuality and the media, are organized around six themes as follows:

- Human development;
- Personal skills;
- Sexual health;
- Relationships;
- Sexual behaviour;
- Society and culture.

Each theme covers knowledge, attitudes and the necessary skills that are age-appropriate for the different levels of education, with special emphasis on ensuring that the FLHE curriculum's content is learner-oriented and pupil-centred, as the many activities are geared towards making learning practical. The content is spirally arranged so that there is continuity and increasing depth of content as the student moves from one level to the other, and the curriculum as structured leads to the comprehensive coverage of the topics listed and achievement of intended learning outcomes.

Over the last three years, Lagos State Ministry of Education, in partnership with AHI and with funding from the Ford Foundation, has implemented the curriculum in 304 public junior secondary schools in Lagos State, trained 90 per cent of the relevant subject teachers and reached 314,666 students aged ten to fourteen years. To evaluate and document the curriculum's effectiveness a concurrent evaluation component is supported by the MacArthur Foundation to track programme implementation outcomes and impact.

Kirby et al. (2005) identified seventeen common characteristics of effective sexuality/HIV programmes and found that programmes with a majority of these characteristics were much more likely to have an impact on behaviour than those with fewer characteristics. Of these seventeen characteristics, fourteen were found to be positive for the FLHE curriculum, two were not applicable and one is yet to be determined.

Preliminary findings from the programme's evaluation also show significant progress in students' knowledge and attitudes regarding their sexuality, particularly on taking care of their sexual health, increased knowledge about pregnancy and HIV prevention, and the rights of girls and boys to refuse unwanted sexual advances. Other important lessons learnt from the programme's evaluation so far are that:

- teacher training equipped the teachers with the right vocabulary and methodology to facilitate students' learning;
- adequate and understandable materials aided students' knowledge; and
- parents and community support reinforced students' learning (Lagos State Ministry of Education et al. 2005).

Participating FLHE-trained teachers attest to the fact that students are active participants in FLHE classes. This is captured in this contribution by a teacher in one of the focus group discussions (FGDs):

> ... they [students] really enjoy the topics though at times when we start the topic they pretend as if they don't [get] what we are talking about. But by the time you [the teacher] become more friendly and familiar they start to open up. (Education District III, Epe Zone, teacher)

The following contribution from one of the young women participants in the programme suggests she finds FLHE beneficial because

> When you start your menstruation you will know what will happen ... even if our parents don't tell us, we know what to do since we've learnt it in school and we can take care of ourselves. (Education District IV, Surulere Zone)

To test students' level of knowledge and understanding of key concepts taught in the FLHE curriculum, at the start of each FGD students were asked to list key words or talk about whatever they could readily remember from previous lessons. In their spontaneous contributions and through the course of the FGDs, 'abstinence' and 'condoms' were the most frequently mentioned words. This strongly indicates that despite the colossal investments made in abstinence-only programmes in Nigeria, young people themselves have consistently incorporated condoms as another sure way to prevent HIV and other STIs.

Challenges

Formidable challenges, however, face the sustained success of the sexuality education programme being implemented in Nigeria.

Underfunded and poor-quality programming: although several other Nigerian states have commenced the FLHE curriculum implementation through the education system, problems are rife with the uneven levels of intervention and the scale of implementation. Limited access to funds has made it impossible to train an adequate number of teachers, produce training aids and provide students with reference materials. In some states funding allocation provides programme coverage for only up to 5 per cent of the school attending population.

Politicization of the sexuality education programme: an ideological agenda is being advanced by the public denigration of the FLHE curriculum in the mass media by a few vocal fundamentalists. Religious uproar from the northern Nigerian, *shar'ia* states led to a change in the name of the initial curriculum from sexuality education to FLHE three years ago. Recently too the federal and Lagos State governments were sued over offering the FLHE curriculum in public schools by two right-wing NGOs.

A divergent approach being exported with international aid: with Nigeria being a PEPFAR focus country, the political and financial pressure to adopt abstinence-until-marriage programming as a condition of receiving US aid is the major battle that advocates and programme implementers are having to deal with right now. Advocates are concerned that the progress made to date with the national curriculum might be undermined as the present US administration doles out funds to a favoured constituency that supports teaching only abstinence, marriage and fidelity as HIV-preventive measures, as well as other groups who may be swayed to toe this line in order to secure desperately needed funds.

The challenges described above are not peculiar to Nigeria; underresourcing, politicization and divergent approaches to programming are common trends in the landscape of sexual and reproductive health across Africa, and this scenario needs to be addressed proactively (Donor Group on Adolescent Sexual and Reproductive Health and Development n.d.).

Conclusion

Assuring a sexually healthy society is a collective responsibility. It involves all units of society, including the family, state and state actors, as well as the international community. At the global level, despite the overwhelming evidence on how the promotion of SRHR will help the attainment of the MDGs, SRHR is not yet considered central to the MDGs. The lesson here is that we must continue to draw inspiration from the work of other activists, especially the feminist movement, as we strive to ensure that SRHR is recognized as being central to the attainment of the MDGs.

To advance the agenda of universal access to sexuality education for young people, funding from the development community needs to address the following strategic areas.

Advocacy in support of sexuality education: sustained advocacy to get governments and other stakeholders to allocate resources and translate international and national agreements to operational programmes in-country. Advocacy is also required to counter the public propaganda and attacks on sexuality education programmes by fundamentalists and well-funded opponents who seek to replace these programmes with their own brand of inaccurate information and scare tactics that research has proved ineffective.

Upholding basic guidelines for content and approach: while recognizing that the content and approach of sexuality education programmes may vary depending on the context and setting, development work must ensure that programmes continue to promote a positive perspective. Programming also has to expand beyond focusing on ill health, violence and exploitation to address human desire, diversity in physical attraction and sexual pleasure as compelling realities for adolescents.

Capacity-building for teachers and education administrators: investments need to be made in quality pre-service and in-service training of teachers to equip them with the requisite knowledge, attitude and skills to teach sexuality. Provision also needs to be made for opportunities for ongoing support beyond the initial basic training because it requires practice, feedback, supervision and refresher training to develop expertise in sexuality education.

Development of resource materials: implementation of programmes will be greatly enhanced with the availability of sufficient quantities of appropriate-quality teachers' and students' reference materials and learning aids.

Scale-up is key to success: improving the sexual health of young people in developing countries requires commitment to large-scale national-level programming. There is an urgent need to move away from piecemeal funding to investing in the scale-up of pilots that have proved effective in the community in order to ensure equitable access to sexuality education and achievement of the MDGs.

Assuring young people's access to sexuality education in Nigeria continues to be a very daunting task, and although much has been accomplished, much more still needs to be accomplished to reap the full benefits of such universal access to ensuring sexual health and well-being.

References

Adetori, O. O. et al. (1999) 'Socio-cultural factors in adolescent sceptic illicit abortion in Ilorin, Nigeria', *African Journal of Medicine and Medical Sciences*, 20(20): 149–53.

Adewole, I. F. (1992) 'Trends in postabortal mortality and mobility in Ibadan, Nigeria', *International Journal of Gynaecology and Obstetrics*, 38(2): 115–18.

Advocates for Youth (n.d.) 'Improving US global AIDS policy for young people: assessing the President's Emergency Plan for AIDS Relief (PEPFAR)', <www.advocatesforyouth.org/publications/pepfar.pdf> (accessed 13 February 2006).

AHI (Action Health Incorporated) (2002) 'Building alliances for sexuality education: the community advocacy project, Nigeria', Lagos: Action Health Incorporated.

Brocato, V. (2005) *Establishing National Guide for Comprehensive Sexuality Education: Lessons Learnt from Nigeria*, New York: SIECUS.

Donor Group on Adolescent Sexual and Reproductive Health and Development (n.d.) *Investing in Youth: A Donor Guide*, <www.fundersnet.org/resources/docs/donorguideASRHD.pdf> (accessed 19 June 2007).

Global Health Council and the William and Flora Hewlett Foundation (2004) *Commitments: Youth Reproductive Health, the World Bank, and the Millennium Development Goals*, Washington, DC: Global Health Council and the William and Flora Hewlett Foundation.

Guttmacher (2004) *Early Childbearing in Nigeria: A Continuing Challenge*, <www.guttmacher.org/pubs/rib/2004/12/10/rib2-04.pdf> (accessed 13 February 2006).

ICPD (International Conference on Population and Development) (1994) 'Reproductive rights and reproductive health', Summary of Programme of Action, ch. 7, <www.un.org/ecosocdev/geninfo/populatin/icpd.htm#chapter8> (accessed 3 March 2006).

Irvin, A. (2006) *Taking Steps of Courage: Teaching Adolescents about Sexuality and Gender in Nigeria and Cameroon*, New York: International Women's Health Coalition.

IWHC (International Women's Health Coalition) (2006) *Get the Facts: Nigeria*, <www.iwhc.org/programs/africa/nigeria/facts.cfm?language=1> (accessed 3 March 2006).

Kirby, D., B. A. Laris and L. Rolleri (2005) 'Impact of sex and HIV education programs on sexual behaviors of youth in developing and developed countries', *Youth Research Working Paper Series*, Durham, NC: Family Health International.

Kolo, S. A. (2002) *Basic Facts about*

HIV/AIDS, Trend in Nigeria and Challenges, Paper presented by Dr Salma Anas Kolo, Lagos: NASCP for Federal Ministry of Health.

Lagos State Ministry of Education, AHI, Phillibers Research Associates and IWHC (2005) *Family Life and HIV/AIDS Education Programme in Lagos State, Nigeria*, Lagos and New York: Lagos State Ministry of Education, AHI, Phillibers Research Associates and IWHC, December.

Okonofua, F. E. (1996) *Critical Issues in Reproductive Health: Women's Experiences of Unwanted Pregnancy and Induced Abortion*, New York: Population Council.

SIECUS (2004) *Making the Connection – News and Views on Sexuality: Education, Health and Rights*, 3(2), <http://63.73.227.69/inter/connection/conn0044.html> (accessed 3 March 2006).

UNDP (United Nations Development Programme) (2005) *Investing in Development: A Practical Plan to Achieve the Millennium Development Goals*, <www.unmp.forumone.com/eng_full_report/TF1mainreportComplete-highres.pdf> (accessed 31 January 2005).

16 | Terms of contact and touching change: investigating pleasure in an HIV epidemic

JILL LEWIS AND GILL GORDON[1]

'sex ... to be desired/to desire/to want someone to desire, to feel desired ... to come to pleasure/to be brought to pleasure/to bring to pleasure ... bodies in motion, people touching each other ...'

Factual information, dire data and warnings, and what *not* to do are often all that people hear about sex. There is little in all this to anchor sexual connections in real situations and real bodies. For many people, pleasure – or concerns and fears about its absence – is part of what they hope to experience when they have sex. So, exploring issues of pleasure is a critically important part of discussions about safer sex. But talking about pleasure means more than just reeling off facts about pleasure zones and sexual acts. It calls for addressing deep-seated cultural norms, taken-for-granted ideas about how the body works, and assumptions about what it means to be a 'real man' or a 'real woman'. It also calls for contextualizing the ways in which women and men talk about, negotiate and have sex in different settings, and in relation to the negotiations and power relations that characterize their everyday lives and intimate relationships.

Western-led commercialization of 'techniques' and the mechanics of satisfaction, and profit-driven media narratives of the quest for personal pleasure, are riddled with problems when set on a wider international and cross-cultural map, let alone within Western societies themselves. In Soweto, with over 80 per cent unemployment, harsh daily conditions of poverty, one in four or more infected with HIV and research showing violence widely normalized in sex with women, television has arrived with Westernized advertising images of sexualized glamour, stereotypes of desirable bodies and a sex-rich formula as the main 'hold' for soaps, films and advertising. In the dry dust of sparse survival among thousands and thousands of barrack-like, apartheid-era dwellings, the good life is imaged with sexy models and scenarios of affluence, where Viagra billboards loom beside Marlboro advertisements. In impoverished, post-Soviet Tallinn in Estonia, fifteen-year-old teenagers reeled off the porn sites they frequented, insisted on setting role-play workshops in a longed-for San Francisco world and dreamed of the *Pretty Woman* film's 'way out', i.e. via sex work, to love and wealth with the unknown Westerner. The free market promises a certain kind of pleasure, with a curious yet insistent absence of sexual risk or sexual safety.

Pleasure is inherently ambivalent. Working with pleasure, but also in ways that bring into question embodied gender prejudices and inequalities, is challenging. But it is also crucially important. In this chapter, we explore how and why pleasure matters for efforts to tackle the spread of HIV and the effects of the AIDS epidemic on social and sexual relations.

Sexual contexts

Context shapes sexualities and sexual encounters; attitudes and images of sexual behaviour are shaped by social conditions, producing self-perceptions that affect people's confidence, their perception of their own desirability, their gender and sexual sense of self, and the way they perceive the agendas of the opposite sex, the sexual agency they feel appropriate, their hopes and their despair. The terrain of sexual experience is permeated by all the other social and human factors that frame the specific encounter where bodies meet. Emotional dynamics around the physicality of sex are affected by the situation people are coming from, the terms of living (or dying) they are navigating, the affirmation of caring or re-enactment of control or abuse, and the relationship that they are in; these in turn are affected by and affect the economics of everyday life.

Pleasure itself can be defined in different ways. If your children or grandparents are starving or ill, if you are unemployed or poor, if you are in a conflict zone far from home, then a paid sexual encounter could be joyful, not because of actual physical or emotional satisfaction, but because you are accessing possibilities of affirmation. If the sex is consolidating the support you need to give you and your children respect in a community, the pleasure can be in the confirmation of the pact. If you are far from home in risky conflict situations, far from the intimacies of family or community, living in discomfort, facing the unknowns of danger, injury or death, under pressure to keep up a 'front' in mostly male company, then the pleasure of sex with a local woman, enabled by financial exchange, may not be just about orgasm, but involve a whole range of reassurances and comfort. If you are living through a civil war, with collapsed social infrastructure, widespread abject poverty and minimal family resources, and violence in the home, your sexual experience with the older sugar daddy (who is enabling your only possible access to education, as a girl) may also be the kindest, most pleasuring relation you have. If the necessity of work or trading takes you away from home, boredom, loneliness and curiosity can draw you into private exploratory pleasures not necessarily condoned back home. If you live in a community scarred by HIV and AIDS, the greatest pleasure may be gained by knowing *how* your exploring sexual pleasure has absolutely no chance of getting you infected, or infecting your partner.

The diversity of reasons why people actually 'have sex' or imagine others having sex surfaces in our workshops in marvellous variety. Satisfaction and pleasure are named by participants everywhere as a key reason for sexual relations. But the list of reasons often expands wildly. In contexts as diverse as the Congo or Azerbaijan, Liberia or Georgia, people have sex, participants have suggested:

> out of a 'natural need'; marital duty or fear of abandonment; owing to the need to perform and prove yourself; because you have no choice; business; education funding; fear of violence; self-esteem-boosting; boredom; kindness and generosity; pity; fear that the man's balls will burst or he will go mad; worn down by constant demand; to be allowed to sleep; to have children; to feel powerful; for exercise; self-affirmation; love; fear of coercion; for revenge; because there are electricity cuts at night; to gain experience; to get work or power; to lose weight; as proof of commitment; to prove trust; for cheap or no-cost enjoyment; to live up to peer pressure; to de-stress and relax the body; to prove you are a real man; because you cannot sleep; to reduce tension in the home; to share intimacy; to get support from your partner; from fear of threats if you resist; for fun; for no reason at all; to keep healthy; out of fear of loneliness; to further your career; to get good grades; to make someone else angry; because of poverty; as a bet; to feel young; to get what you cannot get at home; to feel powerful; out of a long friendship; to get pregnant; to gain stature or prestige; just because it feels good ...

And so the list goes on. Presumably the possibility and nature of 'pleasure' are utterly different in all these situations; equally, the very terms of sexual safety are affected and modified by these very situations and motivations.

Learning about pleasure

Every culture offers maps for learning ways to understand and express desire and ways to project on to or interpret the sexual desire and actions of the other sex. In all cultures, the institution of marriage itself, with the patriarchal and religious traditions, discourses and regulations from which it has evolved, plays a key role in the mapping, categorizing and often disallowing of pleasure. Ideas about what a 'real' woman or man should want or do are rife in all cultures, and affect perceptions of what the opposite sex wants or needs – often in ways that are unhelpful, misleading and unsafe. Unquestioned, taken-for-granted gender systems hold in place ignorance of the body; they create silences between men and women about sexual desire and practice or collaboration in creating pleasure. What individual men or women think of as sexual knowledge is often comprised of a mosaic of half-truths, fragmented information, myths and beliefs, punctuated with doubt and hesitations. These have a huge impact on the possibilities of pleasure, as indeed on the possibilities of condom use or non-penetrative sex.

Notions of sexual pleasure are laced with these half-truths and beliefs. Ancient myths and traditions in northern Norway gave central importance to women's sexual pleasure, with stories of younger partners receiving active instruction from older women. In parts of Zambia the traditional initiation processes for girls take them through demanding, explicit and required learning about exactly what to do sexually with men. The training, run by older women, involves practising rhythmic gyrations with the bodies of other girls, and disciplinary action for getting the movements wrong or lacking enthusiasm. How is sexual pleasure for men and for women being imagined and sought in this context? And what are the men, for their part, learning to do? Women in Sierra Leone, from cultural and social contexts that still enact female circumcision, were, in workshops, full of innuendo and laughter about the pleasures of sex – so what can be learned from *their* map of sexual pleasure? How do American teenagers taking the silver-ring, abstinence-until-marriage pledges backed by the Bush administration's abstinence agenda, in which any discussion of actual sexual practices, let alone pleasure, is silenced, understand sexual pleasure? Or binge-drinking teenagers in Britain today?

The truth of the matter is that you experience pleasure according to what you have heard about it and according to the particular situation within which you seek or achieve – or bluff – it. In workshops involving teacher trainers, ministry representatives, NGOs and school principals in Monrovia, Liberia, the men were unanimous in putting sexual pleasure top of the reasons why people have sex. The pleasure idea was wedded to the idea of climax and release, ejaculation and orgasm. But for them, men's wish for pleasure, many said, also involved women's sexual pleasure (the women watched silently as this was claimed). But when asked when or how a woman experiences pleasure, the only explanation offered and agreed on by the men was: when the man's juices meet the women's juices, she climaxes. While the women shook their heads and laughed (and the HIV prevention educator digested the implications of this 'common knowledge'), discussion opened up about women not having orgasms more often (and faking it). Interest surfaced in more diffuse forms of pleasure through intimacy, not just penetration, as well as a wider curiosity in the group to understand better the ways in which men's and women's bodies work.

It is exactly this kind of talk, and the openness associated with it, which conservative religious forces seek to silence. What percentage of sexual interactions between partners in a lifetime is motivated by the reproductive necessity that religions put centre stage in the marriage pact? Can the abstinence/fidelity pattern meet the ideas of sexual pleasure more creatively? Or do certain religious frameworks need to deny rights to sexual pleasure and regulate all sexual possibilities, since the meeting of sexual desires, the embodiment of sexual pleasure and satisfaction, is not part of the religious, moral and spiritual framework? What alternative, affirming, understandings of sexuality are possible within Christian frameworks? More participants in religion and sexual health HIV prevention work need to be exploring these questions more clearly – and not antagonistically, where possible, but with the aim of real interventions in sexual safety and to meet the real urgency of stemming HIV. And, of course, many are.

From another angle, public norms of marriage and the family coexist often with social banter about sex and flirtation that belies the pressures that work against the very pleasures that the daily banter invokes. Under jokes and media liberalism, innuendoes, rumours and myths lie a plethora of taboos, silences, insecurities, anxieties and policed reputations within youth and adult peer groups. Pressures on sexual behaviours – to do or not do certain things – take all kinds of forms. In the West, there is a taboo in the dominant culture about *not* desiring or liking engaging in sex or in wanting to get married. In some cultures a man abusing a woman with violence is understood as a key part of 'loving' and wanting her. There are prescriptions about 'doing it right', and there can be punishments for not adhering to the rules.

The challenge facing us in sexual health and safety work is that the understanding, anticipation and thus enactment of pleasure are crucially affected by people's sense of self 'as a woman' or 'as a man'. Sexual norms assign different licence, powers, possibilities and constraints for men and for women, positioning men and women in certain ways in relation to sexual interactions. And while there are distinctive similarities across cultures, there are important differences. Imposing Western norms on non-Western cultures not only misses the mark, it may make discussing – and changing – mores and practices that *do* make a difference to sexual safety and pleasure more difficult.

Sexual rights and pleasure

The notion of 'sexual rights' raises interesting challenges in relation to sexual pleasure. Equal rights regarding sexuality can be seen as crucial to establishing conditions for equal access to sexual pleasure. Discussions on sexual rights migrate in two directions, both of which skew the issue. The first involves placing priority on women's right to say 'no', to set limits on what is unnamed, but somehow assumed to be an inevitable male agenda of demands or 'needs'. So for women it is about the right *not* to be sexual unless fully wanting it, holding men in abeyance. But this means that the sexual rights debate does often represent women's sexuality as restrictive and limiting – if not *limited* – in contrast to the assumption of men's 'natural' urges. At an AIDSnett meeting on gender and HIV in Oslo, an Ethiopian man participant asked the haunting question: 'But what are *men's* sexual rights?' It was a question unanswered by the women-centred, traditional gender-equality, development-work participants. Yet the question raised a crucial issue about not only how women's diverse sexual desires are understood (and engaged with) but also how men's bodies and desires are understood; about what is understood to be normal if not necessary for men, and about ways boys and men learn to conceptualize pleasure and to interpret and exploit their bodies.

Whether in England or Burundi, Norway or Zambia, it is often an essentialist biological discourse about male sexuality which is invoked as a given truth – but never examined in detail. 'We all know what men want/need' often feeds an unspoken undertow of assumptions. And this often locks men into the relentless but necessary quest for penetration of women – with the underside being that if you do not do this, do not seek this out, do not situate yourself socially with some kind of proof that you do this, do not go along with the boys' banter that reproduces this assumption, you may not be a 'real man'. And your pleasure depends on you doing this. So does a man have a right to have his sexual needs met; to have his pleasure satisfied? And if so, how are these sexual needs, this pleasure, understood; what shapes them? What compels them to be expressed in certain ways and not in others? Are commonly held and unquestioned notions of male sexual pleasure anchored in legitimizing performance of a masculinity that is in fact predicated on male power, control and naturalized gender inequality – and a performance that in fact limits notions of male sexual pleasure to very narrowly channelled acts?

The other way in which sexual rights discourse is often invoked is to affirm women's rights to have sexual pleasure. This reflects the fact that men's rights to achieve sexual pleasure on their own terms has often prevailed over the neglect or devaluing of women's sexual pleasure. Sexual conventions are often shadowed by silence, taboos and rituals of behaviour that occur without sustained building of intimacy. In a workshop on HIV prevention with male immigrants from Ethiopia and Somalia, the men were deeply interested and engaged in learning very clearly how, where and why the virus circulates, and engaged with the white female facilitators for hours with debate and questions. But at the end, there was a shared lament between them that it felt impossible to open up these discussions with their wives, since cultural taboos on seeing or speaking about the body felt so immutable. Maybe it all just needs more time; after all, effective sexual health and well-being processes always need longer than administrations and funding envisage. In contrast, male security guards, drivers, administrators and teacher trainers in conflict-ridden areas around Goma, Congo, and Gulu, Uganda, and from different IDP regions in Georgia, reported with joy how the gender-focused HIV awareness workshops had in fact generated hours of utterly new levels of dialogue between husbands and wives, parents and children.

The question of sexual rights raises further issues which relate to the institution in which sex and sexual pleasure are socially sanctioned: heterosexual marriage. Conventional marriage expectations are that sexual needs will be 'organized', and met or serviced within the marriage, the supposed lifetime pact. But what happens to 'needs' when relationships develop incompatibility or hostility, when people and situations change, when age and status, strength and confidence shift? Are sexual rights and sexual pleasures simply to be abandoned; frozen? Or is the language of 'needs to be met' and 'rights to be fulfilled' radically off key, dissociating sexual pleasure from social context and insulating it from the tides of ordinary daily lives? Does it foster the notions: She has the right to refuse, therefore I have the right to go elsewhere, or: He does not satisfy me, therefore I can look outside? How can we work constructively and compassionately with the disjuncture between sexual expectations and the contextual realities of real relations, real bodies in real-life situations of survival and children, to maximize the possibility of pleasure being a real and 'sustainable' possibility within human relationships? Or is it important to also argue that sexual pleasure needs to exist on its own terms, for its own sake, irrespective of context and relational dynamic – less as a 'right' than as *pleasure*, in and for itself?

Transforming sexual behaviour – pleasure and safety

How can we invoke the importance of pleasure in ways that are not distant or dissociated from the experiences people face in their actual, lived bodies and lives, and use this to transform sexual behaviour? As Western media globalize the neuroses of Western sex-consumerism culture, this is becoming ever more difficult. In a workshop with Muslim youth volunteer trainers in Azerbaijan, a young man made a telling comment. He said that in his grandmother's time, women were valued for what they could do; in today's world, women are valued (and value themselves) according to their looks. All over the world, women are increasingly driven to valuing themselves and being valued according to stereotypes of attractiveness. Slim girls in Nepal buy slimming pills from the pharmacy. Girls have transactional sex to buy the clothes and cosmetics needed to be beautiful. The sexual health narratives being exported from Western cultures are riddled with problems that risk blocking and disempowering, rather than enabling change.

Addressing pleasure in sexual safety work poses many challenges for working with the mind as well as the body – in the actual contexts people are experiencing. It involves working collaboratively to examine the assumptions that influence people's ideas about sexual behaviour, and creating an interest and a sense of investment in seeing and acting differently which become part of their lives. To realize the potential power of pleasure, sexual health and HIV-prevention work needs to bring alive the dynamic edges between the erotic, the experimental and the exploratory. It needs to open up compassionate conversations about the challenges and gains of dialogue, relationship, caring and empathy. It needs to open up discussion of cultural stories; mapping of sexuality, religious prescriptions and boundaries; the familiar, unquestioned behaviours; traditional approaches to or actual acts of sexual engagement; the realities of socially anchored options, decisions, activities and exchanges. Engaging people dynamically in becoming practitioners of and activists for sexual safety calls for confronting issues of morality in a non-judgemental way, opening up space for dialogue.

We need more cross-fertilization of dialogue and more research about diverse cultural expectations concerning the sexual satisfaction of women. The issue of women's pleasure is still complicated in Western cultures, despite our sex-ridden media. Female orgasm remains shrouded in elusive complexities. Recent research suggests that gendered framing of self-in-the-world is key to women claiming and implementing their own pleasure. Its unresolved inequalities and sexual divisions of labour and power haunt female satisfaction. In the realities of everyday gendered dynamics and domestic worries and tensions, whether in rural Ghana or urban Georgia, women can close down – and men, unable to navigate these domestic irresolvables, can always, it is thought, go elsewhere. This serves to reinforce the polarizations of the domestic and the erotic, where women's sexuality can lose out in more ways than one.

Sexual safety and HIV-prevention work also needs to open up discussion of how the regulation of pleasure is understood in different cultures, how people visualize it and what stories give it meaning. Take, for example, different narratives about sexual fluids in Africa. In some parts of the Congo, Rwanda and Mali, a woman's wetness signifies her arousal and proves her pleasure. In parts of Zambia and South Africa, however, the wetness of a woman's genital area is interpreted not as a sign of anticipated pleasure, but as a reason to not seek sexual interaction with her: as a sign of her promiscuity and her potential for carrying an STI. 'Dry sex' practices prevail, which increase HIV risk through bleeding from insertions into the vagina to dry and tighten it. Resistance to using condoms often invokes the image of liquids needing to meet to achieve 'real' intimacy. Teenage girls in Estonia believed condom restriction actually blocked men's sexual satisfaction, so why would a woman who wants to please her man want to impede this mingling of fluids?

There are data in many countries showing men wanting untrammelled delivery of their sperm into women's bodies, when they pay extra for sex workers not to use condoms. Men in the Congo claimed their delivery of sexual fluid into a woman saved them from insanity, and men in Liberia felt their ejaculation into women's sexual fluids gave women orgasm. A Finnish study showed how men facing age-associated fluctuating impotence and who were insecure about their ability to reach ejaculation inside women's bodies cut off all intimate exchange with their partners – the fluid delivery being the *raison d'être* of intimate pleasure exchange. The fragile edges of pride, anxiety, humiliation and rejection that haunt traditional masculinities bear sad fruit. But semen is also associated with life and growth. In the Gambia, semen absorption during pregnancy is understood to help the fetus to grow, so ejaculative climax is linked to a visualization of life force. In a part of Papua New Guinea, oral consumption of the semen of older fertile men is thought to fertilize sperm in young men.

The ways people visualize the workings of the sexual body are key in the imaginary geography of what sex is or needs to be about, of how and why pleasure needs to or can be achieved – and are thus crucial in sexual safety and HIV-prevention discussions. Taking these visualizations and understandings and turning them into safer acts and behaviours that people can then begin to invest in and act out calls for more than providing information; it requires an approach that can delve into the normative, the emotional, the biological and enable people to come up with strategies that make sense in the context of their everyday lives.

Building capacity for sexual health, safety and rights

If efforts to build capacity for sexual health, safety and rights are to work to mobilize prevention of HIV, then some clear, central agendas need to be developed. There is no substitute for giving people the facts about their bodies in ways that are clear, which allow them to visualize what they are learning and which come to make sense to them in terms of their own bodily experiences and cultural knowledge. Nor can change happen without enabling people to explore gender traditions and reappraise their enabling or damaging dimensions. Learning processes that give people an embodied realization of their own capacity for agency, mobilization, assumption of responsibility and the will to communicate are pivotal. And finally, the work has to include discussions of sex and pleasure, sex and delight, *sex as sexy*, forms of pleasing and being pleased. It needs to acknowledge that pleasure is part of why many people have sex, and that knowing what needs to happen for HIV or other STIs to pass from body to body is a crucial starting point for exploring how to create pleasure without risking infection, and the conscious cultivation of pleasure in diverse ways. To do this involves new modes of communication, responsibility, collaboration, eroticism and caring that *are* at odds with the traditional configurations of the heterosexual pact that is laden with gender inequality histories and contemporary norms.

Embracing erotic diversities has never been a component of mainstream heterosexual sexual safety or HIV training initiatives. But we need to partner greater discussion of erotic possibilities with critical interrogations in order to identify negative consequences of sexuality – health damage, hurt, death and injustice. We need to invent ways to stem the damage and facilitate relational interactions that are on the side of life – well-being, pleasure, happiness, justice, decency, collaboration, affirmation – and the exploration of desire. There is no blueprint for pleasure here. We have to hold in mind an awareness that the sexual exchanges are always within the social realities that pressure them one way or another, but emerge from the conditions, possibilities, (in)securities, fears and incentives, needs and hopes that frame where people are living and what they are aspiring to.

Note

1 This chapter was generated by a dialogue between the authors on the issues and questions that they encountered in their sexual health, rights and safety work in diverse cultural contexts over many years. It is a response to their desire to bring the authentic voices of men and women from many different communities into the discussion on pleasure, rather than a research article. See Lewis (2002, 2003), Gordon and Cornwall (2004) and Lewis and Clift (2001) for more information on this work, and tools that others can use to facilitate their own conversations on sexuality, gender and pleasure.

References

Gordon, G. and A. Cornwall (2004) 'Participation in sexual and reproductive well-being and rights', *Participatory Learning and Action*, 50: 73–80, London: International Institute for Environment and Development.

Lewis, J. (2002) *Mobilising Gender Issues: Report from the Living for Tomorrow Project on Youth, Gender and HIV/AIDS Prevention*, Oslo: Nordisk Institutt for Kvinne-og Kjønnsforskning (NIKK), <www.nikk.uio.no/forskning/nikk/living/1ft_pubtext_e.html> (accessed 24 July 2006).

— (2003) *Gendering Prevention Practices. A Practical Guide to Working with Gender in Sexual Safety and HIV/AIDS Awareness Education*, Oslo: Nordisk Institutt for Kvinne-og Kjønnsforskning (NIKK), <www.nikk.uio.no/forskning/nikk/living/1ft_pubtext_e.html> (accessed 24 July 2006).

Lewis, J. and S. Clift (2001) *Challenging Gender Issues: Report on Findings from the Living for Tomorrow Project about Young Men's and Young Women's Attitudes to Men, Women and Sex*, Oslo: Nordisk Institutt for Kvinne-og Kjønnsforskning (NIKK), <www.nikk.uio.no/forskning/nikk/living/1ft_pubtext_e.html> (accessed 24 July 2006).

17 | A democracy of sexuality: linkages and strategies for sexual rights, participation and development

HENRY ARMAS

Development agencies have traditionally regarded the links between economic growth, poverty and sexuality in very narrow terms, to be addressed through strategies for birth control and HIV prevention. Sexual rights have been regarded as secondary to the important matters of housing, education, employment and so on. Issues of sexuality and sexual pleasure have received barely any attention at all. This chapter asks: what do sexuality, sexual rights and sexual pleasure have to do with growth, citizenship, participation and rights?

In the first section, I will explore the linkages between sexuality, rights and poverty and suggest that the relationship between sexual rights and well-being and development needs to be given greater attention by development agencies. In the second part, I will show how participatory approaches can be a valid strategy for the inclusion of sexual rights, well-being and pleasure in the development agenda. Yet, as I suggest, these issues face conceptual and practical difficulties, and raise a number of challenges that need to be overcome. Making sexuality count calls for a commitment to a democracy of sexuality, one that can make real the promise of participation, citizenship and rights for all.

Sexuality, rights and development

Although sexuality and sexual pleasure are not defined as basic needs, they have echoes in every aspect of life and should be considered in the development agenda. Rights are a clear entry point for talking about sexuality in relation to development; a rights-based approach makes these connections more evident.

Since the 1990s, the rights-based approach has became a crucial element in development discourses, policies and practices, continuing a previous process of work with international human rights, with new actors and strategies. For the United Nations system, a human-rights-based approach implies that:

1 All programmes of development cooperation, policies and technical assistance should further the realization of human rights as laid down

in the Universal Declaration of Human Rights and other international human rights instruments.

2 Human rights standards contained in, and principles derived from, the Universal Declaration of Human Rights and other international human rights instruments guide all development cooperation and programming in all sectors and in all phases of the programming process.

3 Development cooperation contributes to the development of the capacities of duty-bearers to meet their obligations and/or of rights-holders to claim their rights. (United Nations 2003)

Despite the fact that there are many rights-based approaches and practices, some common elements can be identified (Marks 2005: 102):

- express linkage to rights;
- accountability;
- empowerment;
- participation;
- non-discrimination and attention to vulnerable groups.

Sexual rights and rights-based development

What do sexual rights have to do with human rights and the rights-based approach?

- Sexual rights have a clear relationship with *human rights*. Principles of integrality and indivisibility require us to see sexual rights as inter-dependent with rights to health, housing, food or employment.
- Sexual rights enable people to demand *accountability* from power holders regarding the most personal and intimate dimensions of their lives.
- Sexual rights not only *empower* people regarding their own decisions about their sexual lives, but also generate self-esteem, a new perception of citizenship, control over their own lives in other spaces such as, health, education, employment, etc.
- Sexual rights increase *inclusion*, *representation* and the degree of *democratic engagement* people can have with the decisions that affect their lives.
- Sexual rights make visible *discriminated and vulnerable groups* that remain unnoticed by development agencies and governments in general programmes and actions.
- Sexual rights are not only related with sexual and reproductive health projects, but are an important element to take into account in a wider strategy to tackle *poverty*.

211

Sexual rights have a variety of definitions. The Platform for Action from the 1995 Beijing Conference on Women affirms:

Paragraph 96. The human rights of women include their right to have control over and decide freely and responsibly on matters related to their sexuality, including sexual and reproductive health, free of coercion, discrimination and violence. Equal relationships between women and men in matters of sexual relations and reproduction, including full respect for the integrity of the person, require mutual respect, consent and shared responsibility for sexual behaviour and its consequences.

Sweden has used this paragraph as the applicable definition of women's sexual rights (Ministry for Foreign Affairs, Sweden 2006: 7). Furthermore, Sweden considers that sexual rights include already recognized human rights, for example the right to private life (UN Universal Declaration of Human Rights, Article 16) and personal safety (UN Convention on the Elimination of All Forms of Racial Discrimination, Article 5b). It is a fundamental principle of human rights that one individual's rights must not encroach on those of another. In sexual relations or matters concerning sexuality and reproduction, personal and physical integrity must be respected. In light of this, the Swedish government defines sexual rights as meaning that all people, irrespective of sex, age, ethnicity, disability, gender identity or sexual orientation, have a right to their own body and sexuality. There is also the general human rights principle of non-discrimination on sexual or other grounds, such as sexual orientation or gender identity.

In *Sexual and Reproductive Health and Rights: A Position Paper* (DfID 2004) there is no specific definition of sexual rights. Despite mention that sexual and reproductive health is an essential element of good health and human development, and important as an issue in itself (ibid.: 3), this institutional document is basically focused on reproductive issues and HIV/AIDS. In the section 'What do we mean by sexual and reproductive health and rights?' definitions of reproductive health, reproductive healthcare and reproductive rights are provided, but no definitions of sexual rights. When the document appeals to the ICPD (International Conference on Population and Development) approach of reproductive healthcare, however, DFID (ibid.: 4) states that they are:

The constellation of methods, techniques and services that contribute to reproductive and sexual health and wellbeing by preventing and solving reproductive health problems. It also includes sexual health, the purpose of which is the enhancement of life and personal relations and not merely counselling and care related to reproduction and sexually transmitted diseases.

According to the working definition for sexual rights provided by the World Health Organization (WHO), they embrace human rights that are already recognized in national laws, international human rights documents and other consensus statements. They include the right of all persons, free of coercion, discrimination and violence, to:

- the highest attainable standard of sexual health, including access to sexual and reproductive health care services;
- seek, receive and impart information related to sexuality;
- sexuality education;
- respect for bodily integrity;
- choose their partner;
- decide to be sexually active or not;
- consensual sexual relations;
- consensual marriage;
- decide whether or not, and when, to have children; and
- pursue a satisfying, safe and pleasurable sexual life. (WHO 2006)

The integrality of rights

The World Conference on Human Rights (Vienna, 1993) stated that all human rights are universal, indivisible, interdependent and interrelated. The international community must treat different human rights with the same emphasis. Principles of integrality, indivisibility and interdependence lead us to approach sexual rights interrelated with rights to education, health, work, political participation, mobility, and its effects on migration, food, housing, etc. Despite consensus on integrality, policymakers are often unaware of the numerous real and practical linkages between sexual rights and other rights. These include:

In health Female genital mutilation (FGM) is an overt attempt to eliminate women's sexual pleasure. But there are also other non-corporeal mutilations of women's desire: shame, guilt feelings and fixed assigned roles. These symbolic mutilations can be shared by many other people, whether they are female or male, sexual dissidents[1] or not. They have a direct effect on people's mental health and well-being. Heteronormativity affects the health of many men and women and therefore affects their inclusion in economic life. HIV/AIDS is a good example of this: the violence and exclusion experienced by many people owing to heteronormativity discourage them from having safer sex. Men who have sex with men but don't define themselves as 'gay' or 'homosexual' may be more at risk from HIV/AIDS than any other group as a result of the stigma and exclusion associated with openness about their sexuality. Those in same-sex relationships may experience a host of exclusionary practices, from limitations in access to health insurance to discrimination from medical providers. Exclusion in the workplace and social and family environments experienced by those who fail to conform to norms of heterosexuality can create a risk of physical abuse and psychological aggression (see Sardá, this volume). For those LGBT people who have to hide their sexual orientation, depression and stress are a further cause of ill health.

In education There is not enough research regarding the effects of sexual rights violations on education. Yet even the few studies that have been done start to show a pattern. Andil Gosine (2005) cites a 2002 Naz Foundation International study in Bangladesh, which showed that feminine boys were more likely to be bullied in school, drop out and end up in poverty. Teenage mothers have to abandon school owing to social pressure or formal sanctions. Heterosexual sexuality that transgresses established social norms also has effects on education: as, for example, in the difficulties experienced by teenage mothers in continuing schooling, and the risks faced by sexually active young women who are denied access to contraceptive advice and provision. If governments do not incorporate sexuality education as an important element in their national curricula, people (and specially teenagers and young people) will have fewer opportunities to take decisions (regarding parenthood, sexual initiation, HIV prevention, etc.) with proper information (see Esiet, this volume). Sexuality education creates opportunities to give people the capacity to decide over issues concerning their own lives and bodies. Lack of it impoverishes people.

In work Heteronormativity affects labour rights, and limits opportunities for employment (Sardá, this volume). LGBT people may experience problems not only of access to employment, but also of job security. This is especially the case in certain fields, such as education or the armed forces. Transgender people experience greater barriers still to employment. In Latin America, the very limited range of professional opportunities available to transgender people means sex work is almost the only available option. Therefore, there is a negative cycle between lack of opportunities in education and employment. This results in weaker capacities and poverty.

In migration Migration and its economic effects have a direct relationship with sexual rights. Those who are discriminated against on the grounds of their sexuality may need to travel to other countries to seek employment. In around seventy countries in the world, homosexuality is a crime. According to Samelius and Wagberg (2005: 22), Sudan, Saudi Arabia, Afghanistan, Pakistan, Iran and Mauritania have the legal option to issue death sentences for consenting homosexual acts. An organization working openly with advocacy for LGBT rights will be extremely vulnerable as its members risk imprisonment for promoting illegal activities. Conviction may entail imprisonment of up to ten years, forced hard labour, heavy fines or corporal punishment.

The lack of possibilities that LGBT people may experience in their original countries to love, have a family or develop an identity or a sex life is another reason for migration. Cases of family reunification are subordinated to the particular definition of family that certain states adopt. This has economic consequences: there are more barriers for LGBT migrants, and more possibilities to be confined to an illegal status and social exclusion. LGBT may also migrate within their own countries, to cities or places where they can be more anonymous, away from family scrutiny. They may also be thrown out by their families and urged to move away. Women may migrate to escape sexual violence and abuse, sometimes related to a conflict situation. Single women, widows and divorcees migrate to escape social stigma. Young women migrate to escape restrictions on their freedom, or pressure to marry or to remain chaste until marriage.

In political participation Discrimination and prejudice also affect the right to political participation. For example, Lourdes Flores, one of the most popular candidates for president in Peru, was the first woman with a real possibility of winning the most recent elections in 2006. She was attacked by other candidates because she is not a mother and is not married; this, it was inferred, meant that she did not have the maternal sensibility nor the character to administer a country. It is interesting to note that being a *woman* was not considered to be the issue. But not being a *mother* and being single at more than forty-five years old was judged problematic. Women (and especially those who want to participate in politics) are exposed to social pressure in issues related to their sexualities, such as whether they have children or not, or whether they are married. The outcome is decisions to vote based on prejudice rather than on the candidate's proposals.

Perspectives on poverty

For many donors, the rights-based approach is the strategy and the goal is poverty reduction. But who are the poor? If we understand poverty as exclusion, we can find a link with sexual rights and limits to freedom and well-being. As Amartya Sen (2000) points out, poverty depends on capabilities and capabilities depend on freedom. Sexual rights violations imply a loss of freedom, and therefore poverty. The visible loss of capabilities in people is related to education, employment, migration, health and many other domains of people's lives. This affects the lives of countless people: from a transgender who cannot be attended in a public hospital to a woman whose child cannot study in certain schools because she is a single mother, from a heterosexual man who experiences social pressure to lose his virginity with a sex worker without condoms to a man who cannot find a job because he appears in the press as a gay activist.

When we think of sexual rights, we have to think of many other domains of freedom that are affected and are directly related to poverty. If we include sexual rights as part of the strategy to tackle poverty, we would have a core element in our holistic analysis that would enable us to relate intimate and personal arenas with social dimensions of politics and economy. The micro and the macro level of power are closely related. If we think of freedom in relation to the most intimate dimension of people's lives, we can be sure that this process will be reflected in action to address the other dimensions of people's well-being that sexuality impinges upon.

Therefore, we can conclude that sexual rights violations create poverty. If we use WHO's working definition for sexual rights, it can be said that people are poor when:

- they cannot reach the highest attainable standard of sexual health, including access to sexual and reproductive healthcare services;
- they cannot seek, receive and impart information related to sexuality;
- they cannot receive sexuality education;
- there is no respect their bodily integrity;
- they cannot choose their partner;
- they cannot decide to be sexually active or not;
- they are not free to have or not have sexual relations;
- they are not free to get or not get married;
- they are not free to have or not have children when they want;
- they cannot pursue a safe, satisfying and pleasurable sexual life.

If we use this framework, we can analyse certain policies, such as abstinence programmes oriented to tackle HIV/AIDS, for example. They would not only be ineffective, but would also limit people's options. As a consequence, they create more poverty, fewer options and less control over one's own life.

Sexual rights violations create hunger (discrimination leads to lower salaries, underpaid and risky jobs), insecurity (physical aggression against LGBT people, genital mutilation in women), lack of power (police abuse), limitations in access to health (discrimination in hospitals on the basis of sexual orientation, or marital status in access to health insurance) and limitations in access to education (bullying in schools, discrimination, limited access to sexuality education). It is not only gays, lesbians and transgenders who are affected, but also their families. So are heterosexual women and men who diverge from dominant norms in their sexual lives. Not to have freedom in that intimate dimension of our lives affects all of us as society, even at a macro-political level. We all lose.

Participation as a strategy for sexual rights

Participation has different manifestations in different agencies, governments and NGOs. For some institutions, participation is a core element of a rights-based approach. An example of this is the framework that DfID uses, considering participation, inclusion and obligation as components of a rights-based approach (DfID 2000). If participation is the meaningful involvement of marginalized groups in defining their own realities and developing strategies to improve their situation, then:

- sexual rights need to be included in development strategies to tackle poverty;
- sexual rights strategies need to be developed according to the visions of those who are most excluded on the basis of their sexuality and who suffer violations of their sexual rights;
- participating in defining realities and developing strategies should be a transformative and empowering experience for people whose sexual rights have been violated, and, as such, will have a domino effect in many other domains of people's lives.

This implies the following elements:

Participation as an entry right Human rights principles of integrality and indivisibility have as a consequence that we cannot think about civil and political rights as separate from economic, social and cultural rights. The violation of certain rights affects others. Participation is an entry right, absence of which makes it impossible to realize other rights. Eyben argues:

> Deciding which rights are most important, and require priority funding in relation to the state's resources, becomes a political debate in which all citizens have a right to participate. From this perspective the right to participation can be seen as the entry point to realising all other rights. The right to participate is the right to claim other rights. Understanding participation as a right, rather than an instrument for greater aid effectiveness, has been one of the biggest shifts in agency thinking in recent years. (2003: 2)

Thinking about participation as a right and not just as a methodology helps to reframe participation in political terms.

What is the consequence of this approach for sexual rights? If we want to realize sexual rights we need to reinforce participation that could allow inclusion of sexual rights in the public agenda as a valid element. Therefore, participation is an entry right for sexual rights.

Participation and inclusion Participation is a strategy to fight against the exclusion of the weakest groups in society in decision-making. Sexuality has intimate liaisons with exclusion, bound up with the effects of heteronormativity and patriarchy. Normative sexual identities or behaviours for women and men affect many other aspects of people's lives: access to education, employment, health, parenthood, credit and so on. Feminine boys, masculine girls and those with non-conforming sexualities may be excluded as a result.

Chambers asks:

Whose knowledge counts?
Whose values?
Whose criteria and preferences?
Whose appraisal, analysis and planning?
Whose action?
Whose monitoring and evaluation?
Whose learning?
Whose empowerment?
Whose reality counts? (2000: 101)

Similarly we could ask in development discourses: Whose sexuality counts? Men's, women's, transgenders' or intersex? Heterosexual sexuality or also gay, lesbian and bisexual? Whose pleasure? Whose desire? Whose notion of decency? Whose notion of promiscuity? Whose shame?

Whose fears? Whose identities? Whose sin? Whose transgression? Whose liberation? Whose freedom?

Participation is not the panacea for inclusion, but it is part of what inclusion might mean in practice.

A focus on the personal dimension of politics Participation is political. Politics have different dimensions: institutional and inter-institutional, but also personal. It is imperative to consider the personal dimension, because it is the most intimate space of politics, participation, rights and citizenship. To work at the personal level is a unique opportunity for self-reflection and awareness; it is the basis on which wider action and reflection can be supported. Sexuality, the most intimate space for rights and citizenship, when it is linked with rights discourse, is about respect for others, self-respect, dialogue, duties, responsibilities and awareness.

The organization I work with, GRUPAL in Peru, doesn't undertake sexuality training but we run democracy and participation workshops that include reflection on sexuality: Are you democratic with your sexual partner? Do you listen to your own desire? Are you respected when you say 'no'? Do you dialogue about pleasure? What are the power dynamics of sex and sexual orientation and how do these interact with those of gender, race and education? This can be quite a good entry point for getting people to think about democracy. We have sixteen- and seventeen-year-olds who have lived through ten years of dictatorship and think politics is a dirty space they don't want to participate in. Talking about the personal dimension of politics (and sex as a part of it) gets them interested.

Challenges of participation for sexual rights

Participation is not a magic solution for the problems of exclusion. Even participatory strategies may present difficulties for sexual rights.

Participation may represent high costs for excluded people Participation implies costs. For example, the cost of transportation for the meeting venues, the time dedicated to coordinations and deliberations (instead of spending time with family, working or studying) or the costs of political action (campaigns, marches, communication, etc.). This may mean that in participatory policy processes, strong and organized groups are more likely to succeed in pushing their agendas.

What happens with weaker groups? Sexual rights violations imply exclusions at many levels, and those who are excluded face the impoverishing effects of discrimination. How can a sexual rights women's organization or a LGBT group demand agendas, organize a march, lead a debate or present a rights violation case properly if it is dealing with basic issues of survival? Groups formed around sexual rights are usually small and weaker than others in civil society, in a development landscape dominated by less controversial (and more fundable) issues. This element, which is present in a very natural way in a participatory space, is a problem that needs to be faced. The role of aid and cooperation in strengthening the organizational capacities and sustainability of these groups is fundamental to achieving more legitimate and representative participatory spaces.

The costs of visibility A lesbian activist could succeed with her advocacy campaign appearing in public, participating in public debate. But she will have to accept the costs: discrimination at work, in her family, social spaces, etc. This activist could agree to assume all these personal costs in the name of a collective purpose. But when we call for more participation of sexual dissidents, maybe we are not taking into account the costs that this public activity could represent.

Gays are more likely to participate than MSM. What are the consequences of this in HIV/AIDS participatory policies? Can we demand MSM to be gay and come out in order to claim rights? Who will pay for the personal costs of that exposition (which is not the same for every person)? What happens if intimacy and secrecy (and not a public identity) are elements of the desire object? MSM and other sexual minorities (who don't want to be seen in public) are the most vulnerable groups just because they cannot push agendas or claim rights. Aren't these groups the most excluded? Aren't they the poor? We can't say that these persons are bad citizens because they don't participate.

There is an evident tension between the need for sexual dissidents' visibilization in order to push agendas and their right to privacy. On the other hand, representative democracy could ensure the anonymity of those who want to be heard. Otherwise, in a participatory space, someone will talk in their name, or nobody will talk at all. Therefore, could representative democracy be a better option than participation in these cases? What happens with direct democracy alternatives?

Power relationships and representation in different group Groups that advocate for sexual rights are not equal. There is a multiplicity of agendas and relationships. Among them, and within them, there could be diverse forms of exclusion (racism, male chauvinism, patriarchy, etc.). All these elements will be present in deliberative spaces.

Who will talk in the name of whom in deliberative spaces? Will LGBT activists talk in the name of MSM? And within the LGBT movement, which people will be heard? Formally educated, articulated and informed people are likely to be seen as the decent face of these movements. White, middle-class and Northern images are likely to be seen as the prototypes of sexual identities. In this context, representation appears as a problem.

If we base people's participation on their identities (as gay, lesbian, etc.), when representation of different groups is demanded, what happens with the people who base their sexuality not on identities but on fluid desire? What happens with heterosexual men who don't follow traditional social norms and who don't have a specific sexual and political identity? Is it possible to talk about representation without identities? Is there any advantage when people just talk about sexual rights and not about specific sexual identities?

Participation as a mechanism to legitimize moral control Participatory spaces can be used as much as instruments of moral control as tools for transformation. If the strongest civil society groups are conservative organizations with more funding, resources, time, networks, influence and ability to articulate a coherent discourse without criticism, it is possible (as was mentioned before) that these groups could dominate participatory spaces. Therefore, decisions taken in these spaces would reflect conservative ideas, legitimized as participatory decisions or the voice of the people.

Bracamonte and Alvarez (2005) report a case that occurred in Chiclayo, a city in the north of Peru, where activists from LGBT organizations reported that some Neighbourhood Watch groups that depend on the Neighbourhood Councils exercise violence against transgenders in their localities. In a context in which Neighbourhood Watch groups are a response to the absence of the state in its responsibility to guarantee citizen security, these groups (together with the national and municipal police) could mean violence against lesbians, gays, bisexuals and particularly against transgenders who are sex workers.

This problem appears in many other domains of civil society. According to Restrepo (2001: 172), in the name of citizen participation and community participation in justice, there are more popular hangings of criminals in Peru and Mexico. In the name of participation in citizen security, self-defence committees and armed civil associations – which not only dispute weapons monopoly but also involve a growing number of the population in war activities – are encouraged in Colombia. The difference between direct democracy and participation is that the latter has deliberation as a core element. Information, criticism and different points of view are the elements that facilitate deliberation and inform public opinion. Without them, the risk of turning participatory spaces into mechanisms of moral control or even human rights violation appears.

Final reflections

There is an undeniable link between sexuality and development. Sexual rights violations are not just an issue of concern to minorities. They have an economic impact, not only for the people directly affected, but also for their families, friends and social and labour networks. Their impact on impoverishment is a real consequence that we have to reflect about. Social networks are the main bulwark against poverty in developing countries. Prejudice and discrimination weaken these networks and, therefore, create poverty.

Despite these connections, not a single Poverty Reduction Strategy Paper has included sexual rights as part of a coherent strategy against poverty related to human rights. In addition to this, the UN Millennium Development Goals do not mention, specifically, sexual and reproductive health and rights. Which NGO working on poverty or in human rights (not specifically in sexuality issues) would depict a transgender or a sex worker on the cover of its annual report? Why are so many development agencies so uncomfortable working with certain ways of poverty, linked with sexuality? What are the consequences of this uncomfortable feeling?

The discomfort that development agencies seem to experience in relation to sexuality needs to be addressed. Sexual rights are about so much more than sex. That is why it is important to develop not only theoretical but also political and working linkages with other international, national and local actors that are not working in sexual rights, but are involved in housing, health, education, migration and so on. But there are many challenges that need to be addressed. The first of them is the lack of systematic evidence that relates sexual rights with other rights and shows how a lack of sexual rights has a direct economic impact and illustrates the relationship between poverty and lack of freedom. Without this evidence, it will be impossible to formulate, let alone monitor and evaluate, programmes and policies. The second challenge is to incorporate a sexual rights discourse in the existing human rights monitoring instruments, and in international reports. Traditionally, sexuality has been presented in these documents only in relation to reproduction. Non-reproductive sexuality has an important impact on poverty and development, however.

In spite of some theoretical and practical difficulties, participation is an important element in the strategy of including sexual rights in the development agenda. It will not only help sustainability, but also transformation (personal and social). But it is important to acknowledge that not every participation experience is transformative. In addition to this, sexuality is an issue that enables people to work with politics at a very personal level; the very intimacy of working with issues of citizenship and rights through the lens of sexuality makes space for a transformative process of self-reflection that can lead to social action.

To conclude, sexual rights are an important battlefield in our fight against poverty. Our work for inclusion and for the realization of the rights of excluded people cannot be complete if we fail to consider sexual rights as a necessary element that affects many other domains of development work. Taking sexuality into consideration means to have respect for the people we work with and to treat them as citizens.

Acknowledgements

This chapter was elaborated with the invaluable contribution and support of Carolyn Williams, Gustavo Zambrano Chávez, Margarita Díaz Picasso, Susan Jolly, Andrea Cornwall and Ulrica Risso Engblom. I am grateful for their comments, submitted documents, conversations, insights, reflections and friendship. All possible mistakes are the author's.

Note

1 The phrase 'sexual dissident' was taken from Andil Gosine (2005).

References

Bracamonte J. and R. Alvarez (eds) (2005) *Situación de los Derechos Humanos de Lesbianas, Trans, Gays y Bisexuales en el Perú, Informe Anual*, Lima: Mhol.

Chambers, R. (2000) *Whose Reality Counts? Putting the First Last*, London: ITDG.

DfID (Department for International Development) (2000) *Target Strategy Paper: Realising Human Rights for Poor People*, London: DfID.

— (2004) *Sexual and Reproductive Health and Rights. A Position Paper*, London: DfID.

Eyben, R. (2003) 'The rise of rights', IDS Policy Briefing no. 17, Brighton: IDS.

Gosine, A. (2005) 'Sex for pleasure, rights to participation, and alternatives to AIDS: placing sexual minorities and/or dissidents in development', IDS Working Paper no. 228, Brighton: IDS.

Marks, S. P. (2005) 'Human rights in development', in S. Gruskin et al. (eds), *Perspectives on Health and Human Rights*, New York: Routledge.

Ministry for Foreign Affairs, Sweden (2006) *Sweden's International Policy on Sexual and Reproductive Health and Rights*, Stockholm: Ministry for Foreign Affairs.

Restrepo, D. (2001) 'Eslabones y precipicios entre participación y democracia', *Revista Mexicana de Sociología*, LXIII(3): 167–91.

Samelius, L. and E. Wagberg (2005) 'Sexual orientation and gender identity issues in development. A study of Swedish policy and administration of lesbian, gay, bisexual and transgender issues in international development cooperation', Stockholm: Swedish International Development Cooperation Agency.

Sen, A. (2000) *Libertad y desarrollo*, Barcelona: Planeta.

United Nations (2003) *Statement on a Common Understanding of a Human Rights-based Approach to Development Cooperation, as agreed at the Stamford Workshop and endorsed by the UNDG Programme Group*, Paris: United Nations, <http://portal.unesco.org/shs/en/ev.php-URL_ID=7947&URL_DO=DO_TOPIC&URL_SECTION=201.html> (accessed 15 March 2006).

WHO (World Health Organization) (2006) <www.who.int/reproductive-health/gender/sexual_health.html> (accessed 15 March 2006).

18 | Integrating sexuality into gender and human rights frameworks: a case study from Turkey

PINAR ILKKARACAN AND KARIN RONGE

'Our bodies and sexuality belong to ourselves!' Main slogan of the women's march organized by the Women's Platform for the Reform of the Turkish Penal Code from a Gender Perspective in Turkey, 15 May 2004

At the turn of the new millennium, sexuality has once more become a site of intense political struggles on national and international levels, as reflected by the fierce UN debates on issues related to sexuality (Ilkkaracan and Jolly 2007). Sexuality plays an important role in many areas of human rights and development, such as gender relations, health, poverty and participatory democracy, as well as social and political transformation. Yet, until recently, human rights actors and international development agencies have been reluctant to integrate sexuality into their agendas. This reluctance is based on several misconceptions and myths, such as sexuality being a 'private' matter, leading to oversight of its relevance to socio-political and economic spheres or the myth that people are unwilling to talk about or deal with sexuality. Another potential reason, namely the fear of delving into controversial issues of gender or cultural sensitivities, remains to be explored. Corrêa and Jolly (this volume) note that in fact the development world has always dealt with sexuality-related issues, though usually only implicitly and negatively, in relation to population control, disease, violence or exploitation, calling for increased integration of issues related to sexuality into development agendas with a positive approach.

Women for Women's Human Rights (WWHR) – NEW WAYS, an NGO that has played a leading role in the realization of legal reforms for gender equality in Turkey, as well as networking on gender and human rights in Muslim societies, has been concerned with the integration of sexuality into human rights and development frameworks at the local, national and international levels since its inception in 1993. Sexual, bodily and reproductive rights constitute a significant component of WWHR's widespread human rights education programme for women, which has reached 4,500 women living in the most disadvantaged areas of Turkey since its first implementation in 1995. At the national level, WWHR has initiated and coordinated successful advocacy and lobbying initiatives on legal reforms in Turkey which have integrated human rights violations related to sexuality as a significant factor of gender inequality, including the campaign against virginity testing and the campaign on the Reform of the Turkish Penal Code from a Gender Perspective (2002–04). Since 2001, WWHR has been coordinating an international solidarity network of NGOs and academicians for the promotion of sexual and reproductive health and rights in the Middle East, North Africa and South/South-East Asia, the Coalition for Sexual and Bodily Rights in Muslim Societies.[1]

This chapter aims to shed light on the significance of integrating sexuality into human rights and development programmes and agendas for women. It is based on WWHR's experience of more than a decade of integration of matters related to sexuality into human rights, development and legal reforms at the local, national and international levels. It draws on the primary author's personal experience as founder and active member of WWHR in all the initiatives mentioned above.

Sexuality as a crucial domain of women's human rights

Sexuality is a cross-cutting issue, which has political, economic and social dimensions with a big impact on people's lives, especially women and girls and those with non-conforming sexualities. Control of women's sexuality is patriarchy's most powerful tool to maintain women's oppression and the imbalance in gender power relations in most societies, achieved via intricate mechanisms of political, economic, legal and social and cultural manipulation, including coercion and violence. Religion is often misused as a powerful instrument of control in this context, legitimizing violations of women's human rights. The legal regulations in almost all countries of the world – written, customary or religious – play a significant role in normalizing and naturalizing gender inequalities based on sexuality.

Patriarchal institutions and ideologies employ many methods to control women's sexuality, including oppressing women's voices and upholding taboos concerning women's sexual pleasure, sexuality outside procreation, extramarital sexuality, sex work, desire and love between women or virginity. While the practices aiming at control of women's sexuality might vary over time and place around the world, myths of assumed gender differences, such as men being 'naturally' more active or having more sexual desire than women, or women having no sexual desire after menopause while men are sexually active throughout their lives, are almost universal.

For many, particularly women living in poverty, sexuality is often an issue of survival. Examples are many, such as the anti-abortion laws that lead to the death of 68,000 women each year, according to WHO estimates, honour crimes, female genital mutilation (FGM) or stoning for adultery. In fact, these practices often constitute only the tip of the iceberg, as more invisible forms of control of women's and girls' sexuality, such as the restriction of their mobility, education or participation in economic life, in the name of protecting their chastity, lie at the heart of disempowerment and several human rights violations of women and girls. For example, in Turkey, where the enrolment of girls in school continues to be a big problem, the fear that education will facilitate sexual relations in coed settings or increase girls' chances of rejecting arranged marriages – thus costing the family both honour and the bride price, particularly in rural areas – plays a significant role in families' reluctance to send their daughters to school.[2]

Adopting a holistic and affirmative approach to sexuality: the right to sexual satisfaction and pleasure As many experts working on sexuality emphasize, sexual health is more than the absence of disease, and sexual pleasure and satisfaction are integral components of well-being, requiring their universal recognition and promotion.[3] The right to pleasure is also recognized as an integral component of sexual rights in the World Association for Sexual Health (WAS) Declaration of Sexual Rights (1999). The Programme of Action (PoA) achieved by consensus at the 1994 UN International Conference on Population and Development (ICPD) states: 'Reproductive health implies that people are able to have a satisfying and safe sex life' (ICPD PoA, Paragraph 7.2).

Sexual satisfaction and pleasure have, however, remained the most neglected and stigmatized components of sexuality education and sexual and reproductive health programmes. The recognition of pleasure as an integral component of human sexuality in such programmes constitutes the link between choice and responsible sexual behaviour, affecting individuals' healthcare-seeking behaviour.

The sociocultural constructions of sexuality and sexual practices in many societies aim at enhancing men's pleasure, while denying women the right to pleasure. This not only constitutes a blatant example of gender inequality, but also leads to practices that aim to suppress women's sexual pleasure and violate their human rights, such as FGM and laws and policies institutionalizing patriarchal notions of morality or honour.

The notions of 'pleasure' and 'choice' are rarely recognized as being

A case study from Turkey

among the most contentious aspects of female sexuality. Exploring the links between sexual pleasure and power, Patricia MacFadden writes:

> For many African women, even the suggestion that sexual pleasure and eroticism have political implications elicits alarm, and it is seldom recognized that sexual pleasure is fundamental to our right to a safe and wholesome lifestyle. The fears that these concerns often raise constitute what I call 'socio-sexual anxiety'. The intensity of this anxiety is generated by the fact that there is an extremely intimate relationship between sexuality and power, a connection which is manifested in a range of circumstances and experiences. (2003)

Ipek Ilkkaracan and Gülşah Seral also point out that: 'Many women associate sexuality with a lack of control, violence and abuse, and certainly not with pleasure. Therefore, there is a clear need to empower women to take better control of their sexual lives and to build an approach towards sexuality' (2000: 189).

It is very difficult to find texts or materials on women's own experiences of pleasure and desire. This is reflective of the silence and restrictions imposed on women's sexuality, especially when it comes to the exploration and expression of their own desire and pleasure, as well as women's socialization and experience of sexuality as a domain full of dangers. These range from social control mechanisms of gossip, humiliation or ostracization of women who transgress the boundaries of socially accepted norms of sexual behaviour to sexual violence or death (Ilkkaracan 2000). As Carole S. Vance (1992) notes, however, the pleasure we have experienced is as much a guide to future action as is brutality, and is a vital source of energy for the feminist movement.

In addition, from a psychological perspective, a healthy and positive relationship with one's body and sexuality, as well as the ability to experience and express pleasure, are crucial for a healthy and positive self-concept. Thus, integration of sexual rights, including the right to pleasure, in women's empowerment programmes is not only a crucial factor in women's analysis of gender discrimination, but also plays a significant role in enhancing their self-concept, strategies, negotiation skills and empowerment (Ilkkaracan and Seral 2000; Havanon 1996; Cornwall and Jolly 2006).

Integrating sexuality into human rights agendas in Turkey

Sexual politics and women in Turkey: the historical context The founding of the modern Turkish republic in 1923 included the introduction of several reforms aiming at secularization and Westernization, including legal reforms towards gender equality. Turkey constitutes a unique example in the Middle East in this respect. Other countries of the region, such as Egypt or Iran of the shah period, underwent similar attempts at Westernization but stopped short of reforming the code of family laws or introducing changes in the status of women. In 1926, the introduction of the Turkish Civil Code, adapted from the Swiss Civil Code, banned polygamy and granted women equal rights in matters of divorce and child custody. As Tekeli argues, however, women's rights granted by Kemalists were intended to destroy links to the Ottoman Empire and to strike at the foundations of the religious hegemony rather than promoting the actual liberation of women in everyday life (Tekeli 1982). Thus, women were presented as the 'emblem' of secularism and the 'new Republic', just as the conservatives and Islamists used them as symbolic 'protectors' of traditional values and the social status quo.

Despite the apparently opposing views of modernists and Islamists on women's role in society, they competed in their zeal to construct a patriarchal ideal of female sexuality and to maintain and reconstruct mechanisms aiming to control women's sexuality and bodies. The modernists/nationalists attempted to confront the social anxieties triggered by women's participation in the public sphere through the construction of the modern Turkish woman: emancipated and active in the founding of the new republic as mother, teacher and political activist, yet at same time 'modest' and 'chaste'. Ziya Gökalp, the leading ideologue of the Turkish nationalist movement, while strongly defending equality between men and women as a major aspect of the new Turkish identity, asserted that the impact of the new role assumed by women on society would depend on Turkish women's sexual morals, whose principal virtue he defines as *iffet* (virtue, chastity). Claiming that women naturally have higher sexual morals than men, he calls on Turkish women 'to be the responsible and guiding party in protection of sexual [morals] in the new republic' (2005: 143). Thus, as Kandiyoti (1998) notes, a nationalist consensus was created on the terms under which women could be accepted into public life in republican Turkey: as asexual and devoid of their essential femaleness.

The official discourse that the problem of the status of women has been solved by the founders of the nation and that Turkish women should consider themselves lucky, as they were granted specific rights even before their European counterparts, has been internalized by the women's movement of the post-republican era. This movement has been led mostly by women who have been able to benefit from the new possibilities of the young republic, such as professional women living in big cities or women of the bureaucratic elite. Most of the women's groups and associations founded during the republican era concentrated on 'educating' or 'helping' women living in rural areas, instead of questioning the role that the new republic determined for them, gender inequality in the family or gender-specific problems of women, such as domestic violence or women's sexual oppression.

The new feminist movement, which emerged after the military intervention in 1980, was the first movement in Turkey that broke the taboos and the silence around issues that were hitherto considered to belong to the private sphere by bringing them into the public agenda. By questioning and politicizing issues such as domestic violence, sexual abuse in the family and sexual liberation, the new feminist movement started confronting a deeply held state ideology which maintained that the foundation of the new Turkish republic and the transition to a secular state had liberated Turkish women and attracted a large public and media attention. Yet, at the beginning of the 1990s, the activists of the new feminist movement in Turkey advocating for bodily rights and women's sexual freedom were categorized and labelled as 'radical feminists' by the mainstream media, a term used in a negative and humiliating way. This labelling included a wide spectrum of women, ranging from the founders of and activists in the Purple Roof Foundation, the first women's NGO in Turkey advocating against domestic violence, to Duygu Asena, the first popular feminist journalist, who wrote an autobiographical bestseller on the experiences of a woman trying to free herself from the prevailing oppressive sexual norms. Asena's first book, *Kadının Adı Yok* (The Woman Has No Name), sharply criticizing the oppression of women's sexuality, was published in 1987, and became a top seller both in Turkey and later in Greece. The book was, however, banned by the government at the time of its fortieth edition in 1998, on the premise that it was obscene, dangerous for children and undermining marriage. After two years of lawsuits, the ban was lifted, and the book was filmed by the prominent Turkish director Atıf Yılmaz.

The shift of political power to religious right parties in Turkey after the 1994 local elections and 1995 general elections, however, had a restraining effect on the range of discourses and demands of the new feminist movement of the 1980s, especially those related to sexuality, as they lost their initial attraction for many women, who perceived the rise of political Islam as a major threat to their existing rights in the public sphere.[4] Issues relating to sexuality, sexual liberation, critiques of the heterosexual model, sexuality outside marriage, the assertion of female sexuality and the human rights of lesbians, which could have emerged in a politically more supporting environment, were absent from the feminist agenda after the mid-1990s. Thus, after the initial campaigns on sexual violence at the beginning of the 1990s, until the campaign for the Reform of the Turkish Penal Code from a Gender Perspective, which started in 2002, the issues related to sexuality taken up by the feminist movement in Turkey were restricted to virginity tests and honour crimes, though rather in the context of violence against women and without any direct reference to women's autonomy over their sexuality.

Research on women's sexuality in eastern Turkey   Research conducted by WWHR in 1996–97 in eastern and south-eastern Turkey explored the range and extent of various customary mechanisms controlling women's sexuality.[5] According to the results of the research, 16 per cent of the participants were married under the age of fifteen (the legal minimum age of marriage for women until 2001). Although the consent of both the woman and the man is a precondition of marriage according to the Turkish Civil Code, a majority of marriages were conducted by the families and only one in four women had the chance to choose her own husband. More than half of the women (51 per cent) were married without their consent and 46 per cent stated that they were not even consulted about their partner and the marriage.

When asked about their expectations of their future marriages, only 58 per cent of the younger women under the age of eighteen believed that they would be able to have the chance to decide on whom they would marry. Although adultery has not been considered a crime according to the Turkish criminal law since the mid-1990s, 67 per cent of the women thought they would be killed by their husbands and/or families if they committed adultery. Those who reported that they were often or sometimes subjected to marital rape constituted 52 per cent of the participants. It is interesting to note that most of these practices, which lead to serious violations of women's human rights, still exist despite laws banning them passed over seventy years ago.

The research results showed that women's reproductive lives and health were also negatively affected by taboos concerning premarital sexuality, which leads to a significant lack of information on contraception. In eastern Turkey, as in the rest of the country, contraception, like childbearing, is considered to be applicable only to married women, as sex and childbirth are taboo issues for most unmarried women. As a result, many women have no chance of receiving any information about contraception before marriage. Thus, although family planning is strongly encouraged by the Turkish state, the average number of living children per woman in the region was 4.8, and every third woman had more than six children. Only half of the currently married women between fifteen and forty-nine years of age were using a contraceptive method at the time of the research. The least common source of contraceptive information for married women was the family (5 per cent), indicating the taboo nature of the issue within the family. The reasons for not using any contraceptive methods included: having no knowledge of them (15 per cent), the husband or the family not allowing a woman to do so even though she wanted to (12 per cent), and for 6 per cent of the women lacking the financial means (Ilkkaracan 2001).

The extent of violence experienced by women, including marital rape, and the constant threat of violence in case they are perceived as transgressing the boundaries of socially acceptable sexual conduct, not only affects their sexual health and perception of sexuality negatively but also decreases their chances of creating and applying strategies against the violation of their rights, as women often internalize the negative social messages about their sexuality. The internalization of gender roles in a particular culture is often directly related to the impact of specific mechanisms controlling women's sexuality, which are often of a 'collective' nature (Kandiyoti 1987). The rigid codes of conduct for women's sexuality also lead to various restrictions of women by their fathers, husbands or brothers in many areas of their lives, including limitations imposed on their mobility and their right to receive education or to work.

Experience from the ground: women's voices on sexuality (the Human Rights Education Programme of WWHR) Based on the analysis described above, women's sexual autonomy and rights with a positive approach to sexuality, including women's right to sexual pleasure, have been one of the priority areas in the outreach work of WWHR, including in its Human Rights Education Programme for Women (HREP), which was developed in 1995. Below is a short description of the programme and examples of women's voices on their experiences of sexuality.

WWHR developed the HREP, a four-month training programme aiming to reach women living in the most disadvantaged areas, with the ultimate aim of facilitating women's grassroots organizing throughout Turkey. As of 2006, it is being implemented in thirty-six provinces throughout Turkey, reaching hundreds of women each year. The programme is unique in its holistic, comprehensive approach to human rights, linking several areas of human rights both in private and public spheres through a critical gender-perspective lens and an emphasis on personal and social change and methodology (Ilkkaracan and Amado 2005). To do justice to this comprehensive nature, training is organized as an intensive process of four months, a time frame that differentiates it from many other initiatives of human rights education. The programme aims not only to give information to women about their rights, but also to facilitate actual change both at personal and community levels, encouraging women's grassroots organizing. Since 1998, the programme has led to the emergence of fifteen women's grassroots organizations all over Turkey.

It is interesting to note that, despite its strongly feminist nature, the programme has been implemented in state community centres throughout Turkey in collaboration with the State Directorate for Social Services since 1998, giving it the distinct characteristic of being one of the most sustainable, widespread and successful collaborations between a feminist NGO and the state. Initially, this has been possible through collaboration with a progressive director appointed to the Directorate for Social Services in 1998. Although he was later removed from his position, the success of the programme and the immense interest it has received from the social workers and local women who have developed ownership of the programme have been crucial in its sustainability in its later stages.

Among the sixteen modules of the training, two are explicitly devoted to sexuality and sexual rights, in addition to another module on reproductive rights. Yet issues related to sexuality are explored in various sections throughout the programme.[6]

Women's experiences of sexual oppression and its impact on their lives WWHR's experience with over five thousand women who have participated in the HREP over a decade has shown that sexual oppression causes severe problems for women throughout their lives, resulting in deeply held feelings of anxiety and shame, lifelong psychological problems, negative self-concept, despair in their marriages or the violation of their rights in various areas such as education:

> When I was eight years old, I was curious about the sexual organ of our neighbour's son and wanted to see what it looked like. When my family found out about this, they confined me to a dark room. After three days of confinement, I was taken to a doctor for a virginity test, and taken out of school. I still suffer from this experience. I have difficulty in having sex with my husband. I feel pangs of anxiety and shame.

> I had to undergo psychiatric treatment after having my first menstrual cycle as I lost my ability to speak as a result of the fear I experienced. The impact of this dreadful experience continues to this date, despite the fact that I am now a mother of two children.

Unfortunately, in our country, one of the tools most frequently used to repress our sexuality is honour. Honour is deemed to be contained in a woman's body. Her honour belongs to the men; in fact it belongs to the whole society. This is a great injustice committed against women's bodies and sexuality. When you interpret honour this way, many girls cannot get an education, cannot marry the man of their choice or cannot go out to work. This is why we are discussing the concept of honour in our human rights education group.

During the first years of my marriage, I was unable to have sexual intercourse with my husband as I had so much internalized the expectations of my family about the importance of virginity.

Who's afraid of talking about sexuality? In contrast to the widespread myth among the health, development and human rights actors that people in general are unwilling to talk about their sexual lives as sex is a sensitive, private issue, our experience in the programme has shown that women have a great desire to talk about their sexuality. In fact, the modules on sexuality are the modules most favoured by women; they perceive them as opening new doors in their lives:

> One of our friends was asleep during most of our meetings, but as the sexuality came up, she was very alive. I think this shows that she thinks like me. We were all much closed about sexuality. But after attending this training, I started discussing sexuality with everybody. I felt this wonderful change in me after this education programme.

> I wish they had given us all this information that we are receiving now back in school. We all grew up with such little information about sexuality, and most of it was wrong! I don't want my children to grow up the same way.

Women are very aware of the negative impact of the taboos and the silence surrounding sexuality on their lives and complain bitterly about the lack of sexual education:

> When I married, I believed that I could get pregnant by kissing. My husband and I both suffered very much due to my ignorance. I blame my mother for my lack of information on sexuality and I do not want to repeat the same mistakes with my daughter.

> We had been taught that sexuality is shameful (*ayıp*). We opened up slowly, but now we have to overcome thirty years of ignorance. From now on, we have to learn not to take things as they come. I learned and I think I'm also teaching others.

When I had my first period, I even considered committing suicide. Why couldn't they have told me what it was and that it was so normal, so that I wouldn't have been so afraid? Now I think I would like to explain to my daughter such things when she's grown up a bit.

As reflected in the statements above, many women express the strong wish to protect their daughters from experiencing the traumas they had, and find the modules on sexuality very useful in this respect too.

Sexual pleasure? Is that for women too? The sexuality modules of WWHR's Human Rights Education Programme emphasize women's human right to sexual pleasure, which includes the right to seeking sexual experiences and pleasure independent of one's marital status and dominant heterosexual discourses, the right to orgasm, the right to expression and pursuit of one's sexual needs and desires, and also the right to choose *not* to experience one's sexuality.

Many women say that they were not even aware that women are able to have sexual pleasure or that it is a natural right until they have attended this training:

Our sexuality is limited to reproduction. Our organs serve only to give birth. There is no such thing as wanting it or asking for sexuality. It is a luxury for women.

Do girls and women really feel sexual pleasure too?

What is the clitoris for?

Until I participated in this training, I didn't know that girls and women can feel sexual pleasure.

Our experience has shown that discussions of the right to pleasure have an empowering effect on women, and cause a significant shift of awareness and the way they think about themselves and their relations:

Instinctively, I have always felt that sex was a natural thing. It is good to have all this information now, which confirms that what I had thought all along was right.

So, women also feel sexual pleasure, just like men do! I think it's very important to know this at the beginning of marriage, so that you can also teach your husband about it.

The impact of discussing sexuality within the framework of the HREP programme on women's lives One of the main impacts of exploring myths, restrictions and rules of conduct around women's sexuality for women

235

who attend the programme is to gain the ability to say a forceful 'No!' to the oppression they are facing, an experience that goes far beyond opposing sexual oppression:

> After I attended this programme, I gained freedom as an individual at my home. Freedom at home is the most important. Forget about the outside. It is nice to be a free woman at home.

> Since I'm in this training, I started getting angry when people, even friends, want the television turned off when the issue of sexuality comes on. I can't object very much since they are in the majority, but I would like to talk about it. Why should we keep this subject a secret? Is this not how life begins? This is how I see it.

WWHR's Human Rights Education Programme for Women, with its strong integration of women's sexual, bodily and reproductive rights, enables women throughout Turkey to change their own internalized views about sexuality, pleasure and the right to choice, and encourages them to attitudinal changes, not only in their own lives, but also within their family, towards their husbands and children, especially their daughters. They perceive it as a major factor in enhancing their self-esteem and empowerment. Although most of the participants of the programme live in socio-economically disadvantaged regions such as small towns, villages or shanty-town areas, with very little access to social or other services, they become agents and defenders of women's human rights, founding women's associations or platforms around their own needs at the community level, as well as participating in nationwide campaigns of the Turkish feminist movement to make their voices heard.

Bringing sexual rights into the public discourse: the campaign for the reform of the Turkish Penal Code from a gender perspective (2002–04)

> 'Now I say, when women don't want, they just have a right to say no! You want it, well I don't. Men have to respect that. When it is forced, it is like rape. There is something called "marital rape". Women should know that they even have the right to go to court. Even if he's her husband, she has a right to say no.' (HREP participant)

Our field research and experience from our Human Rights Education Programme over the years had clearly shown that there were several human rights violations related to sexuality – the control of women's sexuality was often the underlying reason for these violations (e.g. restriction of women's mobility, early or forced marriages or honour crimes) – and that sexuality played a significant role in women's perceived lack of empowerment. Although our training programme aimed at integration of sexual, bodily and reproductive rights as human rights, we were well aware that the legal framework in Turkey, in particular the Turkish Penal Code of 1926, failed to support the newly gained insights of the participants. In fact the code was full of articles that violated women's human rights.

The Turkish Penal Code was adapted from the Italian Penal Code in 1926, as part of the series of reforms aiming at modernization and Westernization after the foundation of the Turkish republic in 1923. The code included, however, several articles that reflected the traditional notions that women's bodies and sexuality belong to men, family or society and which value women's chastity and virginity, as well as the understanding that linked women's sexuality with men's honour. The underlying philosophy of the law did not recognize women's autonomy over their bodies and sexuality and aimed at regulation of women's sexuality rather than protecting women from sexual crimes. It reflected an understanding of sexuality, in particular women's sexuality, as a potential threat to public order and morality, and thus in need of legal regulation. Sexual crimes were listed under the section entitled 'Crimes AgainstSociety', subsection '*adab-ı umumiye and nizam-ı aile*' (Crimes Against Traditions of Morality and Family Order), as opposed to being listed as crimes against persons. Regulation of crimes such as rape, abduction or sexual abuse against women as crimes against society, rather than as crimes against individuals, was not only a manifestation of the code's foundational premise that women's bodies and sexuality are the property of men, family or society, but was also a reflection of the social anxiety underpinning a perceived need for stricter state control of sexuality in the context of the Kemalist revolution, the abolition of religious laws, the participation of women in the public sphere and the implementation of Western dress codes.

Thus, the reform of the penal code had long been on the WWHR agenda. Throughout the 1990s, however, feminist advocacy and lobbying for legal reform in Turkey concentrated mainly on reform of the civil code, which declared husbands as heads of family and contained several provisions violating both the constitutional guarantee of gender equality and international conventions to which Turkey was signatory, such as the Convention on the Elimination of All Forms of Discrimination Against Women (CEDAW). The reform of the civil code and amendments instituting gender equality had been an issue on the public agenda for decades, yet it did not feature on the parliamentary agenda until 2000. As it finally did, I met the strong opposition of a coalition led by the government Nationalistic Action Party and the opposition Islamist Welfare Party, triggering a dynamic and extensive feminist campaign by a coalition of over 120 women's NGOs from around the country – the broadest alliance of women's groups since the emergence of the new feminist movement in the 1980s. The campaign was successful in getting extensive media and public support, creating an atmosphere where resistance to equality between men and women was viewed with scorn, and finally it was successful in realizing full reform of the Turkish Civil Code, abolishing the supremacy of men in marriage and establishing full legal equality of men and women in the family (WWHR – NEW WAYS 2005).

In 2002, immediately after the success of the Campaign on the Reform of the Turkish Civil Code (2000–01), seizing the opportunity created by the momentum behind the successful civil code campaign, WWHR initiated a Women's Working Group that included NGOs, bar associations and academicians from all over Turkey to work on a holistic reform of the penal code from a gender perspective.[7] The initiative was quite daring, as in contrast to the case of gender equality in the civil code, gender equality in the penal code had not yet been on the public agenda in Turkey.

After analysing the Turkish Penal Code the group concluded that the law embodied a gender-discriminatory, patriarchal outlook and contained numerous provisions legitimizing human rights violations against women. Therefore, it was essential not only to focus on individual articles, such as the article allowing for sentence reductions for perpetrators of honour crimes – which was the only issue on the public agenda – but also to strive for a holistic reform, aiming to transform the entire underlying philosophy of the penal code, which implicitly considered women's bodies and sexuality to be commodities of men, family and society, and reflected a notion that women's sexuality must necessarily be controlled and suppressed by the state.

After identifying all articles violating human rights and the right to sexual and bodily integrity in both the existing code and the draft law, the group undertook a comparative study of penal codes in other countries and prepared detailed proposals and justifications for about forty amendments, formulated as new provisions and articles to be integrated in the new law.

A publication including an analysis of the existing code, the draft law and the amendments proposed by the group was prepared and published by WWHR to be sent to all members of parliament and the government on behalf of the group. While the efforts of the working group were under way, the three-party coalition led by the social democrats resigned unexpectedly after a political crisis in 2002, followed by a declaration of early elections.

The November 2002 elections in Turkey ended with a stunning victory for the newly formed religious right, Adalet ve Kalkınma Partisi – AKP (Justice and Development Party).

The group promptly sent the WWHR publication with the analysis of the existing code and the proposed revisions and amendments to all 550 new members of parliament and the government, along with a letter asking for a meeting with the new justice minister to discuss the proposals. This appeal was ignored for over a year by the minister, despite criticisms by the media of the minister's refusal to meet with women's groups about penal code reform. The minister agreed to a meeting only after the campaign led by the working group put the issue at the forefront of the Turkish public agenda.

Faced with the strong opposition of the government, the women's platform initiated a broader campaign, with the inclusion of twenty-eight women's, as well as LGBT, organizations, aiming at changing the philosophy and principles of the penal code so as to safeguard women's sexual rights. The campaign, which went on for three years, became a major topic of discussion in the media and among the public. It succeeded not only in bringing the discourse of sexual integrity and sexual rights into the public arena, but also in realizing a groundbreaking reform of the Turkish Penal Code in 2004. This reform, achieved despite Turkey's ruling religious conservative government, radically transformed the state's conception of sexuality in Turkey and the code's underlying philosophy. The campaign brought together people from all walks of life and was successful in challenging traditional notions of sexuality in Turkey, with slogans like 'Our bodies and sexuality belong to ourselves!', 'We will not seek permission from the state to make love!'

Major accomplishments of the campaign include the transformation of the underlying philosophy of the law so as to recognize all women's autonomy over their bodies and sexuality; a radical shift from 'the law as the protector of the nation's morality' to 'the law as the protector of people's sexual and bodily integrity'; and the removal of all references to traditions such as morality, chastity, honour or virginity in the code.

The new Turkish Penal Code, accepted in the Turkish parliament in September 2004, states in its first article that the aim of the law is to 'protect the rights and freedoms of individuals'; it recognizes women's autonomy over their bodies and sexuality; brings progressive definitions and higher sentences for sexual crimes; criminalizes marital rape; brings measures to prevent sentence reductions granted to perpetrators of honour killings; eliminates all references to patriarchal concepts like chastity, honour, morality, shame or indecent behaviour; abolishes previously

239

existing discriminations against non-virgin and unmarried women; abolishes provisions granting sentence reductions in rape and abduction cases; criminalizes sexual harassment at the workplace; and considers sexual assaults by security forces as aggravated offences (WWHR – NEW WAYS 2005).

The most controversial debates during the campaign revolved around constructions of honour, virginity, youth sexuality and sexual orientation. While about forty of the women's platform's demands were accepted, the demands that were rejected included designating honour crimes as aggravated homicide; criminalization of virginity tests; removal of an article penalizing consensual sexual relations between youths aged fifteen to eighteen; and the penalizing of discrimination based on sexual orientation – issues related to sexuality outside the framework of marriage. The campaign continues for further progress on these issues.

Conclusion

Our experience at WWHR – NEW WAYS has shown that three factors are crucial in the struggle to promote sexual, bodily and reproductive rights as human rights: adopting a holistic and affirmative approach to sexuality; linking experiences and strategies at local, national and international levels; and adopting a rights-based approach to sexuality.

Issues relating to sexuality are crucial to women's rights, health and overall well-being, lying at the heart of women's human rights in the personal and public spheres. The dominant patriarchal discourses around sexuality have to be challenged on all levels; i.e. at grassroots level as well as at national and international policy and practice levels. Moreover, sexuality lies at the root of many political contradictions and conflicts in many parts of the world, both in the North and the South. For example, in Poland, the debate on abortion between 1989 and 1993 was a central axis of the political struggle for shaping a new state – a democratic and secular one versus a theocratic one – in which, for the time being, the latter has won. The Turkish trajectory confirms that far beyond being a private matter, sexuality has always been a site of political struggles, social anxieties, religious disputes and social transformations throughout history (Foucault 1978; Rubin 1984; Weeks 1989).

As we have tried to show in this chapter, sexuality is an essential domain of women's human rights; it is crucial to women's empowerment and is an issue of political struggles for democracy and development. A genuine commitment to these issues should include the effort to deconstruct misconceptions around sexuality and overcome the fears of delving into assumed cultural sensitivities, which in fact requires only recognition of the efforts of civil society organizations in the South and around the world.

Notes

1 See <www.wwhr.org/musluman _toplumlarda_dayanisma_agi.php>.

2 According to UNICEF statistics, 60 per cent of all girls between the ages of eleven and fourteen living in rural areas are not even enrolled. See UNICEF (2004).

3 See the Montreal Declaration of the World Association for Sexual Health, 2005, <www.siecus.org/ was_declaration.pdf>.

4 The 1994 local elections, which resulted in the triumph of the pro-Islamic Welfare Party in thirty-seven provinces, including the urban centres of Istanbul, Ankara and Izmir, resulted in a drastic shift in the Turkish political scene. The pro-Islamic Welfare Party gained the highest percentage of votes in the 1995 general elections with 21.4 per cent.

5 The analysis is based on data from interviews conducted with 599 women in eastern and south-eastern Turkey (see Ilkkaracan 1998).

6 For more information on the modules on sexuality and sexual rights in the programme, see Ilkkaracan et al. (2006).

7 The members of the Working Group for the Penal Code included representatives of WWHR – NEW WAYS, the Purple Roof Foundation, the Women's Rights Enforcement Centre, the Istanbul Governorate Human Rights Desk and Istanbul Governorate Women's Status Unit from Istanbul, the Republican Women's Association from Ankara, the Women's Commission of the Bar Association from Diyarbakır, the Women's Commission of the Bar Association from Izmir, as well as the academicians Professor Aysel Çelikel, the first female dean of the Istanbul University Law Faculty, and Professor Mehmet Emin Artuk, one of the few male academicians specializing in sexual crimes and law in Turkey.

References

Asena, D. (1987) *Kadının Adı Yok* [The Woman Has No Name], Istanbul: Afa.

Cornwall, A. and S. Jolly (eds) (2006) *IDS Bulletin: Sexuality Matters*, 37(5), Brighton: Institute of Development Studies.

Foucault, M. (1978) *The History of Sexuality*, vol.1: *An Introduction*, trans. Robert Hurley, New York: Random House.

Gökalp, Z. (2005) *Türk Ahlakı* [The Turkish Morality], Istanbul: Toker Yayınları.

Havanon, N. (1996) 'Talking to men and women about their sexual relationships', in S. Zeidenstein and K. Moore (eds), *Learning about Sexuality*, New York: Population Council and IWHC.

Ilkkaracan, I. and G. Seral (2000) 'Sexual pleasure as a woman's human right: experiences from a grassroots training program in Turkey', in P. Ilkkaracan (ed.), *Women and Sexuality in Muslim Societies*, Istanbul: Women for Women's Human Rights (WWHR) – NEW WAYS, pp. 187–96.

Ilkkaracan, I., G. Seral and L. E. Amado (2006) 'Promoting sexual rights through human rights education', *IDS Bulletin: Sexuality Matters*, 37(5): 117–22.

Ilkkaracan, P. (1998) 'Exploring the context of sexuality in eastern Turkey', *Reproductive Health Matters*, 6(12): 66–75.

— (2000) 'Introduction', *Women and Sexuality in Muslim Societies*, Istanbul: Women for Women's Human Rights (WWHR) – NEW WAYS, pp. 1–15.

— (2001) 'Islam and women's sexuality: a research report from Turkey', in M. Hunt, P. B. Jung and R. Balakrishnan (eds), *Good Sex: Feminist Perspectives from the World's Religions*, New Jersey: Rutgers University Press.

Ilkkaracan, P. and L. E. Amado (2005) 'Human rights education as a tool of grassroots organizing and social transformation: a case study from Turkey', *Intercultural Education*, 16(2): 115–28.

Ilkkaracan, P. and S. Jolly (2007) *Gender and Sexuality: Overview Report*, Brighton: Institute of Development Studies.

Kandiyoti, D. (1987) 'Emancipated but unliberated? Reflections on the Turkish case', *Feminist Studies*, Summer, pp. 317–38.

— (1998) 'Slave girls, temptresses and comrades: images of women in the Turkish novel', *Feminist Issues*, 8(1): 35–50.

MacFadden, P. (2003) 'Sexual pleasure as a feminist choice', *Feminist Africa*, 2, October, <www.feministafrica.org/fa%202/02-2003/sp-pat.html> (accessed 21 December 2006).

Rubin, G. (1984) 'Thinking sex: notes for a radical theory of the politics of sexuality', in C. Vance (ed.), *Pleasure and Danger: Exploring Female Sexuality*, New York: Routledge.

Tekeli, Ş. (1982) *Kadınlar ve Siyasal Toplumsal Hayat* [Women and Socio-political Life], Istanbul: Birikim Yayınları.

UNICEF (2004) 'First time Turkish girls see a classroom', <www.unicef.org/girlseducation/index23821.html> (accessed 14 December 2006).

Vance, C. S. (1992) 'Pleasure and danger: towards a politics of sexuality', in C. Vance (ed.), *Pleasure and Danger: Exploring Female Sexuality*, New York: Routledge.

WAS (World Association of Sexual Health) (1999) Declaration of Sexual Rights, <www.siecus.org/inter/inte0006.html> (accessed 2 May 2007).

Weeks, J. (1989) *Sex, Politics and Society: The Regulation of Sexuality Since 1800*, New York: Longman.

WWHR (Women for Women's Human Rights) – NEW WAYS (2005) *Turkish Civil and Penal Code Reforms from a Gender Perspective: The Success of Two Nationwide Campaigns*, Istanbul: WWHR – NEW WAYS.

About the authors

Henry P. Armas is an attorney with experience in human rights and development, with an emphasis on citizen participation, participatory education and gender. He is president of GRUPAL – Grupo de Trabajo para la Participación en el Ámbito Local (the Working Group for Participation in Peru) – and a researcher in the Unit of Rights and Health at the Universidad Peruana Cayetano Heredia, Lima, Peru. He is a member of the International Advisory Committee of BRIDGE (Institute of Development Studies, UK) and has participated in programmes at the IDS, the University of Sussex, Harvard University and Oñati University.

Sumit Baudh works on human rights and law. His areas of interest include the rights of queers, Dalits and undocumented migrant workers in India. Sumit obtained his LLB from the National Law School of India University and his LLM from the London School of Economics. An advocate (Delhi bar) and a non-practising solicitor (England and Wales), he has worked with the Commonwealth Human Rights Initiative (CHRI) and the AMAN Trust, both NGOs based in Delhi, India. Sumit has been closely involved with the Voices Against 377 and is presently located at the South and Southeast Asia Resource Centre on Sexuality, in Delhi.

Deevia Bhana is Associate Professor of Education at the University of KwaZulu Natal, Durban, South Africa. She has published in the areas of childhood sexuality, masculinities and HIV/AIDS. She is currently writing a book on gender and violence in South African secondary schools (with Rob Morrell, Debbie Epstein, Elaine Unterhalter and Lebo Moletsane). She is co-editor of *Sexualities in Southern Africa* (with Rob Morrell, Jeff Hearn, Lebo Moletsane, 2007) and has co-edited a special issue of the journal *Sexualities*.

Giuseppe Campuzano was born in Lima, Peru, where he currently works. He has studied philosophy and for three years has been running a project called Museo Travesti (Travesti Museum), a detailed investigation of Peruvian transgenders, through documents, history dissertations, journalism and art. This project aims to provide a better understanding of who contemporary *travestis* are, to get rid of misconceptions, as well as to offer a useful tool for the empowerment of *travesti* communities and to encourage others all over America to work on similar studies.

Andrea Cornwall is a Fellow at the Institute of Development Studies, where she directs the Pathways of Women's Empowerment Research Programme Consortium, <www.pathways-of-empowerment.org>. She has worked on issues of sexuality, gender and participation for many years and is co-editor of *Realizing Rights: Transforming Approaches to Sexual and Reproductive Wellbeing* (with Alice Welbourn, Zed Books, 2002), *Sexuality Matters* (with Susie Jolly, IDS Bulletin, 2006) and *Feminisms in Development: Challenges, Contradictions and Contestations* (with Elizabeth Harrison and Ann Whitehead, Zed Books, 2007).

Sonia Corrêa is the founder of SOS-Corpo-Instituto Feminista para a Democracia, a leading Brazilian feminist organization. Since 1994, she has closely followed United Nations negotiations in relation to gender, sexuality and reproductive health and has authored *Population and Reproductive Rights: Feminist Perspectives from the South* (Zed Books, 1994). She coordinates the sexual and reproductive health rights programme of Development Alternative with Women for a New Era (DAWN), a Southern-based research and activist network, and is the co-chair of Sexuality Policy Watch. Both programmes are institutionally based at ABIA – Brazilian Interdisciplinary Association for AIDS – in Rio de Janeiro.

Melissa Ditmore is the coordinator of the Global Network of Sex Work projects and a research consultant for the Sex Workers Project. She is the editor of the *Encyclopedia of Prostitution and Sex Work* (Greenwood Press, 2006) and has written about sex work, migration and trafficking for *The Lancet* and *SIECUS Report*. A contributor to *Trafficking and Prostitution Reconsidered* (Paradigm, 2005), *Affective Turn* (Duke, 2007) and *Women across Borders* (Black Rose, 2007), she edits the annual journal *Research for Sex Work*.

Jelena Djordjevic is a feminist activist from Serbia, currently directing the Anti-Trafficking Centre in Belgrade, which she co-founded in 2003. Jelena recently completed a postgraduate degree in Migration Studies at the University of Sussex and a research project for the Urgent Action Fund on Women's Rights, which explores how to sustain and support women's activism globally. Jelena is affiliated with the International Women in Black Network, the V-Day Europe Network for Stopping Violence Against Women and Girls, and the Network of Sex Work Projects.

Adenike O. Esiet, sociologist and youth health advocate, is Co-founder and Executive Director of Action Health Incorporated, Nigeria. Since 1989, she has contributed to building AHI from an idea into a vibrant organization that combines community-based programming with national policy advocacy for sexual health and rights. She led AHI's policy advocacy initiatives which engendered national consciousness and action resulting in the production of the National Sexuality Education Curriculum in 2001. She has also served on WHO's Gender Advisory Panel, the National AIDS and STD Control Programme's Technical Advisory Committee and is currently a member of the National Adolescent Health Working Group and the University of Columbia-based International Working Group on Sexuality and Social Policy. She is a 1992 recipient of the Ashoka International Fellowship for Public Innovators.

Gill Gordon is a Senior Technical Adviser: Prevention, at the International HIV/AIDS Alliance. She provides regular technical support to a project working with young people in and out of schools in six districts in the Eastern Province of Zambia. She has over thirty years' experience of working in the development sector, and is a social development and health promotion specialist with particular expertise in gender, sexuality and community-based participatory approaches. She has previously worked with Family Planning Associations around the world to integrate a broad range of sexual health concerns into their programmes. Gill is the author/ co-author of several publications, including *Talking AIDS* (with Tony Klouda, Macmillan Africa, 1988), and *Choices – A Guide for Young People* (Macmillan Africa, 1999).

Alan Greig is an international consultant advising community-based organizations in sub-Saharan Africa and South and South-East Asia on developing HIV/AIDS programmes that address underlying factors of vulnerability, such as gender inequality and violence. Recently he has worked with MOVE (Men Overcoming Violence) and has trained as an organizer in Generation Five's Community Response Project on Child Sexual Abuse (CSA). With Generation Five, he trained in Digital Storytelling and has used this tool to mobilize more men to get involved in the movement to end child sexual abuse. In his current digital video work, he is working as an activist with Break the Silence Mural Project to produce a documentary on art as resistance in Palestine.

Shireen Huq is an activist in the women's movement in Bangladesh, a founder member of Naripokkho, and for more than twenty years a trainer on gender, rights and development in Bangladesh and elsewhere. She also worked from 1987 to 2001 as Adviser, Women's Development and during 2003–06 as Deputy Programme Coordinator, Human Rights and Good Governance Programme for Danida in Bangladesh.

Pinar Ilkkaracan is an independent scholar and activist who has written extensively on sexuality and sexual rights, women and law, violence against women, Islam and gender, and human rights education. She is the editor of *Women and Sexuality in Muslim Societies* (WWHR–NEW WAYS, Istanbul, 2000) and *Sexuality in the Middle East and North Africa: Contemporary Issues and Discourses* (forthcoming), and the co-author of *Gender and Sexuality* (BRIDGE, IDS, 2007), *The Myth of the Warm Home: Domestic Violence and Sexual Abuse* (WWHR–NEW WAYS, Istanbul, 1996) and *Human Rights Education for Women: A Training Manual* (WWHR–NEW WAYS, Istanbul, 2005). In 2001, she led the foundation of the Coalition for Sexual and Bodily Rights in Muslim Societies, a solidarity network of academics and NGOs working towards the promotion of sexual, bodily and reproductive rights and health in the Middle East, North Africa and South/South-East Asia.

Susie Jolly is a Research Officer in the Participation, Power and Social Change Team at the Institute of Development Studies (IDS). Together with Andrea Cornwall, she is spearheading IDS work on sexuality. She aims to support exchanges between sexual rights activists and to help share their insights with people in the development industry. She writes and manages BRIDGE publications on gender issues in relation to HIV/AIDS, migration and poverty. She is also engaged with local rights struggles, and is founder of Brighton Both Ways Bisexual Group. Susie came to IDS in 1998. Previously, she lived in Beijing for several years, managing poverty alleviation programmes for UNDP and joining in local women's rights and LGBT activism.

Jill Lewis combines teaching as Professor of Literature and Gender Studies at Hampshire College in the USA with work from her home base in the UK as an international gender/HIV-prevention consultant and trainer. Involved in the politics of gender and sexual health since 1972, she has been active in gender-focused HIV-prevention work since 1986 in a wide range of cultural contexts. Recently she has worked on building HIV-prevention capacity for the Norwegian Refugee Council in the Caucasus and many parts of sub-Saharan Africa – and in the USA with youth in a high-HIV-risk Latino immigrant community. She has a particular interest in working with formations of heterosexual masculinity that block HIV prevention.

Sabina Faiz Rashid is an Assistant Professor at the James P. Grant School of Public Health, BRAC University, Bangladesh. She has a PhD in Medical Anthropology/Public Health from the Australian National University. Her thesis focused on married adolescent women's lives and their reproductive health experiences in urban slums of Dhaka city. Since 1994, she has been working in Bangladesh, carrying out research on gender and reproductive and sexual health issues. She has published articles in a number of peer-reviewed journals and has co-authored a book on gender-sensitive delivery care for rural women. She is interested in urbanization, poverty and their impact on gender relations and reproductive and sexual health.

Kopano Ratele is a Professor in the Institute of Social and Health Sciences, University of South Africa. He was previously Professor in Psychology and in Women and Gender Studies at the University of Western Cape, South Africa. His recent publications include, as editor, *Intergroup Relations in South Africa* (Juta, 2006).

Karin Ronge, social pedagogue, has been working as co-coordinator at Women for Women's Human Rights (WWHR)–NEW WAYS, Turkey, since 1996. She has worked as a feminist and human rights activist for twenty years. She is an expert on child and adolescent sexual behaviour and development, non-violent and gender-sensitive education and child-oriented prevention and intervention programmes on child abuse. She is the co-author of a booklet on community-based prevention of violence against women and girls, and co-author of the chapter on 'gender sensitive parenting' in *Women's Human Rights: A Training Manual* (WWHR–NEW WAYS, Istanbul, 2005).

Alejandra Sardá is a renowned LGBT activist who coordinates Mulabi, Latin American Space for Sexualities and Rights. She previously coordinated the Latin American and Caribbean Programme for the International Gay and Lesbian Human Rights Commission for seven years (1999–2006). She was manager of Escrita en el Cuerpo, a lesbian and bisexual women's documentation centre (1994–99). Alejandra is an experienced literary translator specializing in sexuality issues, and a member of the Translingua feminist translation service, a cooperative created by a group of translators living in different continents.

Jaya Sharma is a queer, feminist activist based in Delhi, India. She is a founder member of PRISM, a forum that seeks to raise awareness related to same-sex sexualities and to interrogate the norm. Her work has primarily involved engaging with other progressive groups and movements towards enabling them to recognize and respond to queer issues as an intrinsic part of their agenda. She is also a founder member of Nirantar, a women's NGO working on issues of gender and education. Jaya has been a part of the women's movement in India for the past two decades.

Kate Sheill is Campaign Coordinator on Identity-based Discrimination in the Policy Programme of the International Secretariat of Amnesty International. Her work can cover issues of gender, sexuality, 'race' and faith worldwide and currently includes UN advocacy on sexual rights, campaigning on LGBT rights, and work on the human rights of indigenous peoples and freedom of religion.

Index

freedom of sexuality, 184

Gambia, 207
gay people, 220; organizations of,
   registration of, 110
Gender and Human Development
   report, 28
gender studies, 142
gender: and sex orders, 11–15;
   institutionalization of, 14, 15;
   problematization of, 144
Girl Power Initiative (GPI) (Nigeria),
   35–6
girls: courting of males, 148–9;
   initiation of, 202; rights of,
   81–2; school enrolment of,
   227; sexual pressures on, 35;
   vulnerability of, 81, 82, 84
Global Alliance Against Trafficking
   in Women (GAATW), 165
Global Health Council, 189
globalization, 13
Gökalp, Ziya, 229
Gonzales de Cuenca, Gregorio, 136
Group of Men Against Violence
   (Nicaragua), 38
GRUPAL organization (Peru), 219
Guatemala, 111

hamam, 98
hermaphroditism, 137
heterosexuality and
   heteronormativity, 2, 11, 26, 28,
   35, 39, 67, 68, 71–3, 72, 75, 90–2,
   95, 99, 124, 129–30, 131, 132,
   214, 218, 221, 230, 235
hijras, 93, 95, 99, 185–6; identity
   of, 98
Hinojosa, Claudia, 28
HIV/AIDS, 16, 19, 25–7, 30, 31, 34,
   38, 39–40, 45, 46, 47, 48, 54–66,
   77–85, 98, 161, 168, 170, 175,
   191, 213–14, 220; and sexual
   pleasure, 199–209; awareness
   programmes, 37; education
   about, in Nigeria, 192–5; effects
   of, in Africa, 190; prevention
   of, 3, 8, 62, 122, 126, 188, 189,
   205, 206, 207, 208, 214, 217
   (funding for, 40, 60 (restrictions
   on, 54)); programmes, 194; UN
   resolution on, 50
homophobia, 28, 35, 112, 114, 117
homosexuality, 4, 32, 70, 71;
   criminalization of, 55, 93, 95,
   97, 130; death penalty for, 215;
   decriminalization of, 99–100;
   legality of, 109; repression of, 18
Honduras, 107–8, 112, 116, 117
honour, 17, 227, 237; as tool of
   control of women's sexuality,
   234; killing for, 239
human development, 27–31
*Human Development and Cultural
   Liberty* report, 28
*Human Development and Human
   Rights* report, 28
human rights, 7–11, 31–3; and sex
   workers, 175; and sexuality,
   1–21, 228–36; in India, 93–103;
   in Turkey, 225–42; of sex
   workers, 54–66; sexual rights
   as, 45–53, 226–8; sexuality
   education as, 187–98
Human Rights Watch, 88

identity, issue of, 68–9
India, 4; Article 377 of Indian
   Penal Code, 2–3, 11, 74, 93–5,
   96, 101 (challenge to, 98); HIV
   prevention in, 2; human rights
   in, 93–103; homosexuality in,
   71; sexual rights in, 68–9 *see
   also* Voices Against 377
Indian Association of Women's
   Studies (IAWS), 73, 74, 75
informal settlements, 78–9
Institute of Development Studies
   (IDS) (UK), 1; *Realizing Sexual
   Rights* workshop, 1, 50
International Conference on HIV/
   AIDS, 56, 61
International Conference on
   Population and Development
   (ICPD), 25, 46, 188, 227;
   Programme of Action, 47

same-sex marriage in, 4; sexual rights in, 225–42

Ulka organization (Bangladesh), 183
ultra-conservatism, 8
undocumented workers, 64
unemployment, 149
United Nations (UN), 32; debates on sexuality, 225; Declaration of Commitment on HIV/AIDS, 50; General Assembly Session on HIV/AIDS, 49; Palermo Optional Protocol, 54, 56, 57–9
UN Children's Fund (UNICEF), 77
UN Commission on Human Rights (UNCHR), 46, 49
UN Commission on Population and Development (UNCPD), 46, 47
UN Commission on the Status of Women (CSW), 46
UN Conference on Population and Development (Cairo, 1994), 87; plus ten conference, 51
UN Convention against Transnational Organized Crime, 162, 164
UN Development Programme (UNDP), Human Development Reports, 27
UN Fund for Population Activities, 62
UN General Assembly Special Session on HIV/AIDS, 188
UN Human Rights Committee, 32
UN Human Rights Conference (Vienna, 1993), 86, 213
UN Protocol to Prevent, Suppress and Punish Trafficking in Persons, Especially Women and Children, 164
UN Special Rapporteur on Violence against Women, 32
UN World Programme of Action for Youth, 188
UNAIDS, 64
United States of America (USA): anti-trafficking law, 59–60, 59; National Violence Against Women Survey, 89; sexual rights in, 48; Supreme Court, 96
Universal Declaration of Human Rights, 211
universality, concept of, 48
Uruguay, abortion in, 3
US Agency for International Development (USAID), 60

vagina, nature of, 157
Vike-Freiberga, Vaira, 130
violence, 12, 38; against men, 88, 89–90; against sex workers, 161, 162; against transgender people, 170, 221; against women, 9, 32, 46, 49, 162–3, 166–7, 199, 203, 212, 215, 228, 230, 231, 232 (activism against, 70); among *travestis*, 141; freedom from, 64; of the state, 171–3
virginity, 35, 55, 82, 226, 234; testing for, 233
visibility, costs of, 220
Voices Against 377 (India), 99

women: autonomy of, 239; empowerment of, 127; human rights of, 226–8; humiliation of, 228; imprisonment of, 172; in politics, 215; morality of, 229; status of, 229–30; stereotyped, 206 (as victims, 57); unemployment among, 108; vulnerability of, 154; work of, 151
Women for Women's Human Rights (WWHR) (Turkey), 225–6, 231, 232–3, 240; Human Rights Education Programme, 232–6; courses, 38; Women's Working Group, 238
women's movement: in Bangladesh, 181–6; in Turkey, 229–30
women's organizations, relation with state, 167
Women's Platform for the Reform